The
GREAT
RAILWAY
ADVENTURE

Christopher Portway

The Oxford Illustrated Press

Printed in England by
J.H.Haynes & Co Ltd, Sparkford,
Yeovil, Somerset

ISBN 0 902280 97 X

The Oxford Illustrated Press Limited
Sparkford, Yeovil, Somerset BA22 7JJ

Contents

I am indebted to Robert Hale & Co for allowing me to include material from my *Corner Seat* and *Double Circuit* in this book.

To my friend and colleague, Kenneth Westcott Jones, doyen of railway travel writers — the only man I know capable of quoting the world's train time-tables from memory — who will no doubt tell me that the Montrealer leaves Montreal at 18.55; not 19.15, that my Quetta Express in Pakistan was, in fact, the Sukkur Express, and that the Coast Starlight does not start from San Diego.
Assuredly he'll be right.

Picture Acknowledgements

My thanks go to the following for their permission to reproduce photographs:

The J Allan Cash Photolibrary
page 1: top, left
page 4: top
page 5: bottom
page 6: bottom
page 7: top, bottom right
page 8: both

Christopher Portway/Bandphoto
page 5: top

Alan Hutchison Library Limited
cover photograph
pages 2 and 3: both
page 4: bottom
page 6: top right, middle
page 7: middle, bottom left

O My aged Uncle Arly!
Sitting on a heap of Barley
Thro' the silent hours of night, —
Close beside a leafy thicket:-
On his nose there was a Cricket, —
In his hat a Railway Ticket; —
(But his shoes were far too tight.)

Incidents in the Life of my Aged Uncle Arly
(Edward Lear)

Introduction

Trains. A word spelling the daily grind to and from work for many; the gateway to new worlds for some; a vehicle to adventure for a few. In between can be found a category of person who loves trains simply for the railway's sake and there is the occasional eccentric, like me, who finds in world train travel something of the challenge for which, it is alleged, medieval knights on white chargers were constantly searching.

To travel by train, particularly to a destination far removed from one's own environment, can still evoke a quickening of the pulse unmatched by that of transportation on the ubiquitous aeroplane or the humble bus. Our whole concept of travel has changed dramatically over the last thirty-five or so years. Before then journeys about the world could only be accomplished by train. Yet today the passenger train in some countries — notably North America — is in decline though in others there is a heartening rebirth with new techniques, rolling stock and equipment to match. In South Africa, Japan, India, much of Europe; even Britain where it all began, railways continue to hold their own.

It must be said that on a long-distance train as nowhere else your compartment becomes an observation post of life. Outside there is the ever-changing scenario of the world; inside you are amongst people who can become friends — or occasionally enemies — but from whom much knowledge and understanding of that world can be gleaned. You can stroll in the corridor, visit the bar, eat in the restaurant car. You stop — or can stop off — in towns and cities, cross borders and frontiers, all the while being accepted to membership of an exclusive club. Journey's end can produce a warm feeling of accomplishment.

It took me years to discover that my destiny lay with the railway. Yet over those years a sizeable percentage of the most

5

memorable events of my life were enacted on a train, close to a railway and, more often than not, were directly caused by my interest in and involvement with both. However I am not a true 'railway buff'. I am abysmally ignorant of how the wheels go round and, to me, a 4-8-4 could be a calibre of bullet. I suppose my introduction to the railway game was made during my childhood when I possessed a substantial clockwork model railway layout. But here my interest was retarded by economy and safety-minded parents who denied me electric equipment while my contemporaries dabbled in transformers and electronic magic. From my clockwork Hornby set I graduated, as a 1940 schoolboy in Herefordshire, to playing dangerous games in Kerne Tunnel on the long-defunct Ross to Monmouth line; a kind of lethal musical chairs with oncoming trains as the music and tunnel safety slots as the chairs — a pastime that earned me a well-deserved thrashing. One of my proudest accomplishments as a seventeen-year old soldier recruit was that of effecting a ride from London to Carlisle and back on the same penny platform ticket!

Someone once called me the Don Quixote of the trains and certainly jousting with railway authority — or any authority for that matter — has never lost its appeal. But it was the demands of the Second World War that set me, in earnest, on my great railway adventure.

Capture by the Germany army following the liberation (and destruction) of the Norman city of Caen in 1944 gave me the worst rail journey of my life as my captors transported me and their many thousands of British, American and Canadian prisoners across Germany inside the stifling, putrid, freight wagons of the famous '40 hommes ou 8 chevaux' variety. If we had no horses, we were considerably in excess of 40 men. So cramped were conditions that we had to take it in turns to sit on the bare wood floor and fighting for water broke out amongst us. At Metz we were subject to the attentions of American fighter-bombers who strafed our mobile prison with rockets. Four days and nights of this and the coal-mine slave camp in Silesia to which some of us were eventually transferred seemed ineffably more attractive. But all things are relative. Soon all my energies were being channelled into the single aim of getting away and the

September night when I succeeded in burrowing through three barbed wire fences became my subsequent climax of personal accomplishment.

The Soviet Red Army, our supposed allies, were my only hope of liberation, but walking by night and laying up by day across the flat Silesian and Polish countryside on a diet of stolen potatoes and Red Cross jam, offered small hope of attaining their lines. So I took to the trains.

Freight traffic offered the only practical vehicle at the time since I was not in possession of the sheaf of documents needed to travel in the German *Reich*. But locating the physical conditions wherein advantage can be taken of stowing away on wagon or truck is not that simple I can tell you. The place had to be suitably remote, the track had to go in the right direction, geography had to raise a gradient to slow the train and provide reason for a curve sharp enough to foil vigilance from those already aboard. It was imperative that the armed occupants at each end of the train had no idea what was about to go on in the middle.

It took two days to find the site and another one for the appropriate train to put in an appearance. But have *you* ever tried climbing onto a high-sided steel truck moving at twelve mph? It looks simple enough on the silver screen, with the hero nipping smartly on to an orchestral accompaniment. Unfortunately, the Berlin Philharmonic was on the Russian front at the time so was not available for my little epic. The operation involves doing a lot of things at once with the one set of accessories the good Lord has bequeathed us. The eyes have to be watching the feet, watching the way ahead for signal cables and the impediments of points control, and watching for hand and foot holds on the train. The feet have to run, jump gullies and cables, dodge sleeper ends and, eventually, climb the perpendicular sides of the chosen truck. The arms, besides maintaining balance, have to locate holds, push the body away from the relentless wheels yet lift it when a suitable hold is found. All this, too, on an empty stomach.

My first ride was a disaster. Crouched, frozen to the marrow, against the wet coal-dust-begrimed sides of a truck I sat, helpless, as the train proceeded into a siding, executed an about-turn, picked up speed and delivered me eighty miles in the wrong direction. Two days later another coal and a pit-prop train brought me back to approximately where I had started, a state of affairs that convinced me of the error of my ways. The only marvel was that I had not been caught.

Thus I graduated to the passenger train. With stolen money and my atrocious German I acquired a first-class ticket from a small station near Opole which would take me to Cracow. At least this way I'd have an idea where the train was going while I hoped my first-class status would stall any questions and demand for papers.

At first the only scourge was the ticket-inspector who repeatedly returned to my empty compartment in an attempt to reconcile the sight of my travel-stained person with his pre-conceived idea of what a first-class client should look like. But two hours before Cracow I was joined by a *Wehrmacht* captain and a young German naval lieutenant. For a time they were engrossed with each other and I feigned sleep, but it didn't last. Catching my eye one of them enquired as to my nationality and I was inspired to volunteer 'Ungarish', hoping neither spoke or understood Hungarian. Both intimated a desire to know more about the joys of Budapest and seemed well content with my proferred description of Bristol. For my trouble I was given a bunch of grapes which I attempted to consume with suitable first-class finesse before my two friends departed into the dusk at a Cracow suburban station. I chose to bale out in the marshalling yards of that Polish city since a more civilised disembarkation at a main terminus crawling with Gestapo and police was not recommended. But I forgot the overnight curfew.

It was my undoing. Caught by a German army patrol when breaking into a baker's shop I was apologetically handed over to the Gestapo who displayed, in their usual repulsive manner, a marked lack of enthusiasm for my amateurish efforts to escape. Bruised and blooded I ended up in the cellars of their Cracow headquarters. It was dark and cold and rat-ridden but the rats were better company than the Gestapo.

There's little more of my unhappy wartime saga that touched upon railways. I was to escape twice more and it became a case of third time lucky for I reached the American lines just a few weeks before the end of the war in Europe.

Following the cessation of hostilities it took a surprisingly short time to put the European railways back on their feet and, by 1947, many a famous-named express was running again. The first ten years of an uneasy peace saw great changes on the railways of the world. Much of it was in the unwelcome form of a retraction of facilities and reduction of worked track in face of a rapidly worsening economic situation. Yet in many countries there were notable advances in technology. Apart from the United States of America, whose land had not been invaded nor their cities subjected to bombardment, the railways of Great Britain were practically alone among those of the most heavily involved belligerent nations in having their tracks and workshops intact at the end of the war. Damage had been repaired, although the standards of maintenance of track and rolling stock had, by *force majeure*, been much reduced. But the fact that the railways of Britain were still operating meant that they received nothing in the way of financial aid towards recovery, such as that made available to those on the Continent of Europe and elsewhere (through 'Lease Lend' and similar financial schemes), that enabled the rapid restoration and improvement of services to be made.

The conclusion of the war gave way to a cankerous disease that became known as the 'cold war' which, alas, is not cured to this day. The division of Europe caused a division of the European railway system that could but retard resurrection and growth. However one train that managed to resume its previous route and truly international character was the now defunct Direct Orient Express.

This has evoked many a romantic notion in the world of fiction though factual spies and criminals were probably no more at a premium on that train than any other. I have ridden its routes and ramifications to find it was a little dull in the post-war era in spite of the heightened drama of the borders it crossed. However, on several occasions, this so-called express has led me to an 'Iron Curtain' adventure in a period of history, now thankfully passed,

9

when 'the east was east and the west was west and never the twain shall meet'.

While it was the vicissitudes of war that had pushed me into my first railway adventure it was the post-war policies of militant communism that offered me my second. After the war Europe had entered an unhappy peace; its cities smashed, its territory divided by a lethal frontier of electrified fences, minefields and watchtowers. But for me not all the fruits of war had been bitter. From the welter of killing, fear and hate the spark of love had glowed in the darkness. The girl was Czech, her name was Anna and her homeland was one that fate decreed to be the wrong side of the wire. With the throttling hand of Stalinism in the east the spark could well have died. Entry to Czechoslovakia was inexorably denied me, communication was handicapped by censorship and my distant overtures could only but draw the attentions of a ruthless secret police to a dissident citizen of that unhappy country. But the spark refused to die; from both our hearts it shone the brighter from a panoply of despair. The World War was over. Now my own personal struggle with a new enemy, a new authority, was to begin.

My initial move was by train, the truncated section of what was then the Paris to Prague portion of the Orient Express. Hidden in the lavatory I dodged the well-meaning minions of the West German border police who came aboard the train at the German border to ensure that ongoing travellers possessed both visa and permission to enter the forbidden land the other side. I held neither. At the physical border, amongst the high-voltage and explosive apparatus of repression, pink-faced men with cold eyes and guns searched the train for concealed 'spies' but never asked for papers. Only at the Czech border station of Cheb, ten miles on, did authority see fit to scrutinize my passport, pronounce it invalid and take me into custody. Next day, with a flea in my ear and some useful topographic data in my head, I was expelled and returned to Germany.

My next incursion was on foot, using the single-track line as a banister. Again I evaded the Bavarian patrols and, slinking through the night, came up against the wire. It took me two hours with a pair of insulated cable-cutters to deal with this; another to traverse on hands and knees the ploughed strip (leaving no give-away foot prints) and the minefield. The Czech patrols made more noise than a London bus and were easily dodged and I had the lights of Cheb in my sights before dawn. Then I came to the river.

Carelessness feeds on fatigue. The river was shallow and I could easily have waded it. But, downstream, the railway bridge offered tempting dry passage. I watched it for ten minutes but saw or heard no movement to warn that it was guarded. I succumbed to its lure.

I had reached the further side before the word 'Halt' spat at me. Five soldiers formed a semi-circle around me and they all carried those little carbine things with a prolific rate of fire. I raised my hands slowly above my head. No order had been given but it seemed the expedient thing to do.

Czech communist authority threw the book at me of course and I remained in Cheb for the best part of three months. This was considerably longer than I had intended but the accommodation was free. The town's political prison is a multi-storey structure of unprepossessing appearance and I cannot recommend the food. The monotony of jail routine was broken by the occasional interrogation where the questioning was of the prove-you're-not-a-spy variety and, on the second occasion, I managed to nick my interrogator's pencil. My 'crimes against the state' appeared to carry a total penalty of something in excess of a hundred years' hard labour. The prospects were not encouraging to say the least.

My release was swift, sudden and dictated by the anger of my own government at not being informed of my arrest and incarceration. Returned to the border under escort I was pushed out of the country at an unauthorised crossing point — whereupon the West German authorities tried to arrest me for illegally entering the Federal Republic!

The following Easter weekend I repeated the rail excursion to Cheb. This time I told Anna of my intentions and she was on platform two to meet me. Under the gaze of outraged officialdom I managed to slip an engagement ring onto her finger and plead eight minutes alone with her before the accustomed chucking-out procedure.

My ensuing conflict had little to do with the railways; only

11

once, in fact, was a train directly concerned. This was in East Germany when I unwisely tried to smuggle myself across its border with Czechoslovakia on the Balt Orient Express at Bad Schandau station. Arrested and taken to a police post within sight of the border I attempted to run for it and was lucky indeed to escape being fired upon by my heavily-armed escort. Thus with the added impediment of being classed as *persona non grata* in one state and emphatically unwelcome in others it was four years and many adventures before the girl on platform two was to become my wife.

With the emergencies of a call to arms and the immediate demands of romance at an end I could answer the bidding of the world's railways for little other reason than for the pleasure of travelling the trains and allowing them to show me the world under more pleasurable circumstances. And it is the more adventurous of these that form the core of this book. Some are made on famed expresses crossing the vast expanses of the Soviet Union and North America; others find me on dirty little trains in Asia and South America. One moment I am sweating it out in Pakistan's Baluchistan Desert; the next shivering with cold riding the world's highest railway line in Peru. My fellow-travellers are a potpourri of the globe: friendly Turks, garrulous Armenians, inquisitive Russians, suspicious Albanians, smiling Ugandans, polite Indians, not-so-polite Syrians, 'don't-look-now-but-I-think-we're-being-followed' East Germans. My corner seat is a plush roomette on America's Amtrak, a broken-down third-class wagon on Algerian Railways and standing-room only on India's Frontier Mail. Off the train for a moment and I am being robbed in Kabul, arrested in Kampala and berated in Khaborovsk. The incidents are mine but the main ingredients of track routes and trains that run them are available to all. The journeys described can be repeated, with variations, by anyone in the mind to do so.

The division between experience and adventure is ill-defined. One man's experience can be another's adventure. Not all my recorded rail journeys involve, or lead me, to high adventure. A few are little more than worthwhile train rides plus a little incident that fortuitously came my way. The wider subject of interesting rail routes travelled could fill another book. In this category how can one fail to mention the elegant trains of China especially those on the lines of Sinkiang and Inner Mongolia on which I progressed surrounded by lace curtains, pink-shaded table lamps and potted plants with my overnight bedding tastefully wrapped in a dainty lace coverlet. Or the Royal Thai State Railway's Northern Express between Bangkok and Chiang-mai taking me through the jungle and paddy-fields of Thailand. Nearer home, Switzerland is, of course, a mecca for rail journeying enthusiasts as much for the sheer efficiency of the system as the glorious alpine scenery. And in Scandinavia — particularly Norway, Sweden and Finland — there are lonely lines north of the Arctic Circle that snake excitingly along the side of fjords and lakes. Last but by no means least, mention must be made of the incomparable lines to the Western Isles of our own Scotland. On the Fort William to Mallaig line are views of wild hills as remote today as when Bonnie Prince Charlie hid in the heather in the 'Rough Bounds of Knoydart'. Jacobite history blends with the eternity of the Scottish Highlands as you ride this astounding route. Only in Cuba was I denied a ride on a train in a country that possessed a railway — and this even following a personal request for permission to do so to no less a person than Fidel Castro himself.

These then are just a few examples of railways and trains and their challenge that could set a traveller on the road to adventure. For me on these occasions fate decreed otherwise or maybe I wasn't trying. Adventure has to be helped along a little; goaded or prodded into movement. But once aroused hold on for dear life for, as you will perceive from the following pages, adventure on wheels has a disconcerting habit of running away with you.

1

The Orient Express

PARIS—ISTANBUL

Its very name is a recipe for adventure so let us commence with the Direct Orient Express which I last travelled in 1969 before it was laid to rest with a fanfare of trumpets and a sprinkling of nostalgic television programmes in 1977. No longer is there a through-express from Paris to Istanbul though in spite of that it is still possible to ride its lines if you don't mind a change of train. And then there's the gimmicky — and expensive — tourist train that utilises some of the old rolling stock and calls itself the Venice—Simplon Orient Express that runs between London, Paris and Venice, and only at certain times of the year, in an attempt to recreate an atmosphere long dead. On it I have drunk champagne served by waiters in fancy dress — but the original Direct Orient Express is not for resurrection.

Sadly the last years of this train were, I have to repeat, exceedingly dull ones. Only in France was it an express at all. The expected skulduggery no longer wrapped the train in its aura of adventure and romanticism; one had to take along a sort of 'do-it-yourself adventure kit' if anything remotely interesting was to be generated. Only once, for me, was the famous Express the vehicle that carried me to an adventure of the cloak and dagger kind.

The train that skulked at a badly lit platform in the Gare de Lyon in Paris that summer evening was the Direct Orient Express, the destination boards bearing those evocative place names: Paris—Lausanne—Milano—Venezia—Trieste—Zagreb—Beograd—Sofia—Athens—Istanbul. It left, on time, at the romantic hour of ten minutes before midnight, and was scheduled to arrive eighty-four hours later in Istanbul.

The inaugural trip of the Orient Express in 1883 was a tremendous occasion with many crowned heads of Europe and Asia participating. At its zenith in the early 1900s the great train could accomplish the distance between Paris and Istanbul in fifty-six hours.

From Paris there were two departures for Istanbul the other being routed via Munich. The German section took three hours longer and since a later departure time of 03.00 hours from Paris was frowned upon as an inconvenient hour for a great express to leave from a great capital, a policy of an idling Swiss-Italian section until the two portions could connect in Yugoslavia was agreed upon by the Timetable Committee.

This body also had the onerous task of satisfying the various countries through which the Express passed. This took some doing since every capital along the route of such a showpiece train required it to arrive and depart at a suitable hour. Even the name 'Simplon-Orient' caused disagreement. Liked by the Bulgarians and Turks, it was eventually changed to 'Direct-Orient' and for this the Swiss — a big force in the railway world — were responsible.

In the context of route and timetable it must be remembered that the original Orient Express ran from Paris to Vienna, there to connect with Danube ferries and newly-constructed railway lines towards Romania and the Balkans, to the powerful capital of the Ottoman Empire, Constantinople (now Istanbul). As its popularity grew portions of the same train split at Vienna to serve Budapest and Bucharest. The line through the Alps was by way of the Semmering Pass but in 1906 the Simplon Tunnel was opened so offering a more direct route to Turkey. Thus two entirely separate trains were introduced, the Turkish portion being named 'Simplon—Orient Express' and the original — now boring through the Alps by way of the Arlberg Tunnel — the 'Arlberg—Orient Express'.

Italy was included in the route of the Direct Orient — as the Swiss insisted upon calling the Istanbul-bound train — in 1919 as a result of the defeat of Germany and Austria in World War One. In the 'holier than thou' attitude taken by the Allies at the time of the Treaty of Versailles the idea of a grand express of international repute crossing the tainted ground was repugnant. And with the opening of the Simplon Tunnel between Brig and

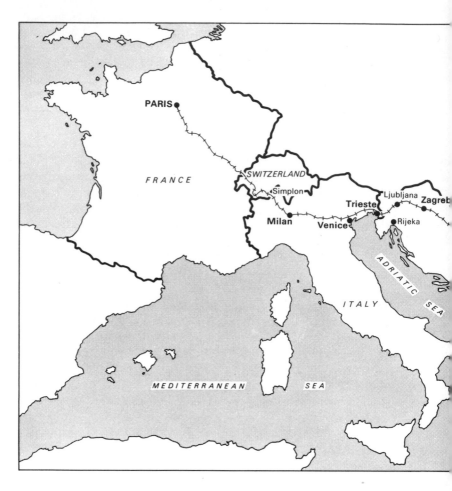

Domodossola the way to Italy was assured. This well pleased the
Italians who were building a gigantic showpiece station at Milan
and wanted a prestigious train to grace it. Beyond lay a newly-
created Yugoslavia with which France was anxious to establish
friendly relations so, supported by the Swiss and the Dutch, the
Direct-Orient Express was born offering sleeping and dining car
service right through to Istanbul and also Athens.

Since then, in spite of another war and subsequent political

PARIS–ISTANBUL   Key

+++++ rail route

BLACK SEA

Belgrade

YUGOSLAVIA

Nis

Sofia

BULGARIA

Plovdiv

Edirne

ISTANBUL

TURKEY

GREECE

division of Europe the ramifications of the Orient Express 'complex' spread to include Prague and today there remains not only a Balt-Orient Express serving Berlin, Prague and Bucharest but also an actual Orient Express following, still, the original lines between Paris, Vienna, Budapest and Bucharest.

I was whizzed through France at commendable speed but at Vallorbe and the Swiss border my Express faltered and shrank to

17

a commuter's special stopping at all stations and, sometimes, in between. The rock-infested greenery of Switzerland ended with the Simplon Tunnel and we came out the other side into a world of powdery white snow. But the pure whiteness soon lost its virginity as the train dropped down to the Lombardy plain and crept for comfort into the great soulless metropolis of Milan, prosperous and commercial, thriving but shivering in a cold drizzle.

At the Franco-Swiss border we had lost our restaurant car and in place of it we had been subjected to an abomination called a 'tray meal service'. As we ambled interminably towards Venice I found the cold fare as tasteless as the plastic tray that bore it.

Trieste, in contrast to Milan, was having a foretaste of summer and as we entered the dry, sullen landscape the chirping of crickets defied the calendar. In sympathy the sea switched from green to blue.

It was with some trepidation that I watched the train zig-zag up the steep incline to the Yugoslav frontier station of Cezana. Hardly eighteen months had elapsed since at this very place I had effected the iron curtain escape of my Czech brother-in-law. In so doing I had 'bent' a number of Yugoslav laws and so had cause to wonder whether authority had caught up with me. If so, here was its chance to pounce. A variety of officials passed in and out of the nearly empty train but only one took close interest in me. Having burrowed in my passport several times he made close reference to a note-book containing, presumably, a list of undesirables. I waited, my fingers firmly crossed, and though the man combed the pages thoroughly my name, it seemed, was not among the legion of the damned. Let me explain . . .

We met, my brother-in-law and I, on the sun terrace of the Hotel Kontinental, Rijeka in Yugoslavia, that sun-drenched Sunday afternoon. The warmth of Paul's handshake spoke more eloquently than his limited English, of his pleasure at seeing me. An exchange of coded telegrams had brought me a thousand miles by Direct-Orient Express from England, and him more than half that distance from his native Czechoslovakia. For Paul the journey was to shape the destiny of his life, and I was the prop to help him effect it.

For twenty years Paul had been dreaming of leaving his country for the security of the West. He had paid for one attempt to turn the dream into reality with the nightmare of a year's imprisonment. Since that time, though a skilled technician, he had drifted from one menial job to another. The fact that he had 'western connections' — a sister-in-law (my wife) living in England — was, in the official files, a further mark against him. But the connection worked for him too and, with the excesses of Stalinism past, his wife, Mary, was occasionally allowed to visit us in England. Paul had to remain behind, a living guarantee that she would return. Yet Paul knew that those few short weeks, when his government irregularly allowed Mary beyond the gates, were his only opportunity for both of them to find freedom. At first he could not synchronise his own and Mary's movements. Either Mary was refused an exit permit to visit England, or Paul's application to visit Yugoslavia with its all-important border with the West was delayed until her safe return. In 1967 restrictions on travel to the Eastern bloc countries were eased still further. By careful planning it was possible to reach Yugoslavia without the immediate knowledge of the Secret Police. And that June Mary had gone to England.

We left Rijeka together in Paul's small car and, threading our way past the hulks of half-completed ships, ascended the heights behind the town. The heat of the sun was beginning to die, and we had two hours in hand to reach Vogliano, a hamlet, seventy kilometres away, that I had designated to be Paul's crossing point into Italy.

The day before, with Tony, a companion who spoke Italian, I had reconnoitred the area behind Trieste, and, in so doing, had come upon Monrupino. From the church that perched atop the dramatic little hill, the border looked unguarded, unwatched, tranquil. An Italian peasant, seeing our interest, had pointed out the invisible line of the frontier curving along the middle of the valley that lay before us. Our eyes had taken in a watch-tower at a rural checkpoint near Vogliano village and another on the brow of a hill. But dusk or darkness and an abundance of trees and thick scrub would hide a trespasser. There was, allegedly, no minefield or wire. No movement of border guards could be seen.

19

With Tony watching from Monrupino church, the plan was for me to accompany Paul to within twenty yards of the border, create, if necessary, a diversion and the job would be done. I would return to the car alone and make my way to Monrupino via the main check point at Cezana. Thus we would all meet up again on Italian territory, the job done.

Paul and I drove towards Vogliano, which we had chosen to be our base for the operation. It was not easy to find, for my Yugoslav map was both out of date and inaccurate. We came upon the checkpoint — the one Tony and I had seen the day before — when we least expected to and hastily turned, and drove back to the cluster of houses that had hidden the junction to Vogliano village.

We left the car beneath a tree and locked it. Vogliano was indicated as '1 Km', the route being no more than a cart track. Taking advantage of the remaining daylight, we decided upon an open reconnaissance of the area to locate a good, well-sheltered section of the border where we would hide up until dusk or darkness. The track ran westwards, roughly parallel with the border. On our left, the silhouette of Monrupino church stood out starkly on its mound against a blood-red sunset. Somewhere up there amid the granite walls Tony would be watching and waiting.

Abruptly we were in the village. But something was different about the small cluster of houses that hemmed us in. The street was empty though we felt the eyes of its citizens upon us. An old man, sucking his ancient pipe, surveyed us morosely from a doorway. A lame dog skulked by to turn and bark defiance — the only noise in a community of silence.

Around the corner we glimpsed a striped barrier pole. We sheered away but not quickly enough. A shout brought us to a halt. A policeman, buckling on a pistol belt, emerged from a house. He asked us where we were going and what we were doing, and taking it for granted that we were both British, told us we were in a forbidden zone and must leave immediately. We retreated hastily.

Halfway back along the track, out of sight of the village, we slipped into an orchard with the intention of concealing ourselves until nightfall. But we had not allowed for the craftiness of the policeman. His suspicions aroused by Paul's dark features, he silently followed to emerge standing over us, a pistol in his hand.

We had fewer explanations this time. Stretched out under a hedgerow within yards of the frontier strip what *could* one say? He ordered us to accompany him. In silence we tramped a mile or more to the checkpoint.

In the office of the customs house we were questioned in turn, our replies being thumped out on a typewriter. A number of telephone calls were made. My answers were intentionally vague and, to my relief, the questioning came to a halt when a home-going Italian, dazed by a surfeit of slivovitz, ran his motorcycle full-tilt into the frontier pole.

In all we remained three hours in the customs house, watching the night blot out the tantalising view of Monrupino. I thought of the unfortunate Tony patiently waiting. It was quite dark when an officer arrived and we were taken first in a police car, and then in Paul's car with an escort, to the township of Cezana. Here, in the barrack-like surroundings of a police station we were questioned again. Only when I intimated angrily that I would report matters later to my consul which would detrimentally affect relations between Britain and Yugoslavia, particularly the tourist boom the latter was enjoying, did the atmosphere become more friendly. Abruptly we were handed back our passports and, to my amazement, released.

Abandoning this initial plan of action I left Paul at a local hotel and, taking his car, returned across the border for the bright lights of Trieste having picked up Tony en route.

With me back on Yugoslav territory next day, Paul and I gazed across the vast expanse of tree-shrouded hills, our eyes roving up and over the double crest. My heart sank at the formidable task that I had set my brother-in-law. He himself was plainly aghast. The early afternoon sun beat down with cruel intensity — an added challenge to the unknown hazards of the frontier that ran along the reverse slope of the second crest.

For the second attempt I had selected a remoter crossing point. Thickly wooded hills off the beaten track seemed to offer the best way out. With a troubled heart and a powerful longing to accompany him, I left Paul on a forgotten dust road somewhere between the hamlets of Vallegrande and Pliscovizza di Madonna. But it was essentially a one-man job. Tony and I would meet him in the Italian village of Sgonico on the other side. We would wait all night if necessary. Paul plainly hated my leaving, and I hated myself for the brutal way I was pushing him into hideous danger. But it had to be done. Either that or surrender. In the driving mirror I watched him, a sad forlorn figure, swallowed up in a cloud of dust.

In the village of Sgonico, a mile and a whole world the other side of the border, Tony and I waited. We were safe and comfortably settled in a vine-sheltered *albergo,* but the waiting seared my soul as the doubts piled into it. Had I sent a man to savage captivity or even death? Had I failed his wife who waited? Had I failed my own whose faith I carried? And fear grew in the abyss of my torment.

In the afternoon I walked deep into the border area as the urge to share Paul's burden of danger stirred restlessly within me. Later a storm broke with violent abruptness. Tony and I finished our umpteenth beer and watched the lightning lash the roofs and walls of Sgonico with vivid hate. Thunder rolled. Our companions in the *albergo* gave up their suspicious attention of us and likewise watched the storm. No rain came to Sgonico that night, but we could hear its angry hiss as it fell on the trees in the hills. There was no sign of Paul so, once more, Tony and I returned, disconsolately to our hotel in Trieste.

It was not until later that I heard how Paul had fared. In the intense heat of the afternoon and on into the refuge of the evening, he had struggled through the dense undergrowth, over two ranges of hills and, in the vicinity of the border, had come upon a telephone line. Foolishly he had followed it and found himself amongst a collection of houses occupied by border guards. An Alsatian dog had caught his scent and jumped to its feet just as the storm struck. That the downpour which soaked him was providence, Paul found hard to appreciate as soaked to the skin, he had slunk back whence he came, a second defeat adding to his misery.

At least Paul was alive and at liberty and a great weight was lifted from my mind. But he was still not free. The direct assault on the border was paying no dividends. A more subtle method would have to be employed.

It was Tony who came up with the third plan. We had already discarded the concealment-in-the-car-boot idea for I had noticed the random car searches at the border. The odds were too high against it. But a 'doctored' passport? We had two identity photographs of Paul, three of my cancelled passports and Tony's talent at our disposal.

With a cheap ballpoint pen, a penknife and a pot of paste he went to work. And as the sun proclaimed mid-morning Tony produced a small miracle. The result was, perhaps, not perfection, but under perfunctory inspection and artificial light the passport would fool anyone. Close scrutiny of that portion of the indented Foreign Office stamp that was on the photograph *might* produce criticism. But it was worth the risk.

I walked through the Cezana crossing point around midday using the 'doctored' passport equipped with my own photograph. It was stamped, given a quick but careful glance, and I was in. So far so good. I met Paul at his hotel, and over lunch outlined the plan to him. He agreed at once with the idea.

The passport of an outgoing traveller was not stamped by the Yugoslav border officials, but the ingoing stamp was verified and the document more carefully scrutinised. It was International Tourist Year and, to suit the occasion, no visas were required. The Italians only glanced at passports and took the registration numbers of cars.

I walked back into Italy without difficulty, still using the same passport. The waiting Tony then substituted Paul's photograph for my own. Hiding it in Paul's car and using his own passport, he drove into Yugoslavia, deposited the car and 'special' passport with Paul and returned.

Again the waiting, and the doubts. Would some smart Alec recognise the car or the driver? I had passed through the checkpoint a dozen times within forty-eight hours. Twice the car had stalled, and its exhaust pipe being punctured caused a sensational noise. But if the car *was* becoming a familiar sight, would a different driver be noticed? And Paul? Would he be recognized by one of the many policemen who had seen him under interrogation two nights previously?

Paul spent the afternoon washing the car. A clean car was a less conspicuous car. As he polished the coachwork, Paul contemplated his emergency instructions.

Tony and I were also thinking of them as we moved up to the Italian barrier. If Paul, waiting in the car, was recognized he was to put his foot hard down on the accelerator and crash the border. Tony would yell a warning to the Italian officials, and I was to place myself directly in the line of fire. I didn't think they would shoot. I had a pathetic faith in International Tourist Year.

It was five to ten at night. 'Zero hour' was ten, but Paul was to wait until a couple or more cars had formed a queue on his side of the border. With a few cars in front he would have a chance to look before he leapt.

The minutes crawled by. I watched one, two, three cars come through. Then a gap. Only one Yugoslav was on passport duty, but others hung around. A machine-gun slit in a concrete blockhouse leered at me. Another car came into the yellow sphere of light fifty yards away. Ten o'clock. The car passed through. Tony and I moved close up against the Italian customs house. The palms of my hands were sticky and my mouth was dry.

Suddenly, like a star-turn in a cabaret, Paul's car was transfixed in the spotlight. I watched him hand the passport to the Yugoslav. The man flipped through the pages, glanced up at the driver, then spoke. I saw Paul nod. A moment of eternity as nothing happened. The passport was handed back with a brief salute. The car leaped forward — and stalled. I heard the starter whine and the engine catch. The Yugoslav turned at the high-pitched screech of the punctured exhaust, but the car was at the Italian barrier. I hardly saw the brief formalities repeated. It mattered no more. Paul was free.

There is no room for sentiment in the communist mentality, and though only a light shade of pink, Yugoslavia had to debunk still further the remaining shreds of glory that clung to the Orient Express after its whistle-stop tour of northern Italy. During the long wait at Cezana a number of very local coaches and even a couple of cattle trucks had joined the train. We had sunk to the level of what the Germans call a *personenzug* and even had to play second fiddle to the connection for Rijeka which left before us.

From the balmy warmth of Trieste we plunged again into thick snow at Ljubljana. It lay, admittedly thawing, heavy upon the ground and in spite of a switch from electric to steam traction the Yugoslav Federal State Railway deemed it necessary to ration the central heating. I sat shivering in semi-darkness until the blaze of light that was Zagreb.

Almost immediately my compartment was invaded by a squad of young soldiers with an arsenal of weapons and implements festooned about them. I gave up three of the four seats along which I had been reclining with little reluctance for it had been too cold for sleep. My new companions eyed me for a few moments discussing my probable nationality amongst themselves. I heard myself labelled German, American, Norwegian and French before the list foundered in a welter of Serbo-Croat. At least they had an answer for the lack of heat. A corporal with an india-rubber face produced a lemonade bottle of slivovitz and passed it round. Each took a substantial swig the last hesitatingly passing the bottle to me. The fire water bit into my entrails and I said 'Danke schön' and then 'Thank you'. The corporal was the scholar. 'Engleski?' he enquired eager to prove his superior knowledge. I nodded and his face broke into a grin. Forthwith I became an honorary member of the Yugoslav Army. Two more bottles followed the first and the swigs became gulps. We held long incomprehensible conversations in which the occasional word that was universally understood became a signal for celebration and therefore more slivovitz. When the heat came on an hour later it didn't really matter for we were all dozing happily on each other's shoulders.

Uninterrupted sleep was effectively denied us however by the repeated incursions into the compartment of the ticket collector. A thin, lugubrious individual, he obviously held a low opinion of the army and smelt a fish regarding the collective travel voucher held by the corporal. For those of us who cared to look, dawn illuminated the most featureless section of the journey so far.

Right up to Belgrade the flooded plain offered a dismal picture of a vast sea of mud. Dotted thinly across the landscape tiny villages, like islands, clung to almost impassable mud roads that were their only link with civilisation.

At Belgrade Central Station my military companions departed and my compartment became as empty as their lemonade bottles. The train gave me a circular tour of the city (an apparently necessary procedure when transferring from one platform to another) but my impressions of the Yugoslav capital were not flattering.

The status of my compartment rose, however, with the entry of an Italian lady and a Yugoslav Airforce officer. They were separate but lost no time in repairing this state of affairs even though both stoutly clung to their mother tongues in the dialogue that ensued. The officer wore a superbly creased uniform and a David Niven moustache while the focal point of the lady was a red gash of a mouth clamped round a cigarette. Plainly the uniform meant more than the budding acquaintanceship to the gallant captain, for a tremendous spring-cleaning operation was put into motion before the sea-green trousers were allowed contact with the seat. Flicking the sparse furnishings with a lace hanky he next covered the seat with sheets of my discarded newspaper upon which I had previously deposited my feet. Various items of outer apparel were carefully folded and stowed on the newly-polished rack before the lesser business of wooing could begin.

From the little snippets of Italian I could understand it became plain that she was not a hundred percent responsive. I watched the blue smokescreen from her cigarette ascend in ever-thickening spirals all but obscuring the no-smoking notices, and coughed pointedly. The officer noticed my stare of disapproval, was obviously in sympathy and handed me a peppermint as a peace offering. It was the first of many from an unending supply.

Whenever he could see his new girlfriend through the fog he would lean forward and dash off an ode in Serbo-Croat. She responded with marked less enthusiasm and eventually it got through to him that she was cold. With enormous chivalry the captain threw caution to the winds and wrapped his overcoat around her knees. I watched his eyes trying to avoid the sight of a sleeve trailing in the dirt on the floor. But it was all in vain. The train rattled into Nis and in Nis lay his duty. Almost despairingly he swept up his coat, threw us each a last peppermint and fled.

Approaching the Dragoman Pass the railway has to bore a way through the northern buttresses of the Balkan Mountains. The pass itself, a winding chasm in which the single track and the flooded tributary of the Nisova river became all but one, was curtained by a blizzard. At Dimitrovgrad the Bulgarian customs had their pound of flesh and, by the simple expedient of turning our bags upsidedown, were able to effect their examination. Italian female and British male underwear lay strewn over the seats like a Women's Institute rummage sale.

I was still struggling to close my bag when the train slowed at the suburbs of Sofia. I was to break my journey at the Bulgarian capital and though I had doubts of its likely attractions — doubts built upon experience of other communist shrines — the city seemed worthy of a visit.

Accordingly I bade 'Arrivederci' to my companion and for the first time in fifty hours left the train. At first I thought I had made a mistake and alighted at the wrong station, so small and rural it was, but I was soon put right when someone rather pointedly, told me that the original edifice had been bombed by the Americans. I have since seen the new station but Sofia remains, in my book, the dullest city in the Balkans.

With no Bulgarian money, lugging a heavy suitcase and with every sign written in an incomprehensible script I would have had difficulty in locating the city centre even by public transport. But every square inch of every tram was occupied inside and out, and with long queues at the stops as well, I struggled along what turned out to be Georgi Dimitrov Street simply on account of the fact that the tramlines looked denser in that direction. I stopped at a restaurant to enquire about hotels and a kind waitress, who spoke a word or two of English, directed me to Lenin Square. She also pressed a tram ticket on me and explained the system by which one purchases tickets — usually in blocks — at kiosks prior to boarding the vehicle. An element of trust is involved since you clip your own ticket, but should a check uncover a ticketless or un-clipped passenger the penalties are severe. I carried on walking.

Suddenly to my joy I was in Vladimir Iljic Lenin Square — though the 'Little Father' seldom inspired such emotion in my heart — and straightway found myself in the centre of a gang-fight. Joy switched to alarm as a squad of pistol-wielding police-men waded into the knot of fighting youths. One of the contestants ran into me and sprawled head first over my suitcase with a policeman on top of him. Hastily I retired to safer regions.

My bleats for assistance in finding a hotel at first met with no response until, at the fifth attempt, a group of citizens abruptly realised that I was British. There followed a rush to claim me. Following much gesticulating and airing of school-book English I was marched off to the imposing if shabby portals of the Grand Hotel.

I had not intended to aim so high but, my squad of chaperons drawn up behind me, I made enquiries about room prices and availability. It was then that I remembered being told of a private accommodation service that existed in Bulgaria. Not only would it be cheaper but a sojourn there would offer an insight into a Bulgarian home.

My further enquiry led me and my retinue round the corner to the still-open offices of 'Balkontourist', the state tourist agency to which I should have reported in the first place.

'English!' exclaimed the girl clerk behind the desk, 'Sorry but I fear we can offer you only a German-speaking host'.

'That'll do fine,' I replied with optimistic trust in my extremely limited German, and no sooner was it said than it was done — for there stood my host at my elbow.

I am quite sure that my escorts would have come to blows over which of them was to accommodate me had they understood what was going on. No doubt some of them had a smattering of English too but probably none was registered as fit and reliable — politically — to play host to a foreigner from the West. As it was, a great deal of bewildered muttering ensued as, paying the small service charge, my host and I escaped into the street. Next I had to change some travellers cheques at the nearby bank but even with that done my new friend insisted upon treating me to a taxi to his home off the Ninth of September Street. I tried to remember who liberated who on the ninth of September but failed.

28

The two days that followed were full of interest. Being a week-end, my host was free and so gave me the complete Cook's tour of Sofia: the vaults of the Alexander Nevsky Cathedral, the nause-ating spectacle of Dimitrov's embalmed corpse in its see-through casket, the museum of the revolutionary movement full of rusty machine-guns and fragments of underground newspapers, the Church of St Sophia and, topically, the finish of a People's Army long-distance relay race at the Liberation Memorial. Here the panting runners were supposedly revitalised by the sight of fresh hoardings extolling the unbreakable bond of Bulgarian-Soviet friendship. One contestant was violently sick at the finishing line but I think this was due to exhaustion.

Only once did I bring up the subject of politics with my host. I asked him what he thought of his own army being amongst those of the Warsaw Pact who marched into Czechoslovakia to sup-press the freedoms offered by the short-lived Dubcek regime. 'The Czechs asked for trouble and got it', he replied with some heat. Though he professed not to be a member of the communist party his sympathy seemed not to be at variance with it. I noticed another thing too. Sofia was the only communist capital I knew of where political slogans continued to be an accepted part of the landscape. But so were packed churches.

For our midday meals we patronised the People's 'Help Your-self' restaurants that appeared to be popular with diners of all walks of life. The food was certainly cheap but exceedingly nasty. Consisting mainly of various types of sausage, beans, shredded onion and chips it was served luke-warm on badly-washed plates. The beer, in unlabelled bottles, might have been what they washed them in. For an hors d'oeuvre we frequented a more classy establishment which appeared to specialise in home-baked bread consumed with a 'dip' of pepper. Too much of the latter and it blew your head off. Whether it was because of the explosive properties of the dip, I'm not sure but the waiters wore masks. Hygiene is taken seriously in the more up market estab-lishments with barbers and food shop assistants invariably wearing masks likewise. Maybe one day it'll spread to the people's restaurants.

Struggling with a little-known language does not bode well for

29

prolonged friendship and I think the feeling of relief was mutual when the time came to see me off on the evening train, the same diesel-hauled express I had left forty eight hours before. As my host watched me go, I caught a wistful expression on his face and in it I saw the bemusement of Bulgaria. It is a country that has consistently backed the wrong horse. Her lost province of Macedonia is a red flag to a bull and Britain was instrumental in the removal of it. Bulgaria thus supported Germany in both world wars though, in 1944, changed sides. Even her life-long friend (if technically her temporary enemy) — the Soviet Union — advanced over her territory as both liberator and conqueror. The shadow remains to this day.

Ensconced in a corner seat, my mind began sorting out the living habits peculiar to train travel. Hard experience has given me an insight into the art of sleeping on trains without recourse to wagon-lit. Coaches vary; most second-class compartments cater for a complement of eight: four to each seat with an arm in the middle. Very occasionally it is only six. Outside the tourist season numbers in a compartment seldom exceed six for long and by spreading oneself or giving an impression that one is holding a seat for a friend it is usually possible to discourage unwanted bodies when mass intrusion threatens. And it is surprising what can be done with a neighbouring empty seat. Padding the hard arm rest in the corner with a jacket or coat for a pillow, some degree of comfort can be attained by curling up like a cat. Three changes of position can be achieved as soon as cramp sets in and a stretch of the legs can be accomplished upwards over the central head rest. But I was still a novice at these procedings as the Direct-Orient Express shuffled towards the Greek and Turkish borders, and I tied myself in knots.

An impressive Russian-built diesel unit led us to Plovdiv and then stole away into the night as if ashamed of having hauled a train brandishing such reactionary names as PARIS, LAUSANNE and VENICE. Thereafter we were steam. Until Bulgaria's second city my travelling companions not only numbered the full complement of eight but were the roughest bunch of cut-throats imaginable. The ticket inspector, on seeing them, raised his eyes to heaven and gave me a pitying glance. Making sure my wallet lay close to my skin I prepared for the worst. Soon I was the object of a merciless interrogation but again, upon learning of my nationality, I became exhibit number one and was treated with a deference that accorded to my status. It was only the acrid smoke of seven stupefying cigarettes that caused me relief when Plovdiv emptied the compartment.

I saw nothing of Plovdiv to send me into raptures on that particular journey but a subsequent visit I made to the city allows me to put the record straight. Roughly midway between Sofia and the Turkish border it was once known as Phillippopolis under Philip II of Macedonia, later the Roman city of Trimontium, the entire central area is built upon Roman foundations. Today it displays with a certain pride the recently-excavated Roman amphitheatre and, in particular, its lion-gateway abutting the main shopping street, now a pedestrian precinct. The Old Quarter remains timeless and is characterised by ancient colour-washed buildings with upper storeys overhanging the cobbled streets, and passageways that lead from one intricately lamp-posted, flower-bedecked square to the next. The houses are lived in too; they're not simply museum pieces, and Plovdiv plainly takes lively interest in her preservation and upkeep as though aware it needs to counteract the numbing standardisation of the regulation square and parade ground loud with crimson poster-art, that mars its heart.

Leaving Bulgaria without so much as a whiff of skulduggery offended my sense of anticipation but other than by pulling the communication cord or throttling the ticket inspector I saw no hope of villainous incident on this trip. Even the train itself bore no resemblance to the Orient Express of popular imagination, its rolling stock reduced to shabby Yugoslav coaches, a restaurant car, a through-sleeper plus two German coaches that would be detached any moment for their defection onto the Athens Line. The lone Wagon-Lit was the only vehicle bearing the slightest aura of grandeur and it stuck out like a sore thumb that no murdered spy would be seen dead on. And, you wouldn't believe it, but the restaurant car was to be taken off at Svilengrad to serve the Athens section of the train thus leaving the residue of its clients meal-less to Istanbul. In this rag-tag condition we limped into the final portion of the journey.

31

The builders of the main line out of Bulgaria could hardly be blamed for the convulsions of history that, in the course of a few years, made Edirne Russian, Turkish, Bulgarian, Turkish again, Greek, and now once more Turkish. Hence the line passed unnecessarily twice through slices of Greece and with no love lost between Greeks, Bulgarians and Turks, the Greeks insisted upon a long and thorough passport and customs check both going in and out of their territory. This was just one expression of a hate that simmered beneath the surface as the three belligerents kicked each other under the table to the detriment of the innocent traveller. Fortunately a new line has since been constructed that by-passes Greek landscape making life easier for all.

Even in a state of semi-consciousness I had been able to tell when we were on Greek soil and not Turkish. The rhythm of the wheels had increased to a rapid tempo — like light infantry on the march — as we passed over short lengths of rail. Laid thus for easy handling instead of being welded and placed by mechanical track-layer the remote areas of Greece were the last European strongholds of this old-fashioned method of railway building.

The dawn made amends for the petty quarrelling of man. Creeping up over the low hills came a gory football of a sun dyeing the barren scrub-covered land an unnatural orange. A profusion of wild snowdrops, crocuses and fluffy tumbleweed gleamed like fireflies through a crimson haze. My latest companions — a trio of Yugoslav students — stirred and rose from their various contorted positions of sleep as the train crawled across the rolling downs of European Turkey. My portable electric shaver went the rounds for which service I was presented with a free breakfast of the previous day's bread rolls, dollops of jam and a shot of slivovitz.

City of a hundred wars, Edirne lay stretching in the cold dawn. The river Tunja joins the Maritza here, the combining streams giving exclusively to Edirne a green belt that makes it the envy of other towns on the edge of the Orient. Against the fleeing night I could see the minarets of the imperial mosque of Selim II presenting a fairy-tale castle appearance amongst the clutter of mean, irregular wooden houses, threaded by narrow, tortuous streets. As a frontier town it is vulnerable to attack, which is possibly the reason why its development was retarded. Very much an outpost of Turkey it is nevertheless fiercely Turkish and the crescent flags in the station wore a defiant air. Until the fall of Constantinople it was the capital of the Ottermans. At the battle of Adrianople — as the city was called — the Roman legions were defeated by Gothic chivalry, a milestone in military history.

The first hamlets with their white sentinel minarets speckled the countryside each supplying a quota of waving villagers to welcome a train that went by three times and more every week of their lives. Their numbers and fervour increased as our panting locomotive hauled us up and over the crest of one of the hills. Below lay Istanbul. By midday we had reached the sea and leaving the International Airport on our left wound our way beneath the walls of Topkapi into the last outpost of Europe.

Istanbul. What can one say about this fabled city that nobody has said a thousand times before. But its magic was slow to filter through to me that warm and sunny afternoon. Maybe I was tired but my first impressions as I strolled through the old city of Stamboul were cynical and unkind. Take away the mosques and minarets and you have a vast slum stretching across seven hills and divided by an oily waterway. A loud, overcrowded slum hooting and yelling and flaunting its poverty.

And then as I walked the spell was woven and through the dirt and squalor I saw Istanbul in all its magnificence.

The magic lies in the people. The slick leather-jacketed traffic police, the Bosphorus ferry captains, the tough, untidy soldiers, the voluble vendors of everything under the sun, the orange-squeezers, the illegal money-changers, the waiters, shop assistants, priests and the vast mosaic of humanity that *is* Istanbul. For three days I explored its labyrinth of streets on foot and by communal taxi and wherever I went friendly smiling citizens, rich and poor, accosted me offering advice and greeting. Even the street vendors of Istanbul have a special quality about them, a transaction being of secondary importance to a complicated conversation with an out-of-season Britisher.

A voyage up the Bosphorus in one of the many ferries hooting their way across the busy straights gave me, for an outlay of little more than a shilling, an insight into the growing spread of the city, its suburbs now licking the Black Sea, Uskudar, Galata-Besiktas, the double fortress of Rumeli Hisar and Anadolu Hisar, Beykoz and beyond. The vessel's captain came over to talk with me and as we sipped our small glass beakers of tea I learnt something of the respect and trust with which his profession is held throughout Turkey. It was raining when we returned to the ferry terminus by the muddled Galata Bridge but the magic could not be doused.

I have been back to Istanbul on many occasions since this journey and it remains an exciting city. But for me it has become a springboard; not a terminal, for adventure. Invariably my eyes turn towards Asia and the Orient for there lies the prospect of truly eventful journeying on trains unburdened with glories that won't quite die.

2

The Taurus Express

HAYDARPASA—BAGHDAD

The Turkish Railway of Europe and that of Asia are, to all intents and purposes, different rail systems. The Bosphorus ensures that the traveller ends his journey at Sirkeci Station Istanbul since there is no such amenity as a through-train rail ferry or even an attempt at a timetable link between the two sections of railway. For Asia and the east the journey starts at Haydarpasa, a twenty-five-minute community taxi ride via the Bosphorus suspension bridge or three-quarters of an hour by ferry if you time your connections right. A footnote in *Cook's Continental Time-table* warns intending passengers in direct transit via Istanbul to allow up to eight hours for connection between trains and I had also been told that the Taurus Express was invariably up to six hours late at its destination. This seemed to me a gross exaggeration. No rail service could be *that* far out in its schedules surely. I was to live and learn.

Haydarpasa Station is an Istanbul landmark in its own right, though the giant building houses quite a small terminus. I made for the ticket office, bent upon requesting permission to make my round trip across Turkey the other way round to that shown on my batch of tickets previously obtained in London. This was too big a decision for the chief ticket clerk and so I was ushered into the august presence of the station-master tucked behind an immense desk attended by his minions. My request was heard with old-world courtesy and the machinery of ticket endorsement put into ponderous motion. Because I would be conveyed an additional 150 kilometres on the outward journey on the Turkish portion of the journey (even though it would be correspondingly less on the return) I would have to be surcharged four lira eighty, or about 25p, which did not strike me as all that scandalous — particularly as, the formalities completed, I was invited to share a

35

cognac to clinch the deal.

Statistics show that the present mileage of the Turkish Railway totals around 5,000 miles. When compared with Sweden which is equally mountainous, considerably smaller but with almost double the track mileage, it will be appreciated that the railway in Turkey is somewhat thin on the ground. But what there is constitutes a considerable engineering feat (in the Taurus Mountains there are 22 tunnels within just over 30 miles), in spite of the fact that much of the network is single track and non-electrified.

A history of the Turkish Railway becomes a study in politics. Construction of the railway began in 1888, when a German company secured permission to build the Anatolian Railway running from Haydarpasa to Ankara via Eskehir and, later, Konya. Following the state visit to Constantinople by Kaiser Wilhelm II a convention was signed between the two countries granting the German Anatolian Railway an extension to Kuwait, on the Persian Gulf. This was but another concession in support of

Germany's *Drang nach Osten* (Drive to the East) that was the frustrated envy of politicians in Britain, France and Russia.

But opinion in Britain at least was divided. Largely out of a dislike for France and Russia considerable support was given to the Germans and their plans to push the railway through to Baghdad by way of two routes. One was the old imperial route of the Romans through Angora (Ankara) and Shivas; the other followed the valley of the Meander river and over the enormous bulk of the Taurus Mountains to Adana and into the plains of Mesopotamia.

The German line had got as far as Basra when the war came in 1914 and four years later Allenby's armies swept through much of the area capturing vast amounts of rolling stock and equipment. Thereafter the dream of economic conquest changes its nationality. But British railway concept was more ambitious still. As well as the link with Baghdad a line south through Beirut, Haifa and Gaza to Cairo was proposed. By 1930 the Paris—Baghdad route by the Orient and Taurus Expresses was a reality and the timetables of the years before the Second World War involved the whole Eastern European and Middle Eastern complex.

Since then the realisation of the dream has withered with the growth of air travel and the post 1939-45 war situation in the Middle East. Turkey has taken over, one by one, the lines originally built with European rather than Turkish money and, in support of her more modest dreams, has built lines linking the Anatolian routes with the Black Sea and the Persian frontier. The Cook's Grand Tour for elegant ladies and dashing gentlemen was discreetly dropped from the agency's brochure and the romance of a journey from Paris to Baghdad has become as faded as that of the destination boards on the Taurus coach sides.

Even so I was scandalised by the state of the present day Taurus Express. Never have I seen a filthier train (this was in 1969). The compartments were thick with grime and soot, the windows opaque with dirt, the seatless toilets an affront to humanity. To cap my disgust I had my first dispute with a Turk who demanded the equivalent of 50 pence for lifting my bag of his own accord onto the train. He got 5 pence and a rude Anglo-Saxon instruction. Gingerly I parked myself in the cleanest seat I could find, weighed up the position of various head and arm rests, and prepared to endure sixty hours of suffering.

By the time we moved out of the station I had with me in the compartment two Syrian youngsters and a quiet studious-looking Turk. A threatened invasion by three companions of the Syrians with a virtual mountain of luggage I successfully discouraged. I didn't much like the look of the ones I'd got with me and we sat glowering at each other as the suburbs of Istanbul evaporated into isolated villages and small towns.

Between Haydarpasa, Uskudar and Izmit the train made good time giving, outwardly, a reasonable imitation of an international express. The thickly populated plateau followed by the Turkish naval base drew all eyes in the compartment and in the general interest our hostility vanished. Forthwith I became the mascot of the Syrians and, one by one, their companions elsewhere in the train were invited into the compartment for an 'interview'. Politics, the topical politics of the Arab-Israeli conflict, quickly became the chief subject for discussion, our exchanges being carried out in a mixture of French and English.

There was no bitterness. For the Syrian Arabs the fact that England was, to them, backing the wrong horse, was simply reason for great sorrow. Nor was there great hate. The Israeli's of course had a right to live in peace. But not by stealing other people's land. I was forcibly reminded of a similar theme of thirty years before. Hitler called it *lebensraum*. Stolidly, as if uncomprehending, the studious Turk in the corner listened in silence to the tortuous debate. His countrymen had played it strictly neutral in *that* conflict, too . . .

One cannot travel far in Turkey without bumping into a mountain. In spite of its twists and turns the single line spanning the wild territory was unable to escape the inevitable and by midday we were in the awesome grip of a million-year-old result of a volcanic convulsion. Through enormous clefts in the rock barriers we crawled following the usual flooded river which had learnt the easiest route long before the railway. Hissing imposingly, its pistons pounding, the big steam locomotive dragged its

38

cargo at a walking pace up the severe incline. Given the slightest encouragement it stopped at the smallest of stations to allow northbound trains to pass. There would follow a frantic competition between thirsty locomotive and soot-covered passengers to take on water, the source frequently being one and the same. Vendors of food disembarked at every halt to make room for others to board the train with replenished stocks.

Food plays a vital part in a Turkish railway journey. In spite of a continuous cavalcade of vendors shouting their wares up and down the corridors every traveller carries huge stocks with him. To my amazement most of the bundles and boxes belonging to my Syrian and Turkish travelling companions contained loaves of bread, fruit, home-made cakes, joints of cooked meat and various bottles of liquid refreshment. Hardly an hour out of Haydarpasa and I was pressed to join the mêlée as Turk and Syrian pooled their resources and made swift inroads into them. As there was a restaurant car attached to the train I had purchased no more than the odd snack so my own contribution was nothing more than a couple of bars of chocolate and some Bulgarian cheese. But I was solemnly warned off the restaurant car. It's dirty, they said. I could well believe it!

Occasionally our rations were supplemented by delicacies from the vendors. These ranged from kebab, the roasting of which was carried out on the spot in little portable home-made charcoal burners, to a kind of Turkish delight and a sweet-meat that looked like cotton wool. Bargaining was surprisingly infrequent though my companions saw to it that in my few dealings with vendors I was not overcharged. One visitor into the compartment was a youth intent upon imparting the word of God. I suppose I looked a likely convert for he loosed onto me an unending torrent from the Scriptures (or perhaps the Koran). I nodded knowingly not wishing to hurt the man's feelings until my Syrians gleefully imparted the news to him that I was unable to understand a word he was saying.

The most un-Turkish city in Turkey is its capital. True, I only saw little of Ankara and this at night, but for the couple of hours I was able to wander in Ataturk Boulevard and Kizilay Square I might have been in Manchester or Milan. The citadel and the old town in the north were hidden by the night and an old woman in the baggy trousers of her country cousins drew stares as she waddled past the fashionable shops.

I arrived back at the station to discover that we had an uninvited guest in the compartment. He hadn't *come in* I was told; he had *fallen in*. Drunk as the proverbial lord my Syrian friends had propped him up in a corner seat, retrieved his spectacles and pipe, and dusted him down. Promptly he rolled full-length on the seat and, finding this to his liking, settled down for the night. Indignant at what we thought might be a ruse to obtain a whole length of seat to himself we pushed him back into his corner from whence the whole performance was repeated. How long this would have gone on had the contingencies of nature not taken a hand it was impossible to say. Suddenly he sat up and asked for the bathroom. We told him that this was not a royal train. 'Train,' he mumbled through his big drooping moustache as if he had never heard of such a phenomenon. 'What train?' We pushed him out into the corridor then drew the blinds and barricaded the door against his return. By this time Ankara was miles away. The poor devil was going to get a horrible shock to go with his hangover in the morning. We never saw him again.

Morning brought a stupendous sight. Looking out of the window and risking the showers of smuts, I saw the railway making a bee-line across the flat Anatolian plain straight for the enormous bulk of the Taurus Mountains. The dawn sun splashed on the vivid whiteness of the peaks, dazzling the eye and reflecting upon the wisps of cloud that hung to their summits.

For the next seven hours halts were numerous, both scheduled and unscheduled. The stations were simply clearings where a double track could be laid to allow for trains to pass. Life for the few inhabitants revolved around the arrival and departure of trains and children ran amok amongst the shunting wagons.

Having made the acquaintance of the engine driver the previous day at Kayseri when I had offered him a beer in the station bar during one of the unexplained delays I was henceforth accorded the special privilege of being allowed to walk alongside the train for much-needed exercise. As soon as the locomotive reached the top of a rise and was able to gather speed the driver

40

gave me two previously-arranged hoots on the whistle thus allowing me to rejoin my coach, an arrangement that gave pleasure to me and considerable amusement to my fellow travellers.

Great blobs of pink and white blossoms softened the sombre background of wild mountain scenery but as we climbed towards the snow-line this gradually gave way to barren rock. Herds of goats and, incongruously, the odd camel, were the only living things in the desolate region while, above, soared the occasional eagle. The train crept at no more than walking pace for mile after mile through ravine and chasm and upon attaining the little summit station an air of festivity infected both passengers and station staff as if reaching this point were cause for celebration.

From here onwards the locomotive became a hound unleashed. It pounded joyfully down the inclines, hissing and snorting, rushing through a series of tunnels, filling everything with acrid smoke and whistling shrilly. Already two hours behind schedule we were, not unnaturally, often held up by signals. This was excuse for the most ear-splitting crescendo of sound it has ever been my misfortune to hear. The mountains threw the echos back and forth and the longer the signal remained at red the more prolonged and angry was the banshee howl. I marvelled that such discord existed and that enough steam remained to drive the pistons before an unfortunate signalman, driven half-insane by the noise, allowed the train to proceed.

With black smoke, soot and showers of sparks from the locomotive pouring *in* through the window and charcoal smoke from our respective burners on the compartment floor trying to get *out* we paid dearly for our meals and each time the train dived into a tunnel complex we were all but asphyxiated. I wondered what Turkish railway bye-law we were breaking, but when the ticket-inspector passed upon his rounds his only action was to contribute culinary advice.

The peace of the Cilician Plain offered as much contrast as that of the fickle weather. Cold and showery in the mountains it was abruptly hot and humid. Our last halt before Adana was at Yenice. Here everyone issued from the train out onto the station for water both for drinking and washing purposes. Sharing the flow from the pump with the sweating locomotive the complement of my compartment stripped to the waist and scrubbed each other's backs, removing at last some of the ravages of travel and cookery. Refreshed and on the move again I watched the distant mountains revert to their picture-postcard remoteness as we ground into Adana three hours late, a state of affairs that worried nobody.

Adana is the third largest town in Turkey but you would never believe it; it is a typical old Turkish town with some brash twentieth century concrete structures thrust upon it. Narrow streets become quagmires when it rains as I know to my cost from subsequent sojourns in the place. Whenever I was to come this way again it was to find myself marooned in Adana.

This time, however, I was to remain on a train that had become my home. And I was especially pleased to do so for, characteristically, it began to rain. By the time we were back in the mountains the downpour had become a deluge. Dry rivers became gushing torrents very quickly indeed and, I think, it was the Aksu that was nearly our undoing. No doubt it was normally a well-behaved little stream, but the rains had turned it into a crazed brown torrent flecked with the saliva of madness. It had burst its banks and threatened the bridge. We stopped and from the windows we watched the driver and his mate issue forth from the big locomotive. Gingerly they proceeded onto the trestle structure and, near the centre, inched forward like nervous skaters on thin ice. A discussion, punctuated with much gesticulation, appeared to produce a decision and, drenched, the two men returned to the train.

Slowly, slowly we crept over that bridge. Nobody dared breathe and children in the corridor were restrained from jumping up and down. White faces watched the engine reach the other side then turned to peer fearfully down at the frothing avalanche of water tearing at the supports. After five of the longest minutes I can remember we were over.

With the exception of the Turk and myself we were a fresh batch in the compartment. I felt like a senior prefect amongst a batch of new boys and my strangeness caused many enquiring glances of the how-far-have-you-come, where-are-you-going variety. The mixture was much as before. But we had a lady amongst us — a young and not unattractive one at that — which could have created problems had she been going further than Aleppo.

The mountains were part of the Amanus range and a prelude to the plains of Syria. These mountains, glowering under the rain clouds, divided one country and way of life from another. Something about them reminded me of Scotland again. But when did Fort William sprout mosques? No, this was Fezzipasa, the Turkish border station and a high-flying Turkish flag was there to prove it. A crowd of men hung about the platform, wearing cloth caps and pre-1940 suits. I noticed only because I was becoming aware of Arab-dressed people in the stations.

Now the land was stilled and flat. A string of camels passed by going the other way. The unchanging East was with us and I never knew when it happened.

At Aleppo we were five hours late, yet the train remained a long and unexplained time in Syria's second city. I think it is because the northbound Taurus meets its counterpart here and the drivers like to swap notes and the current political gags from Istanbul and Baghdad. It has been the citadel that has impressed me most on subsequent visits to the city. With the exception of the pyramids this must surely be the largest man-made object on earth. Abraham may or may not have milked his cows on the summit but his name is the one most bandied about throughout its turbulent history.

The *souks* of Aleppo are without equal in the Orient. Their stone vaults and passages reek of history as old as Saladin. Donkeys and heavily-laden horses come down the narrow passageways as they have for centuries and at every turn there are marvels of colour and variety of wares. These *souks* give to Aleppo an identity of its own that is neither Turkish nor Damascene, and the aggressiveness of the selling has no equal in all the Mediterranean lands.

Hardly had I switched my mind to things Syrian and taken in a desert that encroaches to the very doorstep of Aleppo when, blow me, we were back in Turkey again. And we were to remain in Turkey, skirting the border all night. We were in a tangle of sleep at the second Turkish border village and authority was in no mood to inspect tiresome things like passports and visas. But

43

the second Syrian border was a different story. Furthermore it was the place I ran out of passport. I had often wondered what would happen when I arrived somewhere with a passport full to the brim with mauve ink. There had been occasions when the Soviet Union had refused to place their visa opposite that of the United States, and, once during the McCarthy era, I had been denied an American visa solely because of the presence, within the pages, of a hammer and sickle emblem of someone's people's republic. But I had never run out of space. Now I was to discover how Syrian authority would react to the situation. Nothing could be easier. They simply altered the dates and details of the cancelled visa, re-stamped it, charged me double and gave me a homily on the folly of not having enough blank pages.

More desert and we were at the Iraqi border where the train refused to move for an hour. And I had lost count of the hours we were late at Mosul.

The *raison d'être* of Mosul is Nineveh, the older city that I could see dimly across the River Tigris. The capital of the Assyrian Empire was destroyed by the Medes in 612 BC and nothing more was heard of it until the Sassanid period, when the existence of the town of Budh Ardashir is recorded. Mosul, meaning 'confluence' — that of the Wadi Khosar and the Tigris — first appears in 636 AD, as the name of the town on the right bank. It grew to a great city in the Abbasid period, a centre of commerce and industry, with fine mosques, markets and palaces. It remained so under successive dynasties until the destructive Mongols, and later Tamerlane, came along to spoil things. From these blows Mosul never fully recovered though its position in a fertile belt of oil-bearing land and on a main caravan route from Aleppo to Persia assures it a certain significance.

Before 1918 it had a reputation for dirt remarkable even in the Ottoman Empire, which is saying something. No doubt improvements have been made but I was unable to judge for myself. The railway skirts the city and goes on an excursion round the corporation cemeteries. I stared a long time at the distant mosques and with particular interest at one of them. The Great Mosque has taken a leaf out of Pisa's book and is supposed to lean to commercial advantage. But either the train was on the tilt or my Turkish friend's firewater was more potent than I thought for every minaret in sight stood as straight as a soldier.

The Tigris led us out of Mosul. We had picked up two new recruits at the station, including a massive tribesman of the desert. He looked naked without his camel though he was swarthed in a voluminous *djellabah* over which, for good measure, he had wound a carpet not much smaller than the one covering my dining room floor. It was a typically cool desert night, but this was ridiculous.

'You going far?' I enquired tentatively.

Someone seemed to understand. 'Yes,' I was told, 'we go Samara'.

'I go to Baghdad', this information arrived in the form of a rumble from out of the belly of my sheik opposite. He was afforded instant respect. Here was one of the compartment truly going far. But the small Turk in the corner could cap that one. He mentioned the name of a small place with a proud voice but as nobody had heard of it, his pronouncement fell a bit flat. I wondered where it could be for the train was going no further than Baghdad.

We were diesel-hauled now and the train trotted along contentedly with no gradients to endure. Beside us ran the Tigris like a tame serpent and at Samara we stopped at a station of some reckoning that had strayed from its town.

Our numbers down to four, our thoughts turned to food and the ceremony of the unswaddling of the bundles, and the positioning on the floor of the charcoal fires began. Soon we were feasting communally on joints of veal, pastries and a magnificent tart tenderly prepared by some unseen wife left behind in a forgotten village. A fresh bottle of the home-made liquid that could have been a by-product of petrol appeared from the Turkish quarter. It was shunned by some but not by me. It was night again and I had no desire to remain all that conscious. But at least there were no tunnels here or a steam engine to cause near-asphyxiation during the culinary preparations.

I actually slept that night to awake at the destination. I never even saw the suburbs of Baghdad before we ground into the Iraqi capital's grandiose West Station which looks better from the outside than it does within.

Baghdad: city of the Arabian Nights, of bejewelled caliphs and veiled women, rich in lore and legend. A hot and dusty city, a city of beggars and evil-smelling bazaars, an insanitary metropolis harbouring a hybrid collection of unclean and underfed humanity packed into narrow adobe cells called tenements. I found a little of all these descriptions on my first incursion into Baghdad and, as with Istanbul, its people are the jewels.

In Raschid Street I found the world. Silk-clad sheiks and slouching soldiers, Turks with bright headwear, Kurds in colourful faded robes, Assyrians and Armenians and an occasional American in slacks and a fresh-laundered shirt. The heartbeat of Iraq is felt the loudest in Raschid Street. It is a populous bitumen thoroughfare which runs through the centre of the city, the whole of its length from the southern gate to the northern, parallel to the Tigris, and is considered to be the Piccadilly Circus and Broadway of Baghdad though I'm damned if I could find any resemblance.

I stayed the night in an hotel called Happiness — though it certainly wasn't mine. The European hotels were, I learnt, miles out of town and, anyway I was short of funds, so one of the lowlier establishments would have to suffice. The proprietor had one eye and a gammy leg but a shrewd head for business. 'Two hundred fils' he asked for the best room.

'I'm not buying the house,' I explained.

'A hundred and fifty.'

'Fifty.'

'A hundred.'

'Seventy-five and not a penny more.' I turned to walk out of the door.

'OK, OK, the room is yours. Come and have tea.'

So I joined his friends in a dingy backroom for a most entertaining hour with a delightful bunch of ruffians who never once brought up the subject of money. I spent most of the night scratching and searching for the source of the irritation but I still maintain that I got a bargain. I'd been told bad things about Iraqis but it just goes to show how wrong people can be. Next morning a complete stranger invited me to lunch at his home. You'll find corpses hanging from lamp-posts, insisted my informant, but I found no such thing. Come to think of it I didn't even notice a lamp-post.

I spent another day in Baghdad but by the end of the first I was looking forward to the return journey. Where trains are concerned the coming and the going will always hold more attraction to me than the arrival.

3

The Trans-Siberian Railway

MOSCOW—VLADIVOSTOK

A global network of railways offers rich choice in the field of exploration, and in Russia there lay a challenge that could not be ignored. By its acceptance I set myself not only an enjoyable and formidable task, but one wherein the pleasure lies also in the anticipation. I am not a creature of high ambition but I do hold the opinion that to start at the top instead of the bottom is a time-saving method of attaining an aspiration and I felt able to apply my theory here.

Thus, with my first accomplishment of the Orient and Taurus Express routes behind me I decided to continue with the world's longest railway line in the world's largest country. So I ventured east, to the Soviet Union with my sights firmly set upon the Trans-Siberian Express.

Although a great deal of damage was done to the Soviet railways in the war zones of 1941 to 1944, reconstruction and development continued and today the route length is more than 80,000 miles of which 20,000 is electrified including much of the Trans-Siberian line. My journeyings on the trains of the USSR took place in 1970 when things were not quite so advanced. Since then, too, construction has begun on a second trans-Siberian line north of the existing one which accentuates the worth of this astounding 5,865-mile artery.

For me Russia started on platform 4 of Hook of Holland station. The heavy Russian *wagon lit,* its tory-blue solidness overshadowing the nondescript Polish coaches it led, became my home for forty-eight hours as we trundled by way of difficult and artificial frontiers dividing two Germanies and two Berlins in addition to those of Poland and European Russia. The route was the classic invasion thoroughfare to Moscow in fact and, in 1970, the restrictions on transit were more onerous than they are now.

48

In London's Soviet Embassy I had been issued with a temporary entry visa valid for one week and for Moscow City only. Once there I was supposed to have its validity and scope widened, a project that gave rise to some foreboding.

The trouble with the Trans-Siberian Express is that nobody can find it. Like the Moscow Express — which is called the Ost—West Express, and the rather less-explicit Hoek van Holland—Moskva, Hoek—Warszawa Express, I am not at all sure if such a train exists. That there is a Trans-Siberian *Railway* is not in doubt. A glance at the map proves its existence. The thin black line threads its way across that vast sparsely place-named land mass between Moscow and the Pacific. Sever it and you sever Russia.

There are several trains that cover the full or part length of this titanic line. One is the *Russia* hauling a train labelled 'Moscow-Vladivostok' and they have since doubled it with a nameless Intourist 'foreigners only' abomination that I am glad I avoided. But nowhere in the pages of any timetable is a single unit called 'Trans-Siberian Express'. However my shirt was on the *Russia* and I aimed to make Vladivostok or bust even though tourists are allowed only as far as Khabarousk. But Vladivostok is the end of the line.

Moscow's Jaroslav Station is an odd rambling building that has seemingly come unstuck from its many scattered platforms. These platforms are mostly open to the elements, and I found the administrative part of the station to be a sort of human marshalling yard. Every waiting room, booking hall and arcade was crammed with humanity lying, sitting, standing, laughing, talking, sleeping, eating, drinking and camping. I have never seen a station like it in all my life. To make my way to the platforms I had to walk over inert bodies wrapped in blankets and sleeping bags, past campers making tea at the public samovars, round family groups getting dressed or undressed having been to bed or going to bed. The London Tube was probably like it during the air raids of 1940.

Even when I had eventually discovered some trains there were none that gave the impression of being the great Trans-Siberian

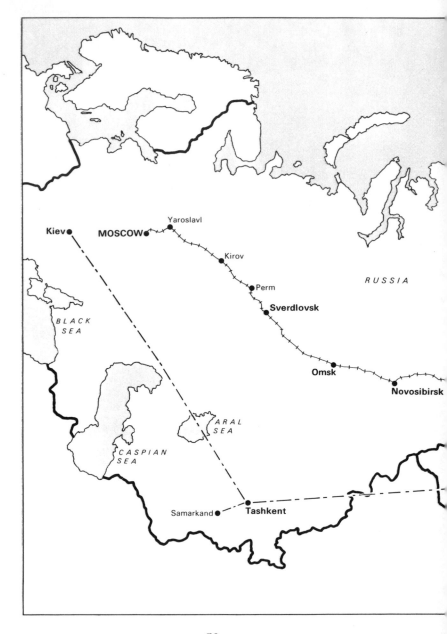

ARCTIC OCEAN

MOSCOW–VLADIVOSTOK   Key

+++++ rail route

----- air route

asnoyarsk

Lake Baikal

Ulan
Ude

Irkutsk

Khabarovsk

VLADIVOSTOK

MONGOLIA

CHINA

Express. I returned to the station buildings to look for a railway official or information bureau and once more had to negotiate the nomads of Jaroslav. Whether they were potential passengers, refugees, homeless citizens or simply railway station addicts I could never learn, but it was a condition I was to find repeated in many other stations and airports.

The only railway official in evidence was a woman selling tickets to a shuffling line of would-be travellers. I switched on my 'little boy lost' look and poked my own ticket at her through the grill. She caught on at once, slammed shut the window in the face of the man at the head of the line and, taking me by the arm hauled me back over Nomad Avenue towards the platforms. I had not the heart to look back at the unfortunate queue.

Train Number 2 — which turned out to be the Moscow– Vladivostok train — had now been advised on the indicator board and was, as we arrived, already backing into the station. The crowd on the platform, most of it with an excess of baggage, promised a full train and I was thankful for my reservation. I had not then realized that most of the crowd were simply 'see-ers off' and that all long-distance travellers on Soviet Railways *have* to be in possession of reservations. Even so, as the line of maroon coaches came to a dignified halt, each was promptly over- whelmed by hordes of people busily intent upon turning the spotless express into a home on wheels.

I found my compartment without difficulty. Straight away I came under the jurisdiction of the girl attendant who was to administer to the needs of her flock and defend it from violation by all gatecrashers. She took away my ticket, presented me with bed linen and a towel and generally fussed about. The compart- ment was roomy, comfortable and spotlessly clean. It held four bunks, the two lower ones of which were now adapted for use as seats. On the table by the window stood four tumblers in their silver-plated holders, a quantity of packaged biscuits and wrapped sugar lumps, and a folder showing the nine-day time- table. There was a carpet on the floor and curtains at the windows. A radio loudspeaker was playing exceedingly harmless music and, contrary to what many writers on the subject have said, this *can* be controlled or switched off — particularly if you have a window seat and learn the hidden position beneath the table of the control knob. A set of coat-hangers and reading matter (of the somewhat limited category that you might expect to be gratis in the U.S.S.R.) is available. If I wanted to be critical I could find fault with the cleanliness of the windows. They were also jammed shut, since the season was officially winter. But, for initial impressions I would award an alpha to that train.

On more general issues the express lived up to its reputation. We were a seventeen-coach train hauled, for the first leg of the journey, by a Czech Skoda electric locomotive. My coach was the oldest, but though somewhat antique it had — I found out later — fewer sharp corners and hard projections than did the shiny silvery interiors of the newer East German wagons. I did not particularly approve of our sombre colour scheme of dark blue and green, but got a kick out of being in the only coach bearing, in silver cyrilic letters, the legend 'Moscow—Vladivostik' along its maroon sides.

My first fellow passenger on the Trans-Siberian was, appropriately, a Russian. He spoke about as much French as I do so we began chatting away understanding little, even before the train had moved. In my hotel I was forever being asked where in England I lived, so when he asked, tiring of giving the proximity of London to my Sussex home-town, I moved it to the capital.

Joining us just before departure was a young mother and, to my dismay, a toddler at what might be described as the messy stage of life. The little girl made straight for my neat pile of bedding and effected an introduction by leaking through her nappy and the mother hardly improved matters when she used my towel to dry her. When I looked up from these absurdities the train was sliding out of the station.

A wave of satisfaction assailed me. An early dream was, this very moment, becoming fact. As the suburbs of Moscow faltered upon the huge plains my mind began to assess the pigments of that dream.

It was in the 1890s that work began on the railway. Motivated by war and inspired, in part, by the Canadian Pacific line, it was opened in 1904 from Moscow to Vladivostok. The terrain it

53

crosses ranges from hot deserts to cold tundra, from rolling steppes to endless forests. Eight giant bridges were built to span the enormous rivers of Amazon dimensions with names that are little known outside of Russia. To match this feat the line was forced through the Yablonovi mountains overhanging the southern shores of Lake Baikal and dropping sheer in great cliffs to the water's edge. In this forty-two miles alone are no less than thirty-eight tunnels. The line was doubled in 1939 and the journey today, serving ninety-eight stations between the two termini, takes nine days, three hours.

These then are the bare facts. Beneath them lies the stuff of history. Together they produce a picture that brought my journey, and the sombre land through which it passed, to throbbing life.

One of the chief social problems of the nineteenth century was the overpopulation of European Russia with its resulting famine and peasant disorder. Hence it was not only military strategy that forced the issue of the Trans-Siberian railway. But combined, its progress was assured. East of Omsk any economic justification disappeared, for, beyond a fishing industry, there is nothing to support the crippling expense. However, far to the east lay a fermenting Japan with grandiose territorial ambitions in and around Manchuria. So the railway proceeded on from Omsk at a pace that became a race with time. It was built in sections, and the first, Ekaterinburg (now Sverdlovsk) to Tyumen, was completed in 1883, to be followed three years later by that from Samara to Omsk. The then Ussuri Railway between Vladivostok and Khabarovsk came into being in 1899 constructed mainly by prison labour. Traversing the great rivers Ob and Irtysh at first by ferries, the Western Siberian Railway was opened in 1895, to be joined by the Central Siberian at the turn of the century.

The Trans-Baikal Railway from the east shore of the enormous lake to Sretensk was begun in 1895. It took five years to build because of the permafrost that existed to a depth of six feet, requiring dynamite in place of the usual excavating methods. Before the continuation of the line round the lake could be attempted, two ice-breaking ferries from Tynemouth, England, provided a water link which was suspended in winter months when the track could be laid directly across the ice.

At first the Trans-Siberian Express ran twice weekly, then daily from 1903. Its first-class compartments carried diners, bathrooms, chapels and reading, writing and music rooms in addition to sleepers. The bathrooms were even marble-tiled. Emigrants travelled in *teplushki* (freight cars fitted with bunks), while special cars with barred windows were provided for the prison traffic of less willing emigrants.

When war broke out between Russia and Japan in 1904 the Trans-Siberian was just a hotch-potch of a railway built to low technical standards and leaving much to be desired. Each section was limited by available funds; it was single track and running difficulties were multiplied with the demands of war.

The 1905 revolution brought anarchy to the Trans-Siberian line. Government control lapsed as mutinous soldiers returning from their dispiriting campaign against the Japanese revolted *en route*. Fatal collisions and disasters occurred as troops and unqualified drivers took over locomotives. Chaos was the order of the day, and only a special operation, probably unique in military annals, restored the situation. Two troop trains, each commanded by a general, set out simultaneously from west and east. With frequent halts to suppress, flog, execute and generally discourage rebels and mutineers along the way the two trains met at Chita, where the railway was declared open once more for business.

But the subsequent Civil War of 1917, had a still deeper effect. While British, American and Japanese troops had landed at Vladivostok, the White Army under Kolchak was advancing along the railway from Omsk, and for a while the line fell under the control of the Czech Army.

The Czechs were on their way home to Europe via Vladivostok having fought with the Russians on the Austrian front. With the Bolsheviks in command of all cities on the line between Irkutsk and Vladivostok, a confused situation arose and before long the movement of Czech troops came to a halt, leaving them distributed on railway sidings all along the line. There was little love lost between the Czechs and the Austro-Hungarian occupiers of their country, and when west-bound trains of released

Hungarian prisoners began to pass the delayed Czechs it only needed one flying half brick to start real trouble. Chelyabinsk was to supply the half brick which started the Czech revolt against the Bolsheviks.

News of the revolt spread swiftly along the line and, since they were the only disciplined armed force in Russia, the Czech soldiers were soon in charge of the railway and using it to continue the move eastwards, routing any Bolshevik garrisons attempting to stop them. An anti-Bolshevik government was then set up in Vladivostok and, joining forces with Kolchak's White Russians, the Czechs swept back again, turning Siberia, politically speaking, from red to white. The tide turned, of course, and the Czechs and the Whites were eventually halted. Control of the Trans-Siberian was then fought over by Reds and Whites and, to confuse the issue still further, by powerful bands of terrorists under Semeonov, who had established a base at Chita. The latter controlled the junction to Peking and would grab any freight they required from either Red or White sources.

Recovery was understandably slow and a series of five-year plans were needed to put the railway on an economic footing. But against this chequered backcloth of history, and even though the Soviet government has neglected the significance of the line until comparatively recently, there is no doubt that the Trans-Siberian remains the greatest railway project the world has ever known.

'But of *course* I can go to church when and as often as I like'. The words were thrown at me with the lilt of challenge, as if the speaker was convincing himself as well as me.

It was my French-speaking Russian talking and if I have oversimplified his words, it is because our discussion on religion went floundering on for more than 100 miles. We were alone in the compartment, the mother and child having been discreetly and conveniently banished by the attendant to another further down the coach.

The discussion had been given impetus at Zagorsk. Zagorsk is the Canterbury of Russia, though its name is that of a communist big-wig. Formerly it was Sergievo or Sergius, and the fame of its monastery can be traced back to the miracle whereby the original abbot's body was found unmarked after a disastrous fire. By the sixteenth century Sergievo was rich as well as famous.

Like the Moscow Kremlin but on a smaller scale, the pink and white outer walls surround a complex of monasteries and churches. A vision of onion-shaped domes, spattered with golden stars, hang above it, and a magnificent rococo tower of superb Byzantine rises from the St Sergius monastery. Beneath the Cathedral of the Assumption with its own five bright-blue baubles lies the grave of Boris Godunov.

It used to be the ambition of every Russian to come to Zagorsk at least once in a lifetime. Many still do, but in the guise of tourists instead of pilgrims. Religion is far from dead in Russia even though there have been many attempts to suppress its influence. At first it suffered at the hands of the revolution when communists saw it as a rival to their own new 'religion' — especially since the Orthodox church was closely connected with the hated Czarism. Then it suffered savage persecution in the excesses of the Stalin era, but persecution is a double-edged weapon that breeds faith as fast as it destroys it and people have continued to practise it even if not overtly.

But the present régime is more subtle. The anti-God campaign has ceased and there is religious freedom in the sense that people wishing to worship may do so. However, the severely practical inducements to stay away are emphatic, and I was to hear, time and time again, variations on the theme 'to be seen in church would be more than my job's worth'. And yet the Russians are by nature an emotional and mystical people. They have proved in World War Two that they can be Christians and still remain loyal to their country in spite of its communist government. They are genuinely sad that the present-day celebration of births, marriages and deaths falls short of what, in their hearts, they would wish. Not easily can the country shake off its historic title of 'Holy Russia'.

From mid-morning until late at night the dining car was always full. Sometimes you had to queue, but if you chose unorthodox meal times this could usually be avoided. My first excursion to the diner was at midday and though the coach was far from empty most of the occupants congregated round the counter of a small store selling anything from vodka to ballpoint pens.

I sat down at an empty table and was promptly moved to another. The move was without rhyme or reason, for no special comforts or separation from the common herd resulted. On subsequent visits I stayed put.

The menu was in four languages and extensive. It listed a great variety of items, but only those with a price scribbled against them were available. This knocked the selection down to one soup, about three main courses and a few sweets. I started pointing out my wishes to the waiter when I noticed someone at an adjoining table eating caviar. Quickly I scotched my order for borsch and substituted caviar, even though its presence was not indicated by a price. It was well I did so for that was the first and last caviar I saw in Russia. A small amount comes aboard the train at Moscow and at a few other points along the line — to be swiftly snapped up by knowledgeable travellers. My portion, when it came, turned out to be the pink variety, which is supposed to be more succulent than the black. But the rest of the meal could hardly be called exciting, though, like all the meals I had on the train it was adequate and wholesome. Mostly I stuck to Wiener schnitzel accompanied by a bottle of lukewarm Russian beer and experimented with the sweets, which were usually disastrous. The price of such a meal was surprisingly modest, in spite of a chronic rate of exchange.

At Jaroslav town we crossed the Volga. It provided adoration from the Russians in the corridor, but all I saw was a mud-coloured river no wider than the Thames at Richmond, washing the backsides of factories. My friend wasn't so uncritical as his compatriots and talked of its exploitation rather than its symbolism. According to him its waters have been so dammed and diverted that there is grave concern for its future.

I had made the acquaintance of a Swiss couple in the next compartment and resolved to join them for an hour or so when my companion left the train at Jaroslav. I helped him with his bags onto the platform, for which I earned an excruciating handshake and a gem of a prepared speech in English. With a broad grin he carefully pronounced 'God be with you, Comrade' and was gone. Who says all Russians are without a sense of humour!

His place was taken by a stern-faced man with bushy eyebrows and an impressive lapel badge. Even before he confirmed it, I had tabbed him as an engine driver. Intent upon learning more about the man I postponed my visit to the neighbouring compartment.

Jaroslav faded into the autumn landscape of fine-drawn larch and birch sparkling with light. It had been that way since the last environs of Moscow and would remain so for hundreds and thousands of miles with only very slight variations in light, tree-density and the swell of the ground. Tiny villages of wooden houses grew, like the trees out of the black earth, their mud streets speckled with hens and big white geese.

These villages of square wooden houses *(izbas)* were dying, I was told. Indeed some did remind me of a film set for a derelict gold-rush town in the Klondike. The *izba* communities, it seems, are being rehoused in the new towns with their ugly standardised blocks of flats that would wipe all individuality out of any human. No doubt this is progress and a better life for those involved. But another aspect of Russia will surely die. Even now there was something missing, and as each village passed I racked my brains in puzzlement. Suddenly it was obvious. There was never a church to provide a hub of life, a centre for the little community. Its absence added to the desolation.

Trains throughout the world allow a sort of visual eavesdropping that is notorious for its intrusion into the affairs of back gardens and kitchens. That there are no back or front gardens in Russia was particularly noticeable in these clannish villages of the steppes. Through the little wooden windows, framed by neatly parted lace curtains, could be seen the simple warm little rooms beyond. Each was a bedroom, a living room and kitchen combined, a strictly functional one-room suite given a touch of longed-for refinement by the pot of flowers on the sill.

Hundreds of miles out of Moscow and there were still no hills. I began to long for a sight of the Urals, the mountain barrier that lay dormant in my imagination. 'Behind the Urals' was a phrase that, for me, signified either protection or dread. I found myself getting exasperated with the endless forests, the streams and the timber villages with their men and women living out a hopeless existence that had been thrust upon them.

I found solace in my fellow-passengers. The Swiss couple were not alone in their compartment. With them was an extraordinarily pretty Ukranian girl called Katerina *en route* to Komsomolsk, beyond Khabarovsk, to join her jet-pilot husband. She spoke a little English and the three of them had spent the day hard at work improving upon and learning each other's language. Katerina came from Kiev, and the prospect of living among Russians in a pioneer town hundreds of miles from anywhere, was only softened by that of a reunion with the man she had married. Her age was no more than twenty. The two Swiss came from Geneva and he was president of the Association of the Swiss Alpine Schools. Though both were in their late thirties I gained the distinct impression that they too had not long been married.

Back in my own compartment my new companion turned up trumps. I had heard him ask the attendant my nationality and for a period we sat engrossed in a kind of optical sparring match, looking for an opening. Russians are less inhibited than the British and he got in first. Things began with the usual cross-examination in a *pot pourri* of languages until we found our common denominator to be German. He was not just an engine-driver but an engine-driver *de luxe*. He was going right through to Vladivostok to take over a west-bound Trans-Siberian Express on a steam section of its journey. He was amazed and delighted at my interest in the workings of the line, and though we frequently got bogged down by misinterpretation we had all the time in the world to hammer out the sense of the discussion. In spite of the fact that he was a hero of labour or something equally formidable I found myself liking himself immensely. The coach attendant treated him with great respect, bringing him (and me) copious glasses of tea, despite the fact that he barked at her unmercifully.

From him I learnt the routine of the Trans-Siberian staff. Coach attendants, dining-car waiters, guards, cooks and the like do a full nine-day stint. They then have a week off alternately in Moscow and Vladivostok. The pay is good and so it should be, for they work like beavers. Though there are two attendants to each coach — one off duty and one on — the young girls never let up. At least three times a day they vacuum-clean the compartments and corridor, rub down the walls, and at every halt nobody is allowed off the train until the door handles and brass handholds have been thoroughly wiped clean. Furthermore, there are the never-ending pilgrimages to attend the samovars which, throughout Russia, are coal or wood fired and various additional duties that are thrust upon them at stations. In the crowded dining-car the waiters were on their feet morning, noon and night. They were not very refined, and none too clean, but were always pleasant. I got to know one of them quite well and frequently passed him an English cigarette, which he appreciated greatly. One of their more unpleasant duties was the attempted removal of Russian youths who hogged the tables for card-playing and beer-drinking. Rows were frequent and loud arguments often rent the air. Sometimes the arithmetic of the waiters when they were compiling the bill was, to put it kindly, original. Everywhere in Russia — whether it be on a train, or in the most sophisticated hotel, shop or restaurant — a calculation has to be carried out on an abacus. I could never understand how the thing worked and as they flicked the beads up and down the runners at great speed I think they knew this, and so erred to their advantage! However, I was to learn this to be a very general Russian weakness, and I held it against those long-suffering waiters least of all.

At dusk we were joined by two short-haul travellers going only as far as Buy, three hours away. The engine-driver introduced me and it was discovered that we were all soldiers, in, what Russians term 'The Great Patriotic War' (World War Two). We promptly told each other our tallest war story, doubling the number of Germans we had killed and acting out our individual epics with a pantomime of staccato machine-gun fire. Exhausted, we deemed it to be supper time, and from the many parcels and bags that littered the compartment came a procession of victuals. Since it seemed that the restaurant car was to be passed over on this occasion I started to dig in my bag for a contribution of tinned meat but was told to desist and help myself to the piles of

61

sausage, fish, bread, cake, cheese, cherries and plums overflow-
ing the table. From an unlabelled bottle the engine-driver filled
my tea glass with a cherry-red liquid that I took to be a mineral
water I had already sampled in Moscow.

I should have known better of course. Half a tumblerful had
followed some salty, thirst-provoking fish before I realized that
the liquid was home-made vodka. Quickly I sank a tumbler of
beer to extinguish the flames in my stomach and fell back
gasping, while my companions, seeing the half-empty glass,
topped it up again.

The meal was a feast and, though I am a non-smoker, I was
persuaded to accept a Russian cigarette. Half the cigarette was
simply a tube, a holder for about an inch of loose black tobacco.
Choking over the acrid smoke I blew most of the tobacco onto
the opposite seat, nearly setting fire to the train.

Buy was upon us all too soon, and in the welter of hugs and
back-slappings, the two companions departed. Before settling
down for the night the engine-driver insisted upon a nightcap of
home-grown tomatoes and another dose of the hard stuff.

In a comfortable bed of sheets and bolsters I slept well. We slid
through Kirov in the night, and I have vague recollections of
white smoke from tall chimneys scrawling words in the dark sky.
With dawn we were rambling towards the Urals.

Everyone rises late on the Trans-Siberian. The samovars are
stoked up, the first glasses of tea are poured down sleepy throats,
while yawning men and women in pyjamas parade in the corridor to view the new countryside. I was told half a dozen times by
complete strangers that we were passing through such-and-such
an *oblast* (county) or that in the night we passed over so-and-so
river. One can feel the immense pride the Russians have for their
giant country. It is a pride that does them great credit, though it
also blinds them to the shortcomings.

The toilets on the train were a pleasure to use. Spotlessly clean
they never lacked for soap or toilet paper though mysteriously
there was never a plug for the basin. With me I had a book, *One's
Company* by Peter Flemming, in which he too observes the
Russian allergy to plugs and indicates the reason as basically
religious. When I pointed this out to various Russians, even

showing them the relevant passage in a book written by so distinguished a travel writer, they simply laughed. I never could get to the bottom of it.

At Perm and subsequent stops the passengers tumbled out of the coaches to exercise by parading up and down the stations, many still in their uncovered pyjamas. I was to find that some Russians lived in them all day and they became a common sight in the dining car. My Swiss friend rather unkindly suggested that this display of night attire was a badge of emancipation, a sort of proof to the outside world that Soviet people no longer sleep in their clothes. If so I fear I let Western culture down badly by going to bed in my underclothes. It was pure laziness on my part, while it was easier than dressing and undressing should our male exclusiveness be invaded. Mixed sexes in sleeping cars seemed to be another Russian contradiction for in most matters concerning sex they are complete prudes. The Russians love badges denoting their accomplishments, interests or political prowess, and on one occasion I noticed a man sporting a double row of campaign stars on his pyjamas!

Perm is another of those unfortunate towns that has undergone a series of name-changes. Although it was originally called Perm it was renamed Mololov in 1918 until Stalin and his Foreign Minister went out of fashion and it reverted to Perm in 1958. For this reason Kirov was lucky to escape the same inconvenience, since it was renamed, only once, in honour of Stalin's greatest friend who was assassinated before the political wind of change could blow his name into the black book. Perm is the gateway to the Urals, and before we drew into the station the train rumbled majestically across a great river. A dozen voices proclaimed it as the Kama.

I took a series of photographs on the platform. My engine-driver was pleased to pose for me against the background of the train, but when our girl attendant noticed that she was being included in the picture she scowled and scuttled aboard the coach, refusing to emerge even when the driver bawled at her. By and large Russians are exceedingly camera-shy and not only, as down in the more primitive south, on religious grounds. Once upon a time the very sight of a camera in the Soviet Union labelled you as a spy. It was the same in the satellite countries where I was frequently in trouble for taking the most harmless of photographs. Old suspicions die hard and I was still the capitalist foreigner made more deadly with a camera. I had heard of many Soviet regulations regarding the taking of railway photographs — just two of which were that photography *from* trains was forbidden and that trains themselves could be photographed but not the track they were on! Intourist made it sound all very matey. 'The taking of pictures in the Soviet Union is entirely unrestricted except, as in any country, where military objectives are concerned.' But what is not made clear is the fact that in communist countries all manner of innocent objects are classed as military objectives. Bridges, for instance, are out for a start, and when I later went through the motions of filming from an aeroplane I all but caused a riot.

After Perm a slight lift of land wrapped in a cloak of birch and red pine announced the approaches to the Urals. For an hour or more the gentlest of downs played a discreet game of tag, with the railway hardly bothering it at all. A river called Chusovaya I never noticed. Yet we were now out of Europe and into Asia, out of European Russia and into Siberia and, as we drew into Sverdlovsk, the Urals were behind us. It was all very casual and I was disappointed that they hadn't been the dramatic mountains of my expectations.

Sverdlovsk has been in the name-changing game too. In the eighteenth century it was Ekaterinburg after Catherine I, wife of Peter the Great. Following the 1917 revolution it was one of the places captured by the Czechs with the White Russian Army, and it was this action that led to the murder of the last Czar of Russia and his family. It is all too easy to get emotional about this particularly obnoxious assassination; but though, as individuals, the Nicholas II family might have been decent people, they headed a harsh and repressive regime.

A city of a million souls, Sverdlovsk spreads its black industrial might over a landscape that reverts to a deadpan flatness as if exhausted from its manifestation of the Urals. It was the end of a journey for many on our train and the commencement of one for others. Our compartment became crowded with a youth and a middle-aged woman.

The youth was a soldier, a driver in the Red Army. He was a pleasant fellow, full of laughter and life. We conversed at length on matters military with the ease of two soldiers anywhere. The woman hardly spoke but smiled frequently. She had the submissiveness I found in many older Russian women, a trait that dismayed and baffled me intensely. At intervals along the line women in boots, grey shapeless overalls and woollen headscarves were to be seen doing heavy repairs on the track. I had already seen them carrying out traditionally male tasks at stations and again found it a mournful and unnatural sight. The faces of the woman in my compartment and of those I saw beside the track showed an indomitable patience and a resigned acceptance of the absence of special recognition by their men and their societies. One of the saddest sights in the whole Soviet Union is that of the uniformed women with long old-fashioned skirts who stand with unfailing regularity by each signal cabin or wayside halt solemnly holding up their tiny yellow flags as a sign that the way ahead is clear.

Having eaten well for lunch at the expense of the engine-driver I managed to entice him into the restaurant car for the evening meal. It was not without interruptions however: the train was being hauled by a steam locomotive over this particular portion of the journey and my driver kept dashing off to offer advice or encouragement to his associates on duty. I enquired if there was any chance of my being allowed to drive the train under supervision and was told that if I remained with him he would arrange it. This was the nicest *niet* I got in Russia.

When our two new companions left at Tyumen, the soldier pressed upon me a cigar as black as the Siberian earth, as a farewell gift. I shrank from sampling its pleasures this time, and added the thing to my own stock of duty-free cigarettes I had with me for any eventuality for which they might prove useful.

Sleep came with more reluctance the second night and Omsk was simply another noise at two in the morning. Yet it was broad daylight and when I looked at the station clock it confirmed the time. Confused I pondered upon the delayed reactions of the brandy I had consumed, until I remembered that all rail and air schedules in Russia worked on Moscow time. On many subsequent stations was a pair of clocks showing both Moscow and local time, which did save the inevitable confusion that arose. During the night an ethereal newcomer joined us for a few hours on the top bunk and was gone by daybreak. What sex it was I'm not sure, but in the faint glow of the compartment's blue night light I had an impression of a man in a white peaked cap.

The third day brought hardly a change in the scenery. The vast flat lonely horizon was with us still, and only the glorious gold of the autumn birch foliage with its silver pillars injected beauty into a scene of utter gloom. I felt the first twinges of loneliness not so much for myself but for the little people of the tiny forgotten villages that, with every mile, grew farther and farther apart. The *izba* houses became more rugged and hugged the ground even closer. Munching bitter Russian chocolate, Katerina and I spent an hour in the corridor watching the sad countryside unwinding from its endless spool. We spoke little, she apprehensively wondering how she would live in the great outback and I thanking God I didn't have to.

The train speed never lessened. Moving at a steady forty-five miles an hour it neither hurried nor dawdled. It arrived at stations exactly on time, remained never longer than fifteen minutes, sometimes only five, and departed to the scheduled second. A sneaky train when electric or diesel hauled, it slunk out of the stations in silence to send jay-walking passengers skipping over the tracks to regain their seats. Never once did it emit even a mournful whistle. The Trans-Siberian Express is a serious train burdened by its responsibilities.

For breakfast we had sausage, hard-boiled eggs and a huge slice of cherry pie donated by my companion. It was a farewell breakfast. In a particularly serious mood the train trundled ponderously between the steel knitting that gave strength to the slender bridge crossing the gigantic Ob river. And on the east bank was Novosibirsk. Here, I had a scheduled stop for twenty-four hours when I would have no wheels beneath my feet.

My friend the engine-driver helped me out of the coach with my bags and gave me a great bear hug. As the few other tourists congregated on the platform to be fussed over by a new Intourist guide, the train rolled quietly out of the station. I felt a strange sensation of loss as I watched it go.

While I am happy to wax eloquent on the subject of the Trans-Siberian Railway, I can find little to praise in the cities it serves. Since only three (Novosibirsk, Irkutsk and Khabarovsk) are in bounds to foreigners, judgement is of necessity limited, but the mere fact that we were told that the others offer 'no facilities' and so are barred, speaks for itself. Of the three 'open' cities I rated Novosibirsk bottom.

The Hotel Novosibirsk was, however, a considerable improvement upon the establishment in which I had stayed in Moscow. With a total of five foreign tourists to document, the hotel reception still managed to keep us hanging around in the foyer a full twenty five minutes, its staff making no attempt to hide the fact that we were a confounded nuisance.

My passport had preceded me to the Intourist service bureau on the third floor and the shortcomings of my visa were being ogled over by its staff of three when I reported there. 'Why didn't you have things rectified in Moscow?' they asked, so I told them, truthfully, that I'd not been given the opportunity. But though the system was seen to be hanged by its own petard it wasn't going to get me a new visa. I was handed my onward rail ticket to Khabarovsk for the morrow. 'Have it done there,' they said, passing on the buck. But I was fast losing interest. 'What chances are there of going to Vladivostok from Khabarovsk?' I enquired with recharged enthusiasm, and the ode to no facilities was still ringing in my ears as I made my way to the next floor.

One of the two lifts worked, but I found the stairs quicker. My bedroom was fresh, new and comfortable and had a bathroom attached. There was, however, no water. A plug existed for the bath but not the basin. I wandered downstairs with a vague notion of lunching, only to discover that it was late in the afternoon. Somewhere I had lost a meal in the limbo of time.

Needing exercise after a surfeit of sitting I made for the river as the spot likely to show Novosibirsk in its best setting. But the great river with its nine-span bridge was almost totally ignored. Except for a poorly designed formal garden where the steamers tied up, the Ob got the cold shoulder from the city. The town was dreary in the extreme — a big brawny rolled-shirtsleeves kind of place. The main square, a copy in miniature of Moscow's Red Square and the same as in a hundred other towns in the Soviet Union, gave a fine notion of space but nothing else.

The streets themselves were unfinished and displayed a patchwork of repairs that were obviously never going to be completed. The pavements were death traps, full of holes and open drains. Broken curbs and weed-infested uneven paving stones offended the eye. A drunk lay dead to the world in a gutter and I was to see others before I left the city. Drunkenness is an affliction that affects all countries but the people I saw in the Soviet Union were more profoundly drunk than I have seen elsewhere. Maybe living in a place like Novosibirsk one gets drunk for sorrow instead of joy.

Shop windows were blind eyes in the high street. We in this country are sometimes sickened by the sheer volume of high-street advertising, but Russian shops are drab, colourless places without it. The best buys, material-wise, in communist countries are books, which are cheap by Western standards. In Novosibirsk the bookshops were full of people searching for simple down-to-earth information amongst a welter of Marxist-Leninism.

Few people would speak to me beyond answering my directional enquiries. There is still a reluctance to be seen talking to a foreigner and, though partly a legacy of the Stalin era, the fear of becoming branded as a cosmopolitan is ever present. Like going to church, the first, second even the third time produces no unpleasantness. Then suddenly it is reported and the word 'unreliable' appears on your file. Labelled thus, little things like promotion, going abroad and being included in the waiting list for a car, start becoming difficult to attain. In Stalin's day you knew where you stood. Life was black and white, but grey is a very indeterminate colour.

Except for someone else's early call on the telephone it was a quiet, pleasantly interruption-free night after the noises of the train. While our little band of five tourists were breakfasting a vivacious lady from Intourist swept in to announce that the car for our sight-seeing tour would be ready at ten. There was no asking whether we would *like* to go on it — not, I think, through any discourtesy — but simply because, in Novosibirsk, she could conceive of nothing else we might want to do.

Our guide's name was Tamara and she did her stuff charmingly. She seemed to enjoy our company too so we behaved ourselves by not asking 'difficult' questions. The lecture on Novosibirsk occupied about three minutes and was delivered as we gazed at the railway bridge.

Founded in 1896 the town owes its existence to the bridge and to Michal Garin-Miklailovsky, a famous engineer and novelist, who built it. Refusing bribes by local merchants to erect it elsewhere, he stuck to his assertion that it must go where the river was stony-bottomed and comparatively narrow. During the three years of construction Novosibirsk came into being and grew, spreading to both banks. A list of industrial achievements followed and the lecture ended with the hoary quip that the Ob was the longest river in Russia with the shortest name.

Some of the party brought out their cameras but were sternly rebuked by a wagging forefinger. And because the smaller road bridge upstream got in the way of the view-finders even a picture of the steamers and timber barges going about their business was forbidden. To me it didn't matter. I had already got mine.

In the minicoach we sped southwards for about 15 miles on good tarmac roads to Academgorodok, known as 'Science City'. Though no doubt a fascinating place for the scientists who live there, the long rows of flats, tower blocks and institution-like buildings hardly constitute a tourist mecca. The place reminded me of Welwyn Garden City as it was a quarter of a century ago, with its self-conscious statuary amidst brash avenues of concrete lamp posts.

Our enforced tour at an end, Tamara saw us off at the station, smarting under the studied insult of the minicoach driver who preferred to go to sleep over the wheel instead of helping with our luggage. In the train corridor she hugged us all individually.

Back on the train it was as if Novosibirsk had never happened. I was again in the oldest coach with the same blue and green colour motif, while the girl conductor who took away my ticket might have been the other's sister. With me in the compartment was the Swiss couple. Also in the coach were two elderly Australian ladies, a thin lugubrious American and his wife, and the three other members of our Novosibirsk group. Of these one was an American journalist from Alaska with a sense of humour; the others a Swede and his Japanese girlfriend. All were stopping over at Irkutsk before continuing to Japan. I was the only foreigner *not* going to Japan, a fact that caused some bewilderment. Nobody wanted to believe that I was only there for the ride.

It was interesting to note the proprietary attitude of the established passengers to us 'new boys'. It is the same in any long-distance train, but probably more pronounced on the Trans-Siberian. Even for Russians it is generally a once-in-a-life-time journey and, whereas in Europe and America people travel in a train fully aware that it belongs to a state or a company, in Russia people simply view it as their own. During the period of occupation it is their home, and a Russian's home is also his castle. Many hours pass before you are 'accepted' and, you in turn, are soon frowning upon fresh intakes. I was to have five days and four nights as king of *my* castle.

A reconnaissance showed that the new train was again spotlessly clean and that the previous one was not just a happy accident. And, glory be, there was a plug for the washbasin.

So the refreshingly aimless routine of life on the Trans-Siberian commenced once more. To me travel on this train is the very essence of a holiday. You wake up in the morning, your watch tells you it is eight o'clock, but you know it doesn't matter a hoot since, moving east, it will alter anyway and not just with the passage of time. Your berth is comfortable. There is no need to get up and no incentive or reason for doing so. You have little to look forward to, nothing to avoid. You lie on your seat, justifiably inert, seeing all there is to see without the slightest effort. Mostly there is nothing to look at, but that is no reason to stop looking. You are living in a vacuum and there is something rather novel in the experience.

As a break from monotony there is the restaurant car full of noise and movement. Whether you have a meal or just a beer it is a social event. In addition to the restaurant car there is a system of vending where bread rolls, soup, apples and yoghurt are continually hawked along the corridors. A third source of food and drink exists in the market stalls run at every station by wizened old women in huge spreads of aprons. The stalls get bigger and better the farther east you go and, oddly, each of these sources supplements the other — which is just as well since there are periods when the restaurant car is virtually out of stock of everything.

At Marunsk the central heating came on. While at the station a band of uncivilized looking Mongolians tried to board our coach, but the girl attendant was ready for them. Bristling with self-righteous indignation she repulsed the invasion on the steps and waving her arms towards the rear of the train diverted them to someone else's coach. I began to revise my opinion of the sub-missiveness of Russian women.

A drunk managed to get aboard the coach at the goldfield town of Achinsk. But he wasn't with us for long. He fell into the little control room of the coach — the place where all the light switches are — and aroused a hornet's nest. A uniformed engineer, the coach girl and her off-duty companion in a night dress combined in their wrath to fling him bodily off the train.

At all stations incredibly long slow trains had drawn up to make way for our maroon express. Most were goods trains of oil tanks and construction-material trucks, with occasional flat wagons laden with military equipment. Traffic was intense and train after train roared by us at intervals of very few minutes. One could feel the beating pulse of Siberia as riches beyond imagination were being gouged out of its black earth and perma-frost. In the other direction go young Russians full of enthusiasm and pioneering spirit. No longer are they slaves. But it wasn't always like that.

The movement east started hundreds of years ago. The first organised push beyond the Urals began in 1581 when an expedition under a Cossak named Yermak routed the forces of the Siberian khans and pushed on to the foothills of the Altai and

71

to the River Ob. But it was Peter the Great who started the banishing of people to Siberia that was to give it the name that made it stink in the nostrils of the world. In 1710 he despatched a group of undesirables into its inhospitable wastes. Cheaper and more fruitful than simple imprisonment, the exile idea caught on and succeeding Tsars followed suit. By 1823 a continuous stream of convicted criminals was to be found trudging eastwards to the living death of the Siberian labour camp. Before the end of that century their numbers were augmented by political deportees, and soon 18,000 people a year were being disposed of in this way.

Though some of the exiles were hard-case criminals, very many had committed no crime at all. Siberia became the easy solution to problems of unwanted minority groups, non-conformists and simply those individuals who had incurred the displeasure of somebody in authority.

Before the railway came into existence the way to exile was on foot. The journey sometimes took as long as four years with less than half the prisoners surviving it. Fettered by leg irons, with heads shaved and a list of their crimes stitched to their backs, the poor wretches were herded in convoys through blizzard, rain, dust and mud; lashed by brutalized guards; sick, hungry, and lice-covered, and without hope to the purgatory of mines and camps.

There are, no doubt, old men and women still alive in the Soviet Union who will remember the song they sang; the terrible *Miloserdnaya*, 'Have pity on us, O our Fathers, have pity. O our Mothers, have mercy for Christ's sake.' Death by typhus and scurvy ended the misery for thousands whilst others succumbed more slowly to exhaustion and malnutrition. Attempted escape brought retribution in the form of years of solitary confinement on bread and water.

The fate of purely political exiles was different. For them it was only compulsory emigration. With their wives and families they could pursue their professions and take part in an active creative life. Many were men and women of culture and intelligence who brought these attributes to a largely barbarian land.

At first these political exiles formed a minute percentage of the deportees to Siberia. But after 1905 the picture was to change again. Following the abortive revolution, 100,000 suspects and sympathisers landed up in Siberia. Included among them were Lenin, Stalin, Trotsky and others who suddenly found themselves with time to think, learn, organise and plan. Thus the future leaders of Russia received their political education, gratis, at the hands of the Czar. And when in 1917 the next revolution came, the knowledge they gained lost him both his reign and his life.

Had all this been a fairy tale, the new order of Lenin would have given a fresh deal to the masses and the iniquities that had made Siberia what it was would have been swept away with everyone living happily ever after. That indeed was the idea so far as the masses were concerned. But it is one of the awful paradoxes of history that what the revolution had aimed to sweep away it soon restored. With unparalleled ruthlessness the new régime of modern Russia increased its prisoners more than thirtyfold.

The highest number of persons in prisons and camps throughout the country during Czarist rule was 184,000. This figure was exceeded after only ten years of Soviet rule. In 1937 it was 6¼ million; thirty years after a revolution had freed its nation from servitude some 16 percent of its male population was enslaved.

During the 1930s the movement east owed much to Stalin. With Lenin's far-sightedness he saw clearly the danger of having the bulk of Russia's vital industry concentrated near the invasion routes from the West. He knew the vulnerability too of the Far East, which was dependent upon a single railway line. Hence the enforced development of industry east of the Urals to make that vast and neglected hinterland self-sufficient.

A free working population was hardly likely to be persuaded or even gently coerced into carrying out this policy. So, where the Czars had failed to develop the Siberian wilderness because of inefficiency he would succeed by methods totally basic to the task. Thus the grotesque nightmare of the Stalinist labour camps began.

Never in history had there been terrorism on such a scale. Entire races, entire communities were decimated. Millions were sent east to dig for ores, build roads, railways, harbours and air-fields, new towns, powerhouses and dams. Even those not directly caught up in this frightful project lived on the edge of an abyss of fear.

Between 1932 and 1941 the original labour force was augmented by huge influxes of Latvians, Lithuanians, Poles and other discredited nationalities, together with the survivors of the Stalinist purges. It is said that had it not been for the energy and ruthlessness with which this recruitment was carried out, Russia may well have succumbed to the Germans in the Second World War. But he who sits in judgement over us could hardly accept this as an excuse. However the war had one vital side effect to the advantage of the Stalin régime. It brought more labour in the form of captured Germans, Italians, Japanese, Finns and Hungarians.

At the time of Stalin's death a total of some 15 million souls lay in camps in Siberia and beyond. Gradually they were released to fumble, broken and bewildered, back into a normal life. There must be many millions of these ex-slaves in the Soviet Union today. One wonders what the comforting slogans in the streets, and the platitudes of Moscow Radio, mean to them. Can they, even under a ruler with a new name, support a régime that basically is the same as the one that banished them to hell? But Russians will always remain Russian, and for Russia they will endure anything.

Today one of the penal sentences of Soviet courts is exile to construction sites in Siberia, but most of the work is undertaken by young and enthusiastic volunteers, freely recruited, from European Russia. There were a number of them in the hard-class section of my train and, to judge from their excited eyes and earnest faces, they were *en route* to paradise. Compared with the Siberia of their fathers, they were. The pay is good, there is freedom from ideological pressures and a sense of liberty. The foundation of the new Russia east of the Urals has been laid, even if at a certain cost. Progress can now continue in a more normal fashion. Whatever he was, Lenin, with his henchman Stalin, was no fool.

74

And what of the Siberia of today? A few statistics provide a rare eloquence. It is more than 4,000 miles long and 2,000 wide. It is one-and-a-half times the size of the United States of America and it stretches over 8 million square miles. Its contrasts of temperature are no less sensational: at Verkhoyansk the temperature falls to minus 70°C and human breath becomes ice, yet in the Kuzbas it is temperate enough for all-the-year-round wine production. In the Siberian tundra in the north, the larch trees take a century to grow, yet down south there are tiger-infested jungles.

In a sense, much of the Siberian earth is a gigantic deep freezer. Within its depths is fossil ice dating from the Ice Age, that preserves for posterity, such extinct forms of life as the mammoth. Though the species died out fifteen thousand years ago, remains in a remarkable state of preservation are still to be found. Rumour speaks of dinosaurs in a mountain called Labankus but then so it does of Loch Ness.

Siberia too is a land of untapped riches. Locked in its territory are diamonds, coal, oil, ores, gold, tungsten, uranium, lead, zinc, mercury, and copper in inexhaustible quantity. It is the greatest potential world producer of grain. The enormous rivers supply eighty percent of the hydro-electric power of the Soviet Union, the Lena alone producing as much electricity as the entire output of Great Britain. Much of the territory is covered with unbroken forest or taiga. Pines, cedars, larches, silver firs and spruces combine to shut out the sky. The forests are alive with stoats, weasels, squirrels, sables, badgers, otters, chipmunks, wolves, bears, foxes and lynxes. In the more open tundra there are reindeer, polar foxes and swans.

Siberia too is the home of Russia's nuclear energy and her launching pads for satellites, spaceships and rockets. It is a land that in an over-sophisticated world can still provide mystery, dread and excitement. There is also the railway . . .

The great plain upon which Novosibirsk lay like a speck of dust was beginning to falter. With every mile the trees pushed even closer and soon the forest crowded arrogantly round us, jostling the train. Krasnoyarsk and Kansk, with more goldfields, had passed in the night. In the early dawn we halted inexplicably in a village hemmed in by solid barriers of trees. Its earth road was a broken mirror of shining mud and puddles leading optimistically into the trees, there to be extinguished. In the tiny wooden station was the inevitable statue of Lenin, spick and span in a square-mile battlefield of existence. The tiny *izbas* in their little rows reminded me of a neglected cemetery. A place to live and a place to die.

Propaganda had never so earnest yet crude a champion as in the Soviet Union. Whether it be the enormous hoardings concealing whole buildings in Moscow or this pathetic Lenin statuette in a forgotten village, the writing on the wall seems to have a meaning. In the more advanced communist republics of Czechoslovakia, Poland and East Germany the few remaining slogans in the streets are simply a sop to their Soviet masters, the citizens themselves having long since ignored their existence. In Russia these enticements to be good productive citizens were stuck everywhere, though whether they were there as a reminder or because they weren't already good I could not be sure.

With a woman now in the compartment some of the niceties of civilized behaviour had to be observed. Somehow it seemed out of place in this primitive land. Discreetly I waited out in the corridor as my Swiss friend's wife made herself 'decent'. On this particular morning it seemed that everyone had hit upon the 'decency hour' at the same time. The Alaskan was also hovering in the corridor as was the lean American. We held a male conference. The Alaskan spoke some Russian, so, with an eye to dodging my reception committee at Khabarovsk, I got him to jot down for me the Russian for 'A return hard-class ticket to Vladivostok please'.

The 'decency hour' came to an end with the emergence of the ladies: the Russians were dressed as if for the Olympics in track suits, the foreign community in creased and impractical creations.

The hint of a change in the earth earlier was confirmed by sight of the distant foothills of the Great Mongolian ranges. Everyone rushed to the corridor windows, exclaiming loudly, like shipwrecked mariners having their first glimpse of land.

Soon that land was rolling heavily and, though the tenacious forest still clung to it, crests of rock began to break through the golden surf. Rock. I had almost forgotten what the stuff looked like.

We would be at Irkutsk soon after midnight (18.00 hours Moscow time). There was plenty of rock there too, but more important to the community of the train, it was a replenishment centre. In the restaurant car nearly everything was 'off'. The new waiter was a big florid type who had a bad habit of saying that something was 'off' even though it wasn't. *'Pivo, Neit'*, he would pronounce when I asked for beer, ignoring the guzzling going on at the next table.

For the evening meal that day I was reduced to an item called beluga belly flesh, which, surprisingly, tasted like fresh salmon. It looked more like the hide of that dinosaur I was talking about and the Swiss couple played safe and stuck to borsch. For a sweet the waiter recommended *stolichny*, which was the only sweet available anyway. It turned out to be a Russian copy of our own castle pudding and I appreciated the waiter's desire to get rid of it. The crust was as hard as the permafrost! The meal ended with the usual battle of the bill, the waiter beating a rhythmic rumba with his beads and supplementing his calculations with equations written on the tablecloth.

For exercise I made regular hikes the full length of the train. It wasn't the ideal setting for a constitutional: the swaying corridors and inter-coach connections were made more difficult to negotiate by the unconscious rudeness of Russian transitees who were inclined to walk at instead of past you. Hard class was at the rear and, though well-filled, was perfectly adequate. Much more open and communal than the soft-class compartments, the hard bunks were well padded with the bedding supplied. There was a deadly hush and cessation of all activities as I passed through.

The impending arrival at Irkutsk broke the routine of the night. Ignoring my bed roll I watched the great Angara River flickering in the darkness and, as we drew into the city, catching its lights to jostle them playfully in its huge paw.

It might have been the middle of the night to me but it was well into the working morning so far as Intourist was concerned.

I was whisked off the train and pushed off on my compulsory city tour even before I could see my hotel or contemplate breakfast. A mousy little girl of Japanese extraction was my escort as the taxi of 1930 vintage rattled me through the tired-looking town.

In the event it was a useful tour. It was hardly enjoyable for the morning was bitterly cold, but I was beginning to see more in these Soviet towns then just their superficial drabness. Between the lines of the production achievement recital from Valya (I think that was the girl's name) and the inevitable Lenin statue pilgrimage I could glean points of interest.

Chekhov had some kind words to say about the place. In 1890 he wrote: '(It) is a splendid town. Thoroughly cultured. A theatre, museum, municipal park with music (and) good hotels.' Since then it has grown into a city boasting large factories, a university, a library housed in the one-time Czarist governor's residence, and a lot of sedate nineteenth-century public buildings set amongst tree-lined, wide-pavemented streets of residential *izbas*. In the central square, on the site of the former Kazan Cathedral, stands the pretentious House of the Soviets, itself almost dwarfed by a new Intourist hotel for visitors holding luxury-class vouchers. Nearby are three churches, all charming in their day but now in use as museums or storehouses. Only one, the two hundred-year-old Spasskaya, is being physically restored, and it was caged in a network of scaffolding. The eighteenth-century Russian Orthodox Church of the Risen Cross at the other end of Irkutsk was one of only two remaining places of worship and, to my surprise, Valya recommended me to attend a service there.

My hotel turned out to be the hardly originally-named Siberia. Its charms (or lack of them) were gloomily similar to those of the Novosibirsk.

I slept well as one does after a heavy dose of train travel. Seating myself in the big dining room next morning I refused to be segregated to a stuffy little room with a thicker carpet. While I waited for breakfast an East German party sat down at their group table. I listened to their gutteral chatter, watched them eating their yoghurt and worked myself into a private hate over

Germans in general and red Germans in particular. Suddenly a woman in her middle fifties detached herself from the group and came over to my table. Her action was prompted entirely by kindness and a desire to welcome a lone foreigner. We spoke a mixture of English and German and our exchange of pleasantries ended with her inviting me to join the group on the day's outing to Lake Baikal. Shame and gratitude combined to make me feel extremely humble.

The previous day I had asked Valya about the chances of a visit to Baikal, but she had shrugged and looked uncomfortable. I was a lone tourist and therefore was not to be encouraged. So there were 'difficulties'.

The German group's Intourist guide was made of sterner stuff, even providing me with a packed lunch. There was room on the coach, she said, so of course I could come.

It would have been a pleasant day anyway, but a brilliant sun in a cloudless sky made it doubly so. We spent an hour atop a snow-bound rocky mound, a trig point and a landmark, from which opened out a stupendous view across the taiga to the white-capped Mongolian mountains beyond. At Port Baikal, near the original lake station that was the terminus of the old Trans-Siberian Railway, we picnicked amidst the marching trees.

Suddenly it was there, a gigantic scar of water stretching to far horizons. Except for the Caspian, which is described as a sea, Baikal is the largest lake in the world. It is 390 miles long and up to 50 miles wide. Eighteen hundred species of plant life, many of them unique, live in its crystal-clear waters, 5,500 feet deep. Fed by 333 rivers, and emptied by one — the titanic Angara — it broods in a silence that is uncanny.

He who hasn't seen Baikal, they say, hasn't seen Siberia. The name is derived from the Turkish *Bai-kul* meaning 'holy sea'. The lake resulted from a fissure in the earth's crust caused by an earthquake. Even though 2,000 miles from the sea it contains salt-water fish and is subject to sudden violent storms that whip its placid waters into a frenzy. Its uncharted bed is a graveyard of railway engines, trucks, lorries and motorcars — among them the rotting skeletons of men. This jetsam is the legacy of those who failed to negotiate the lake's treacherous winter ice through the

79

centuries. And with their death were born the stories which are woven into the legends of Baikal. One much older legend concerns the Angara. According to the Buryats, Lake Baikal is the father of his 333 river daughters including, of course, Angara. She was restless, poor soul, because she had heard rumours of the Yenesei, that bold warrior river in the west. So one night she broke out of her mountain nursery, cutting a deep cleft as she threw herself towards Yenesei. Father Baikal, aroused by her escape, hurled a rock at his erring daughter but too late. She had gone to join the Yenesei 600 miles away. The rock remains, the great Sharman Rock now 20 million years old. It is a sacred rock, as befits one from which doubtful criminals were flung, chained, into the torrent in which it stands. If they drowned they were pronounced innocent; if they survived to reach the shore they were guilty and had their throats cut! We threw pebbles to ripple the surface of the dark water, hunted for mica on the shore and I even braved a swim in the chilly waters.

Next day I took myself to church in Irkutsk. It is actually a cathedral, the Russian Orthodox Krestowosdwishenskaya, to give it its full title, and it stands among trees, a piece of old Russia, near the centre of the city. It is a white solid building with green copper domes. A police check was in progress as I entered and was besieged by several beggars hidden from view behind the walls. In the big porch old men and women sat packed together on a bench listening to the service through the open door. The body of the church was heavily ornamental with paintings on the ceilings and candelabras, ikons, pencil-thin candles and gold-painted effigies leaving little room for a largely peasant and middle-aged congregation of about thirty. The shawled old women and *tolstofka*-clad, peak-capped old men came straight out of a Tolstoy book, and a young couple who had come in out of curiosity seemed more embarrassed by the surroundings than by the act of religion taking place.

By Siberian town standards Irkutsk is an old city. It was founded in 1652. For a period it was an administrative centre for the surrounding region, staging post for exiles (including Trotsky) and headquarters of the gold-mining industry. In 1920, Kolchak was executed here in the Civil War. The network of streets are flanked by chocolate-coloured single and two-storey wooden houses, some with their original raised sidewalks of wooden planks. Nearly all of them, large and small, had beautifully carved baroque window frames outlined in green and white or blue, colours that the Russians use with genius. After the hideous modernity of Novosibirsk, Irkutsk is a place to explore with rapturous abandon.

My last night in the city, and with the German group departed, I was refused service in the main dining room and though I held out, simmering with rage, for almost an hour time alone forced me to the 'foreigners room'. I hope it was bugged, for, if so, someone got an earful.

Back on yet another Trans-Siberian Express my existence was to undergo a change after Irkutsk. I left in the dusk of evening and I could only hear the train passing through the granite bastion along the southern shores of Lake Baikal. We were to be exclusively steam-hauled from Irkutsk onward and the echoes of the mighty locomotive in cutting and tunnel made a satanic lullaby.

I came to life in the morning to find the train was accompanying a wide river which my map indicated as the Selenge. Unlike earlier no-nonsense rivers it zig-zagged violently along valleys and between hills, while in the background the Khangai Nurv mountains of Mongolia loomed ominously close. It was cold in the coach until somebody up front switched the heating on.

At Ulan Ude, capital of the Buryat Autonomous Soviet Socialist Republic, I joined the more hard-up members of the community for a picnic breakfast in the station. The melancholy old women had got themselves organised here and were installed in a long stable-like shed with their wares before them. On sale were eggs, milk, yoghurt, gherkins, tomatoes, blueberries, home-baked pies, cakes and batter puddings, and I joined the throng of pyjama and underwear-clad customers.

After Ulan Ude the pace of the train noticeably slowed down. We stopped more frequently, sometimes in the middle of nowhere, and the stature of the places served decreased. It was at one of these lesser stations that I met the colonel.

81

He strode up to me as I was photographing something that was probably forbidden to photograph and I braced myself for trouble. He was a big burly fellow and, in what he presumed to be English, invited me to his compartment for breakfast; a 'Red Army breakfast' he said.

Any visions I may have conjured up of fried eggs and bacon evaporated when I perceived the huge flagon on the table of his compartment. The 'Red Army breakfast' opened with a mild interrogation by the colonel, whose jacket carried a veritable array of medal ribbons, as to what a lone *'Anglicki'* was doing the far end of Siberia. And, yes, he knew I was a soldier too by my martial steps as I exercised on the platform. He then went on to list his battles of the 'Great Patriotic War' in crisp military fashion and then at dictation speed. With each action he spilt a generous portion of home-made vodka into our two tea glasses and I caught onto the idea, though my few Normandy skirmishes soon gave out. But to keep the Colonel happy and my glass topped up I delved into history a little and borrowed a few earlier campaigns and their battles. The last thing I remember before I fell asleep was the Colonel covering me with his greatcoat and offering me a handsome salute. I hoped I'd upheld the honour of the British Army.

There was also Peter. A student, he was on his way to Komsomolsk. I told him that he was the second person I had met who was going to Komsomolsk and he replied, of course, the hard-class was full of them.

Komsomolsk is a new industrial city north-east of Khabarovsk and likewise on the Amur River. Founded in 1932 it was built on a site hacked out of dense forest by idealistic communist youths and is still growing. Another such project is Bratsk and its great dam south of Irkutsk.

Peter told me of his hopes and fears for the future. A native of Lvov close to the Polish border in the Ukraine, he could hardly have found a destination further away and still remain within the Soviet borders. He was immensely proud of his home town and, though far too young to have known Polish rule, he had a fervent love for things Polish.

After the third English cigarette in my compartment he invited me to meet his friends in the more austere portion of the train. This subsequent visit to the hard-class coaches was a friendlier affair and, escorted, I had to go around shaking everybody by the hand and patting children's heads. Many of these people were emigrants with all their goods and chattels and I could sense the strong community and pioneering spirit.

That evening Peter and I dined together, mostly on beer, in the restaurant car. We were joined by an older man who wanted to bombard me with questions, mainly of the kind not likely to endear him to his régime. But popsies or politics, he got the answers and, full of beer and vodka, I found myself lecturing the entire coach on the rights and wrongs of the East-West situation.

Another night, another dawn. Again that incredible horizon of trees rose to circumscribe the sky. I saw off my friend of the 'unprogressive' views at Chita station. A town of the *oblast* of the same name, Chita is singularly unromantic-looking, in spite of its close connection with the precious stone industry. Crystal, topaz and amethyst seemed odd companions of this grey little town of square-box houses.

It was on this train that I learnt to play chess. I never have been one for games of this sort but because it is the national game I felt obliged to accept the invitation to learn. I sat miserably moving pieces about the board having them taken away with every move. About the third game I think I learnt the general idea, and all the while my cigarette supply took a beating.

And so another day ground on. At the slightest pretext or at no pretext at all I was either visited in my compartment or invited to others. Sometimes it was my dwindling supply of 'hard' cigarettes that was behind it, but more often it was basic Russian courtesy and kindness to a lone foreigner on their train, together with a unique opportunity to make contact at no risk.

There was a tremendous community spirit on the train and before long everybody knew everybody in their coaches. But on the station platforms I was a leper: ignored by most, stared at by the locals and befriended only by the stalwarts such as the Colonel and Peter.

Peter was my most frequent visitor. And as frequent were our hikes down the long narrow trail to the hard-class coaches, with him speaking loud English to impress the natives. Another student monopolized me for a considerable period simply to compile a dossier on my person, commencing with my wages, and working right through my possessions. Everywhere in the Soviet Union I was to find that such individual possessions as a house, land or car created either incredulity or extreme respect.

I put to Peter my Vladivostok problem giving him sight of my reduced cigarette hoard as I did so, and suggested he might like to help. Yes, he would get me the ticket and the reservation. He too was alighting at Khabarovsk and he would contact me at the hotel. He seemed to know which hotel. There would be no problem at all.

I slept well for the last full night before Khabarovsk. The landscape was as flat as a pancake again, with just a hint of strained-out mountains in the far distance. Around mid-day we crossed another mammoth river, which might have been the Bureya, a tributary of the great Amur which formed the border with Manchuria only a cannon's shot away. I noticed that each and every bridge was guarded by soldiers. Somewhere in the night we had passed out of Siberia to enter a region called the Soviet Far East.

Lack of proper exercise was affecting my appetite. Pilgrimages to the restaurant car became rare, and meals turned to snacks. A furtive little man came in to offer me a string of anti-Soviet jokes of the 'What Lenin said to the bishop' variety. I couldn't understand any of them but laughed politely. It came to me that these 'new Siberians' tended to take the State less seriously and tragically than other Russians. With Moscow thousands of miles away they were 'off the leash', more suspect of authority and able to rely on their own judgement and assessment of a situation. In a way they are like the Americans; convinced that their forests, rivers, lakes and towns have no equal in the world.

The joke merchant was my last caller. Though the train was not due at Khabarovsk until midnight I was left severely alone as if by intention. Not since Irkutsk had I a resident in the compartment, yet the other compartments were reasonably full. I began to view the coach attendants with deep distrust. It could only have been they who diverted potential occupants. Yet Intourist it was that made the reservations and surely even their deviousness could not ensure my segregation when such reservations were being made over the whole length of the line?

An early sunset coincided with a return of the hills, and the beautiful autumnal gold of the trees tempted me to the rear of the coach to take some last photographs. Hardly had I focused on a scene I wanted when the camera was knocked sideways and I received a severe castigation from a blue-uniformed policeman who had appeared from nowhere. And then I understood the reason for the shunning I was receiving. The line ran very close indeed to the Chinese border and, being in a restricted zone, police patrols were on the train. And with authority came fear, or at least prudence. I stalked back to my empty compartment.

The final halts were fun no longer. The sculptures of Lenin and the absurd slogans became oppressive. There was little food left in the restaurant car and the station stalls could produce only potato mash and pumpkins. I began to long for a sight of something luxurious. Only the train itself maintained a splendour and a dignity in the face of an atmosphere gone sour.

It was after one in the morning when we crawled into the city of Khabarovsk. The fact that we were an hour late was obviously an exception and the tannoy was making a meal of it explaining the reasons. For the first time since I started the journey I was glad to leave a Russian train.

Khabarovsk grows on you. The growth in fact was rapid from the moment the Trans-Siberian Express steamed off into the fog of its own anticlimax, to the moment I saw the pretty girl from Intourist who had come to meet me. I was even dazzled into an apology for having kept her waiting though it did occur to me that *I* hadn't asked her to do so. She was beautifully uncommunicative as we raced through the blacked-out streets of Khabarovsk.

My hotel was the AMYP which I thought an odd kind of name until I realized the word was Cyrillic for Amur. It being two in the morning and there being only one tourist no excuses could be found to prolong the agony of reception. I bid my Intourist guide and Chinese chauffeur good night, arranged to meet them later in the morning for my compulsory tour and made the expedition to my bedroom. Hardly had I dumped my bag when I found myself being solicited by a weird, unshaven individual who barged in unannounced. His first request was for a cigarette; his second was less explicit but it concerned the fact that his bedroom was next door! With some difficulty and gentle force I got rid of him.

My bedroom was, again, no more than adequate, except that someone had forgotten to finish the toilet which was full of broken bricks and dust. I locked the door and went to bed.

I was awoken by the telephone. A woman's voice said something in a questioning tone and I was about to answer '*Ya neponimayu*' when I realised I *did* understand and changed it to 'Niet'. The second ring was an early call I had not ordered. I left the receiver off the hook and flung the bedclothes over my head. But I couldn't win. The last inmate of the room had left the radio on full volume and at five am an exalted rendering of the Soviet national anthem hit me like an electric shock. This set off my passionate neighbour who started banging on the wall excitedly.

It was another glorious day of sunshine in spite of the nip in the air as I introduced myself to Khabarovsk. Once more I made a bee-line for the river. One cannot miss the Amur. It is one of those rivers that makes itself felt. Slowly and majestically it flowed to its reunion with the Ussuri less than a mile away. There, like aristocratic giants, they wound against each other before becoming one. And behind the green on the opposite bank, plain to see, were the blue hills of China. Against all this Khabarovsk hasn't a chance. It is considerably older than Novosibirsk, but only comparatively recently, in 1922, was it resurrected and given prominence. Since then thousands of tons of concrete have been poured into what was virtually an overgrown village. Amongst a concentration of *izbas* and barefoot children I sampled Soviet ice-cream, which has to be laboriously weighed out on scales, and a glass of non-alcoholic beer called *Kvas* from a tank on wheels before returning for my tryst.

My guide was late, as I knew she would be. Her name was Jane and her irritation now receded, she even laughed when I told her of my all-night cabaret. She started off, like the others, with the usual roll of local industrial triumphs, and threatened a visit to the Amur Cable Factory. But her personal interest in Britain —

and particularly the Royal Family — proved her undoing and soon our roles were reversed with her asking the questions and me providing the answers. There was a French film in town to which foreigners had immediate access as opposed to the locals who had to reserve seats weeks in advance. So, in lieu of the cable works, we went to the pictures. As a sop to her conscience I allowed Jane to tell me a little about Yerofei Khabarov, how he erected a fort on the site of the city in 1652 and how in 1858 the Russians settled there under Count Muraviev. We had a quick look at Yerofei's statue and then queue-barged the cinema.

I would have bet very little on the chances of my student friend keeping his appointment. And I'd have been wrong for there he was in the crowded foyer of the hotel that afternoon. We greeted one another prudently and caught a bus to the railway station. He left me outside while the deed was done and came out wielding both ticket and hard-class berth reservation, this having been applied for early that morning. I paid the amount owing him, as well as donating the remainder of my cigarettes for his trouble. I also invited him to spend the rest of the afternoon with me, but he declined with reluctance. Maybe the enormity of his crime was enough to bear without the stigma of being seen in the company of an imperialist warmonger.

Subsequent examination of the ticket revealed it to be valid for only a single journey to Vladivostok. This would mean applying for a return berth reservation — compulsory on long-distance journeys in the USSR — in Vladivostok, an action which filled me with dread. The less people who knew I was on forbidden territory the better.

In the light of the *fait accompli* of the ticket I made my plans. With four days in Khabarovsk, one of which was now expiring, I had time to reach Vladivostok, spend eight hours in that city and return to Khabarovsk before my scheduled departure on the fourth day. Both the outward and return journey would be made overnight and I'd still be back for my last night in Khabarovsk. If all went well nobody would know that I had been away.

The train was, again, the 'Russia', the same east-bound express that had brought me to Khabarovsk just twenty-four hours earlier. I left my luggage in my bedroom, slunk out of the hotel at midnight and arrived at the station to see the great express slide into its allotted platform in a cloud of steam.

I found my more humble coach at the rear with difficulty. The girl attendant gave me an odd glance and twice checked my ticket. I thought she was going to start asking questions, but a scuffle the other end of her domain sent her scurrying off. With more difficulty I located my berth amongst the prostrate, snoring, smelly bodies. An old woman was sleeping loudly on the numbered space that corresponded with that on my ticket but the one above was free. I clambered up amidst a chorus of grunts. As soon as the train moved the attendant appeared with my bedding which I spread with difficulty. I didn't bother to undress.

On the whole it was not a bad night. At least my mattress was soft. The class of travel refers to the bunks, 'soft' indicating four sprung bunks in a closed compartment, 'hard' describing a more crowded wooden-bunk-filled open coach. But since bedding is issued to both classes of passenger the texture of the bunks themselves is immaterial. The 'hards' are more communal which can be either an advantage or disadvantage depending upon individual outlook.

From my vantage point on the top bunk I watched the coach come alive in the morning. Children's voices, in laughter and complaint, rose in volume as parental control laxed and big women contorted themselves replacing or tightening garments removed or loosened in the night.

I lay contentedly dozing and reading until quite late. My bunk was too high for me to see out of the window and I did not want to draw attention to myself until it became necessary. The train was not scheduled to reach Vladivostok until early afternoon so I had the whole morning to lie low. When the coach attendant began collecting bedding I was forced to emerge.

There was a flurry of excitement as it flashed through the community that an Englishman had joined it. There was amazement, too, for tourists never travelled hard class. I tried to tell a hushed audience that this was no fault or choice of the tourists and that their own organisation — Intourist — was to blame. I hope they got the message, for the compulsory segregation in

88

hotels and elsewhere was a source of bitterness among simpler Russians.

I was invited to share breakfast with the owners of the bunks around me and soon was replete with salami, hard-boiled eggs, fish and cheese. I was fussed over by old men and women of peasant stock whose gnarled hands kept passing more food every time my own were empty. A refusal did no good, only provoking noisy indignation.

Outside, the grey morning was increasing the sombreness of rolling countryside that reminded me again of the lowlands of Scotland. Uncultivated grasslands rising above the undulations were, in turn, overlooked by higher hills and a narrow road ran for miles alongside the railway. Later the hills became slag heaps, universally ugly, and some birch trees offered the illusion that we were back in Europe. Yet China was but five miles distant across that dew-laden grass.

We stopped at Nadejdinskaya, the junction for Nakhodka, and among my fellow-passengers strolling on the platform I noticed that police were more in evidence than usual. They were infesting the train, too, and my bunk began to live up to its class as I retired, subdued and mattressless, to its bare refuge.

The few minutes it had fallen behind schedule the train made up in the last thirty miles and we drew into Vladivostok station exactly on time. I felt a glow of satisfaction. With the last 500 miles from Khabarovsk I had, no matter what happened next, accomplished my goal. I was nearly six thousand miles east of Moscow, nearly eight thousand miles from home. I had reached the Pacific on the other side of the world and, except for the English Channel — not much larger than some of the Siberian rivers — it had all been done by trains.

Vladivostok means 'ruler of the East'. Count Muraviev, who had a hand in the colonising of Khabarovsk, selected the site of the port after the treaty of Aigun in 1858 by which the district was ceded to Russia. In 1860 the first settlers arrived and the port itself came into being twelve years later — to the discomfort of Japan who had no great desire to have a Russian naval base on her doorstep. But Vladivostok is not only a naval port. Its four-by-one-mile harbour, kept ice-free all the year round, is home to the Soviet whaling flotillas and her far Eastern fishing fleet. The town itself is heavily industrialised.

It is also overpopulated with soldiers as well as sailors. I found this out before I had left its rambling station as a battalion of fully armed troops disgorged from a train on the same platform as us. I went in search of the ticket office. If reservations had to be made I thought it wise to get mine done early. I got out my piece of paper detailing the Russian for 'a return hard class ticket to Khabarovsk, please', and pushed it at a face behind a grill. The face spoke words to the effect that I must obtain reservations from an office in the town and my paper came back with an address scribbled on it.

The town I discovered to be exceedingly awful. Even Novosibirsk had beauty and charm in comparison. Ports anywhere can rarely boast of exotic surroundings but those of Vladivostok, even with its backdrop of hills rising behind, were truly functional. I found the office with the help of a middle-aged citizen muffled up as if it were already midwinter. He walked with me a considerable distance out of his way and refused my thank-you offering of a caramel.

The office seemed to be a department of the railway. It was pillared, high-ceilinged and full of travel posters — mostly of places unattainable to Russians. No one spoke English. I didn't think they would. My request for a reservation was understood but something seemed to be required to support the application. It was not a passport and anyway I had no intention of giving mine up unless strictly necessary since the visa was now weeks out of date and I was six thousand miles off course. It could only confuse the issue. They kept invoking the name of Intourist which didn't help for they knew as I knew, there was no Intourist in Vladivostok. Then I had a brainwave and mumbled the word 'diplomat' not quite certain if I wasn't making things worse. From my wallet I withdrew and displayed my driving licence, regimental association membership card and credit card. Each came under interested scrutiny, the credit card scoring highest points. Shrugs followed, but they were constructive shrugs — the kind that says 'what the hell anyway'. Came the capitulation, and the indication that I was to return for both ticket and reservation that evening, and I felt like cheering. Thankfully I fled.

I have never been able to hide a guilty conscience. And the one I bore as I skulked down those depressing Vladivostok streets was the most monumental ever. The fact annoyed me for I could not accept that I was doing wrong. 'Don't go and do anything silly', had been the refrain from my loved ones as I left home and here I was flouting the rules simply to satisfy a whim. In my heart I knew the source of the conscience.

Certain elementary precautions had been taken. My camera, for instance remained in my Khabarovsk hotel. I looked reasonably nondescript Russian in a pair of thick fawn slacks and leather jacket. I had not shaved that morning. But I still jumped at the sight of the expressionless little man standing in what was almost certainly Karl Marx Square. I had long realized the significance of the Lenin-style cloth cap and ill-fitting overcoat. I sheered away but when I stopped to tie a shoe-lace he wasn't following. Later I thought one was and led an imaginary watchdog circuitous route through a department store. But I suspect that the only person I was tiring was myself.

Suddenly I saw the sea. It was brown and lifeless but the moment was a milestone in my life. I have seen the Pacific many times before, but that glimpse between an unfinished building block and a sheaf of dockside cranes will shine the brighter in my memory.

To approach the sea I had to walk along the harbour front. Shipping of every description jostled the docks which hummed with activity. I watched deck-swabbing on trawlers and whalers and the unloading of crates from cargo vessels. All the while, in the background, the gaunt forms of cruisers and destroyers were outlined starkly against the sky. Seamen and sailors, all speaking the language of the sea in spite of their contrasting dress, thronged the dockside. Soldiers, out of place in maritime territory, lounged around a convoy of heavy lorries and I felt their eyes following me as I walked stiffly by. Red slogans announced: LENIN — OUR TEACHER AND OUR FRIEND from wooden hoardings.

I had a meal in a stand-up buffet serving frankfurter-type sausages, cabbage and potato. It was a rough dock-area kind of place but its exclusive supply of sausage and mash offered a minimum of chat. Late in the afternoon I walked around the corner of a back street into a funeral cortège. A double row of men in white shirts escorted an open coffin carried shoulder high; they walked purposefully and looked neither left nor right and I strained ghoulishly to see the head of the corpse which lay against a pillow of flowers. Behind them followed a gaggle of women with no apparent sense of the dignity of the occasion.

Some of those back streets housed families living in poverty pure and simple. There is no other word for it. Many left-wing writers on Russia do not recognize that poverty can exist in a communist state and it gives me no pleasure to prove them wrong. Perhaps it is a reason for the exclusion of tourists from Vladivostok.

With dusk I entered a bookshop to browse around the shelves as I invariably do when at a loose end. Most of the literature was political and deadly dull. A man recognised me as English (so much for my efforts to look otherwise!) and from behind the pages of a large volume he told me something of his years in both a Hitler and a Stalin camp. My heart went out to him. Now he was a man without rights and without hope.

I left to return to the railway office and then to the station. I'd seen enough of Vladivostok. On the way I passed a cripple, horribly disfigured. On the man's jacket was a treble row of medal ribbons and I realized that he was one of the legion of maimed ex-servicemen who had fought for a country that exiled its broken ranks to places not visited by foreign tourists. To me this was perhaps the ugliest facet of the Soviet Union; one that never reaches the pages of the glib Intourist handouts.

The collection of my ticket produced no incidents and I offered no arguments even when I noticed it was for soft-class travel. I still had two hours to wait before departure of the train but in the station I felt on safer ground. Hadn't I made a simple mistake and come to Vladivostok instead of Nakhodka and was now waiting like a good citizen for the return train? A bit thin perhaps but it sounded better here in the station that it would have done in the vicinity of those battleships.

I immersed myself in my book propped up against a pillar and was thus engaged when I felt someone staring at me. I changed position and caught sight of my watcher. He was another member of the Lenin cloth cap brigade. Forcing myself to read a couple more paragraphs I stood my ground, then, as if tiring of the book, closed it and ambled off towards the platforms. A convenient lavatory, masked by the left-luggage room, offered sanctuary and in I went — straight into a vast woman, arms akimbo. I had a split second to choose between the female mammoth and the secret policeman. I chose the policeman, executed a smart right about turn, and emerged discomforted from the ladies toilet. But the sleuth was not in sight having either failed to follow me or, as I intended him to, passed by. Tiring of cops and robbers I took refuge in the pungent tobacco fog of a waiting hall.

My soft empty compartment was a treat. The coach girl gave me bedding and a long, hard, but not unfriendly look to go with it. I thought ruefully of my £30 of bed that had gone for a burton in my Khabarovsk hotel. But my dismal little excursion had not been wasted. Maybe it had been cheap at the price.

Back at Khabarovsk, Intourist gave me what could almost be described as a royal welcome. I was obviously the first tourist they had 'lost' and the return of the prodigal son had them rushing over to my hotel full of the joys of spring. I could tell that the carefully guarded questions were not simply a personal interest in my welfare. The hotel had reported my absence, I was told, and all the staff of the Intourist office had been *most* concerned. What *had* I been doing? They were in an unfortunate position. To have demanded an explanation would have put Intourist in a wrong light. And as I wasn't telling they could only jump to conclusions. My answers were evasive in the extreme, giving the impression possibly of shame so they jumped to the wrong conclusion. Firmly convinced that I had spent a couple of nights with a girl they next wanted to know *who*. I made no denials and as their concern was obviously centred upon some female 'deviationist' whose political education I may have corrupted all the more at the expense of my own morals I let them stew. Finally I got a mild lecture on inconsiderateness.

The rest of the day I spent behaving myself in Khabarovsk. Next morning I flew west. I had not asked to fly but Intourist had designated it and that was that. Back at Novosibirsk I changed direction and flew south across the barren corrugations of the Kirgiz Steppe to Alma Ata — City of Apples — grovelling at the foot of the Tien Shan — Mountains of Heaven — and onto Tashkent; a new Tashkent of modern concrete that had arisen from the earthquake-stricken old town. There is a perfectly adequate railway line covering the southward route but its trains — if there are any — are not for the likes of you and me. 'There is no railway; there are no trains', insisted Intourist when I pushed the point and expressed a desire to make my journey that way. Yet even Soviet railway maps show the 2,000-mile stretch of line between Novosibirsk and Alma Ata though without a single station. One, however, I must have flown over. It was Karagunda, where the penal camps are not just memories.

From Tashkent a short-haul monoplane made a poor substitute for a golden road, but the byways of legend were also barred, so I had to make do with an air corridor to Samarkand.

The impact of Samarkand is staggering. It speaks to one of Tamerlane and Ulug Beg. I spent my allotted hours amongst its treasures before shuddering on to the city of Emirs and carpets that is Bukhara. And here you have history breathing down your neck as you wander, deliciously oppressed by ghosts of generations past, along streets unchanged from the dawn of time.

From Bukhara back to Tashkent and the long flight across the time zones of the incredible Kizil Kum and Kara Kum deserts, the swamps of the Murghab River, the ruins of Merv — oldest of all cities — the Aral and Caspian seas until a long overdue night finally catches up to curtain a mind that is drunk with wonder. But the darkness could not blot out a city sitting squarely on the Volga. The atmosphere in the aircraft was heady with emotion as we passed above the twinkling lights. Few Russians had not lost a son, a husband, a dear friend at Stalingrad, and their blood-soaked land they loved the more for it.

From Kiev I managed to get back to the railway again and caught the Danubius Express from Moscow to Bucharest. A steady rain was falling to lay tears on the great black Ukrainian

Plain that is also drenched in soldiers' blood and is therefore the more terrible. Sad little villages swept by, their houses a contradiction of white paint, their tiny gardens tended as of gestures of despair.

At Ungeni, close to the border with Romania, some of my misdemeanours caught up with me. An irate personage wearing the starred epaulettes of an officer bore down upon me in the station while I was dutifully changing my remaining roubles into a mixture of Western currency. He waved my passport which had been taken off me by the lady of the coach. 'Are you Mister Portway?' he demanded in a voice that showed he knew damn well I was. 'Do you realize your visa is out of order?' he went on and the anger was tinged with awe.

I said the last place they had promised me an extension was Tashkent.

'*Tashkent!*' The voice rose an octave. 'Where else have you been?'

Seeing no point in holding back I gave him the full list but carefully omitted Vladivostok. I was unable to understand what the fuss was about for I was following my confirmed itinerary and was now on permitted ground.

The officer's face became a dark thunder cloud as I reeled off each city.

'And now Ungeni', he ended for me. 'Don't you know your visa is for Moscow and *Moscow only* and that it is already weeks out of date?'

'Oh *that*,' I replied gaily, 'Intourist never gave me time to get the thing altered.'

The man all but burst a blood vessel. His voice rose even higher as he recited the regulations I had apparently broken.

I said nothing. Sometimes silence is golden.

I was to get to know Ungeni. For eighteen hours I was forcibly tethered to its dismal station overlooking an overgrown village. Here my crimes came home to roost. My visa, of course, was the root of the trouble. Vladivostok never came up. Moscow had to be informed of my deficiencies and I suspect that it was poor telephonic communication that was behind much of the delay. I spent a night in a border guards' hostel listening to a lullaby of bogie-changing as trains arrived from or departed to Romania.

There is a myth still going about that the wider 5-ft gauge is evidence of traditional Russian suspicion of the outside world. Actually it was an American called Whistler — the one with the mother-in-law — who recommended the wider gauge. The strategic significance is negative, since it is easier for an invader to relay one rail on a broad gauge track than it is to widen the gauge on standard gauge track in the opposite direction. At daybreak I watched the bogie switching operations with some interest. They had the job down to a fine art and the most common articles to be seen on Soviet border stations are discarded bogies.

Next morning I wandered into the town and along a road out of it. By so doing I came face to face with the physical border of the USSR; a conglomeration of electrified fences and watch-towers into which the little road petered out into a rash of concrete dragons' teeth. It all looked depressingly familiar. Across the river Prut I could see Romania, its territory ending in a mine-laden river bank.

Even the stroll cost me a reprimand but I really dug in my heels when told that I would have to pay for my overnight accommodation. The cheek of it. After all *I* didn't ask to stay in a damp barracks! Refusing point blank the demands of the Intourist official who had been summoned all the way from Odessa, we finally negotiated a compromise. I would surrender one accommodation voucher if the Soviet authorities purchased my onward rail ticket to Bucharest. And, you know, they did just that!

They gave me the green light that afternoon. A soldier with an automatic rifle escorted me onto the Bucharest-bound express, proffered an unsmiling salute and waited pointedly in the corridor. The train belched and trundled out of the station. Close to the wire entanglements marking the frontier it stopped for the customary search. As we rolled towards the bridge, at the last moment, the soldier jumped off. Having forced me to remain on Soviet soil for eighteen hours authority was determined to ensure I remained no longer of my own free will. They needn't have worried.

Above: A meal stop on the line between Ibarra and San Lorenzo, Ecuador (chapter 9).

Left: A snack stop on the Quito to Guayaquil line in Ecuador (chapter 9).

Below: An Ecuadoran *Autocarril* skulking in a tunnel mouth on the Ibarra to San Lorenzo line (chapter 9).

'I felt a strange sensation of loss as I watched it go' — the Trans-Sib

ess about to leave from Novosibirsk station (chapter 3).

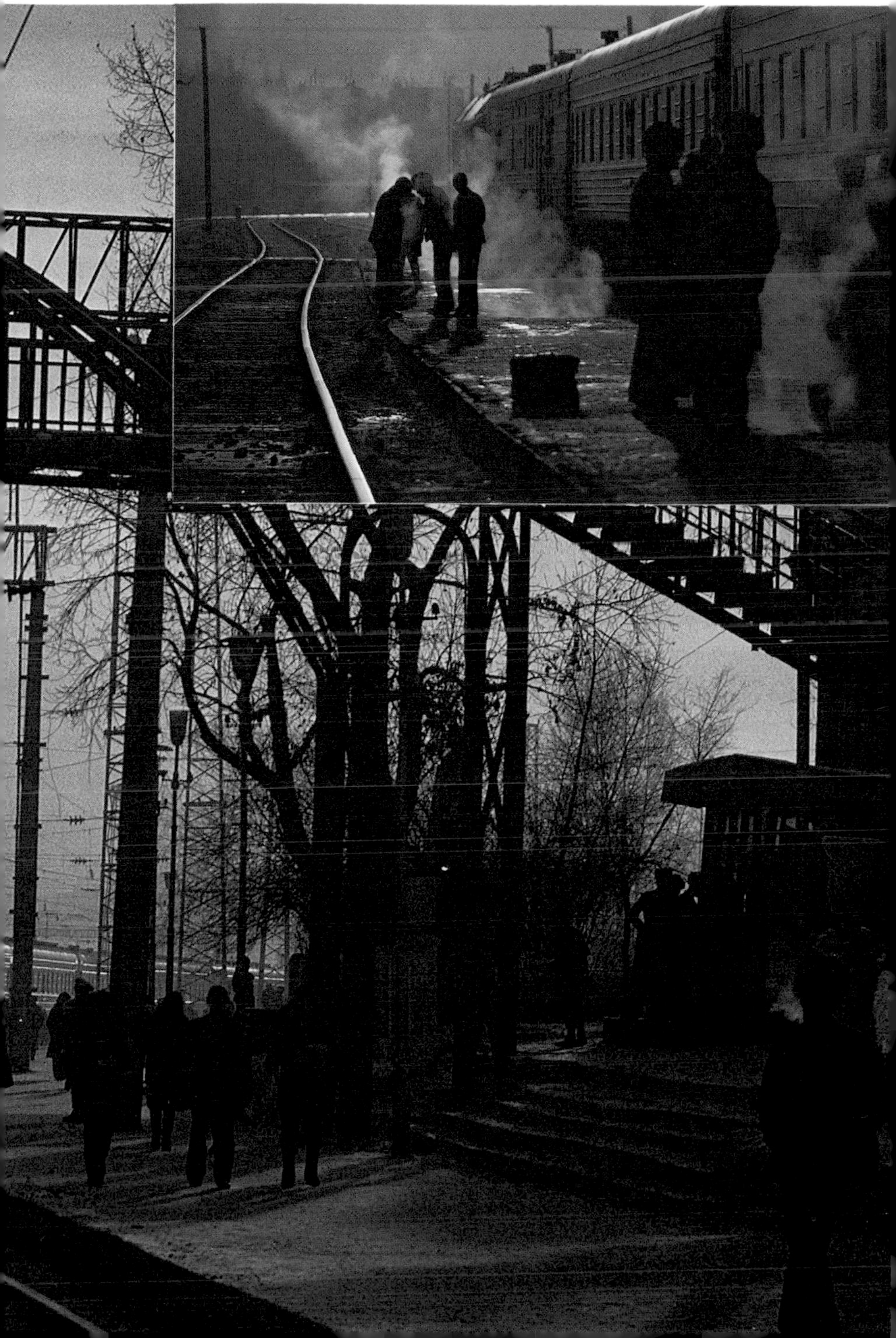

Right: 'My personal struggle with a new enemy, a new authority, was to begin' — railway lines at Leipzig, East Germany (introduction).

Below: 'The Trans-Siberian Express is a serious train burdened by its responsibilities' (chapter 3).

Opposite page, top: The train arriving at Elbasan, Albania (chapter 4).

Opposite page, bottom: A passenger train striding across the great empty plains near Castle Bran, Romania (chapter 4).

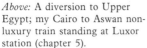

Above: A diversion to Upper Egypt; my Cairo to Aswan non-luxury train standing at Luxor station (chapter 5).

Top right: 'The crack Taj Express which took me to Agra and the Taj Mahal to see how the other half lived' (chapter 6).

Right: The crowded station at Delhi (chapter 6).

Below: Shunting operations in the railway yards of Jaipur, Rajasthan (chapter 6).

Above: 'Observing Africa from the comfort of a train' — the view from Matathai station over the Rift Valley to Longonot volcano (chapter 7).
Left: Kisumu railway scene (chapter 7).
Below left: A delayed train on the Nairobi to Kisumu line (chapter 7).
Below right: Dining in the restaurant car on the Nairobi to Mombasa Night Mail (chapter 7).
Overleaf: The VIA train and observation coach, Alberta, Canada (chapter 8).

4

The Balkan Rail Circuit

TIRANA—BELGRADE—BUDAPEST —BUCHAREST—SOFIA—ATHENS

I suppose it was a kind of reaction. From the longest railway in the world it was, to me, but a logical step to try the shortest: Albania. In 1970, the year of my visit, the total rail network was about 135 miles but, by dint of volunteer student labour reinforced with more technical help, lines now run between Fier and Vlora in the south, between Elbasan and Lake Ochrid, and north to Lac. The track is Czech made but Albanian laid with Chinese assistance. Diesel locomotives are from Czechoslovakia, shunting engines hail from Poland and other contributors of rolling stock are from East Germany, Hungary and China. The Albanian State Railway might not be the most sophisticated of systems but, at least, it is truly international.

My journey commenced in Montenegro. It was to lead me not only across the closed borders of the People's Republic of Albania but, subsequently, through all the people's republics of the Balkans. South from Dubrovnik, my vehicle had to be a bus for no trains run this way. Once a narrow-gauge railway wound through Montenegro, and its ghosts — mysterious empty cuttings and embankments — still haunt the northern end of the Montenegrin littoral. Since my journey the Yugoslav Railway's new Bar to Belgrade line — an engineering marvel of multiple tunnels and bridges — has been completed but there remains no link whatsoever between the Albanian State Railway and the main European network.

The geography of Montenegro fits its history. The barren rock, or Karst, of its mountains is more savage than beautiful. It is easy to see how the Black Mountain, as the region is called, was never subdued by force of arms. The territory is typical of that of Albania and, in a more general way, displays many characteristics of the Balkans as a whole.

THE BALKAN RAIL
CIRCUIT

Key

+++++ rail route

.... road route

BUDAPEST

Szoln

HUNGARY

Subotica

Novi Sad

YUGOSLAVIA

BELGRADE

MONTENEG

Dubrovnik

*ADRIATIC
SEA*

Lake Shkodra

Durres **TIRAN**

Elbasa

ALBAN

Though the Balkans form part of our continent, the fact does not immediately register, for the violent, irrational temperament of the Balkan countries is alien to our conception of an ordered Europe. For centuries men and nature have conspired to make this territory a hell on earth: Goths, Romans, Avars, Huns, Slavs, Magyars, Byzantines, Tartars, Turks, Venetians, Austrians, Russians and Germans have all fought for its inhospitable terrain. The history of the Balkans is a chronicle of atrocity interwoven with a fierce pride in the dark and bloody hills of a land sanctified forever by a burning love. These men of the Balkans have not had luck on their side. They have been brave but have all too often been beaten in battle. They have been industrious only to be broken by the terrible reversals of nature and human affairs. Prosperity invariably eludes them.

The region is a kind of microcosm of the universe. The modern states that have now emerged from the ancient empires hold within their grasp diverse cults, ethnic minorities and a passionately proclaimed uniqueness. Only in the last century has a vision of larger national loyalties been put to any account. Each nation has forged itself into an uneasy political entity proclaiming a grandiose destiny that tumbles over the rock-strewn path of archaic national politics.

With the exception of Greece, each of the countries is a communist state. True to form, even their communism is of an intensely nationalistic brand and there is not one that will blend with the other. Yugoslavia flirts with capitalism, earning hatred from Albania and distrust from the rest of the communist world. Bulgaria is a loyal appendage of the Soviet Union. Romania, while seeking ties with the West, craftily continues its ideological ties with the East. Albania has become an enemy of Moscow, a short-lived ally of Red China and flaunts a hatred of most of the rest of the world. Even the exception — Greece — conformed to type for a while when she replaced her monarchy by a military dictatorship only recently shaken off.

History has not been kind to the Balkans. Perhaps least of all to Albania.

There are two problems ahead of the intending traveller to Albania. The first is the basic one of getting into the country.

100

And, once in, there arises the second which is to see the country through one's own eyes instead of through the blinkers applied by a forceful state propaganda machine.

To attempt a lone visit to Albania is a waste of time. You can write letters to her embassies in Paris and Rome (the country has no diplomatic mission in Britain) until the ink runs dry in your pen but there will be no reply. So the visitor has to go with a party of not less than fifteen which is deemed a worthwhile number for the Albanian authorities to shepherd about to the places *they* want you to see. Because of this, a chronic lack of hotel facilities, and complicated visa regulations few travel agencies bother with this small country which, geographically, is little different from her less troublesome neighbours.

For thirty-five years Albania has been 'out in the cold'. Increasingly she has banned religion and engaged upon a 'hate thy neighbour' policy which is remarkable for its venom. Her list of 'undesirables' remains formidable and includes all nationals of the Soviet Union, the United States, Yugoslavia, Israel, Spain, and South Africa.

Not surprisingly, the two million Albanians who reside in their native land (there are another two million outside it) have lost much faith in human nature under the fanatical inwards-looking leadership of President Enver Hoxha. With many of their former friends suddenly pronounced enemies and everybody else labelled a spy, deviationist, imperialist or revisionist, life must be very bewildering indeed and so it is hardly surprising that strangers are looked upon with suspicion; even open hostility.

This gives rise to another problem for the traveller, that of making contact with the man in the street in order to learn how he ticks away from the gaze of ruthless authority. A purely natural barrier is that of communication. The Albanian language is understood and spoken by few foreigners though, fortunately, English has taken over from Russian as a second language in the schools while older folk can, if pushed, fall back on Italian and German. The country (its proper name is Shquiperia, Land of Eagles) is no larger than Wales and much of it barren rock. In it, any kind of foreigner stands out like a yeti in Oxford Street while every visitor, upon arrival, is preached the 'riot act' in support of

101

the edict whereby it is a crime to stray from the fold.

I therefore could be excused for wondering what the Albanians would make of my little bunch of fifteen good men and women true. We certainly were an odd collection, comprising a self-confessed anarchist, a trade unionist who refused to share my hotel room because I read the *Daily Telegraph,* two elderly ladies from Worthing and a middle-aged Marxist carrying around a weighty biography of his idol, Karl, which he never let out of his sight.

We arrived at the border in a Yugoslav tourist coach. The Albanian border stands a hundred yards back from that of Yugoslavia and we had to lug our own baggage across the bleak strip of no-man's land that separates them. Right from the start Albanian officialdom made it plain it doesn't suffer fools gladly. The literary omniscience of the group was probed by an inspection of our reading matter which netted a worthy assortment of undesirable works ranging from *The Spy Who Came In From The Cold* to *Mein Kampf.* The Marxist only just managed to hold onto his biography, the inspecting officer being uncertain as to whether or not he was having his leg pulled.

In our new Fiat coach, a magnet for all Albanian eyes, we cruised along the shore of Skadar Lake, the same as in Yugoslavia only now it was spelt differently. And at Shkodra, the town, we were introduced to an Albanian phenomenon, the Law of Lek. Almost everyone wears a weapon in northern Albania as casually as we in Britain don our pin-stripe trousers or denim jeans. The vendettas of Sicily and Corsica pale into insignificance with what goes on here in matters of family honour and, although the authorities will deny it, the average killings work out at two per valley per week. Of great force, however, is the *besa,* a word of honour or exemption, which comes into effect on saints days and harvest thanksgiving. During the validity of *besa* you can merrily drink your rival's wine and, at the moment of expiry, shoot him dead. Unless he gets you first. Never have I seen such a trigger-happy lot as the good citizens of Shkodra.

Where the Albanian government does stamp hard is on the question of religion. At least in some atheist-guided countries Sunday is associated with the church but not in Albania. Or at least not if the present régime can help it. I lost count of the number of times I was told, hysterically, that it was the people themselves who decreed the banning of God. And to make sure their resolve does not weaken, any building that remotely resembles a place of worship is vigorously guarded. But I had no overpowering desire to attend an Albanian Evensong; instead it was time to consider just how I was going to break away from my cosy party and achieve a ride on the Albanian railway.

I had already blotted my copy book with our tour guide and protector by alluding to King Zog and the fact that I had seen him during his exile in Britain. Anything picturesque in Albania is usually pronounced unprogressive and hence 'inherited from the Zog era' and I suppose steam locomotives are laid at his door too. So my politely-phrased application to ride Albanian Rail was met by stern admonishment, together with another reading of the riot act and a list of penalties of horrific consequence including the death penalty. It all seemed a bit drastic and made the railway the more intriguing. However, my pre-departure application to the Albanian Ministry of Communications had, predictably, evoked no reply and it came to me that Albania, was the only country in which I had to apply to a government for a railway ticket.

A traffic warden would have a cushy number in Tirana, the midget capital. In the vast Skanderbeg Square a lonely policeman went through the motions of directing non-existent traffic while whistling shrilly at pedestrians daring to cross within sight of the slowest ox-cart. Skanderbeg, the national hero, horsed and armoured, stares down in bronze disbelief whilst in a lesser position astride a central highway, the last remaining Stalin statue in Europe metaphorically raises two fingers to Lenin opposite. The minaret climbs from a miniature Turkish mosque (a museum of course) to hold its own against an impressive façade of concrete that is the pride and joy of Tirana: the People's Palace of Culture. 'Glory to the P.R.A.' screams an enormous slogan on the roof, which is hardly an original statement for a country like Albania.

These are the high-spots of the premier city and are compulsory viewing. The guide is hard put to expand further on the sights so falls back defiantly upon a run-down of the production records of the local factories. The two-platform railway station is omitted from the itinerary since it stands, isolated, in a ploughed field.

Had we been lucky we would have stayed at the Hotel Adriatik, the best of the foreign hotels in the complex near Durres, the port that is Albania's second city. The building is Italian (and therefore well constructed) and, like the others, stands close to the water's edge. Its rooms are spacious; there are comfortable lounges and it contains what *Albturist* (ever out of touch) calls a 'cosy tavern' which is actually a ballroom. But we stayed at the Apollonia which, if nothing else, produced some quaint customs. Water seldom emerged from the taps except in the middle of the night when we discovered we had left them, so, for washing, we relied on the sea. Albanians stare at foreign tourists anyway and never more so than at this peculiar group of Britishers standing among the breakers solemnly brushing their teeth. Balkan food at any level is not considered everybody's cup of tea and that of the Apollonia was some of the worst. The 'ersatz' coffee came in handy for shaving, however, and if you liked grapes you were happy.

In the neighbouring hotel, protected by heavily-armed militia, were the members of the Peking Revolutionary Opera Company, 'The Red Detachment of Women' doing a stint at Tirana to show a then solidarity. It is always a little difficult to determine sex in those unisex tunics the Chinese wear but I could have sworn many of them were not women at all and was able to confirm so later when, using the unguarded back door, I paid an evening call. However, both men and women were charming and made me feel very much at home as, together, we made light of this minor point of discrepancy.

The sea was faultless but my sights were still fixed upon those trains. Railways are great levellers of people and none promised more humanising qualities than those of Albania. Vainly trying to look like a Tosk peasant I presented myself at Durres station one morning and joined the press for tickets for the 09.17 third class to Tirana.

I was to note that this railway tolerates either a second- or a third-class train but not a mixed one. Why first class doesn't come into it I cannot say. Maybe it sounds too bourgeois, and since Albania abhors the Soviet Union she refuses to ape them with a hard and soft class distinction. So, for my first excursion on an Albanian train I would join the proletariat.

At the ticket window, heavily screened, I mumbled 'Tirana' in what I hoped was the local inflection and tendered a soggy 10-*lek* note. But my fair hair was too un-Albanian even when viewed through the grid and ensured a yell that could be heard all over the station. This brought the policeman I had successfully dodged to get into the building and, while the crowd grumbled fitfully, the law and the ticket official perused my passport, copy letters to the Communications Ministry and a cornflakes packet gift coupon that had accidently got into the sheaf of papers. Expecting a minimum of ten years hard labour for my indiscretion I was amazed when I was saluted and given both ticket and change.

The train that awaited my pleasure would have earned a fortune in a railway museum. Any fittings that may have graced the oblong boxes on wheels had long since been ripped away. The destructive elements of Fulham FC Supporters Club still have much to learn. All aboard we moved off in a direction we were not expecting and everyone fell in a heap. Resetting his gears the driver got himself organised and we sat ourselves down as best we could on bench and floor which, comfort-wise, offered little difference. Except for someone wanting my autograph the one-hour trip was uneventful.

On arrival at Tirana Main I was confused by the rural setting and enquired, in some disbelief, if this indeed could be Tirana. Everyone shook their heads so I returned to the floor whereupon everyone walked over me to leave the train. Alone in the coach I remembered. Albania is one of those countries where a nod means no and vice versa.

I almost missed my return train three hours later through the same error and, in spite of a second-class fare, got no seat on either bench or floor. But conversation blossomed and reached higher planes as I was questioned extensively upon the health or otherwise of Mister Edward Heath.

Becoming something of a commuter there was no nonsense about passports or permits at Durres Station next day as I set out for the excursion to Elbasan in the other direction. The driver got his gears right first time round as behoves one of a second-class train though I noticed that the toilets were worse than third. On this longer journey provisions were deemed necessary and I was pressed to accept a lemon-curd pie following its rejection by a nose-dribbling baby who, twice, had flung it to the floor.

The army were involved in my procurement of a ticket back to Durres. I had no need to spend long in this pleasant town for a close examination of it featured on the tour agenda. So I returned to Elbasan Station in good time only to find a rugger scrum besieging the ticket office. My look of helplessness must have been more obvious than I thought because a detachment of a People's Cavalry came to the rescue and scythed a path through the crowd to emerge triumphant with my ticket.

In the corridor (there wasn't an inch of space in the compartments), I came into close contact with half a battalion of lady soldiers, all armed to the lips with carbines, bayonets and wicked-looking grenades draped about them like some exotic form of jewellery. It doesn't pay to get fresh with ladies in these circumstances so, instead, I chatted up the men. We ranged over our respective life histories, swapped our silliest army stories and all the while the lady soldiers, hugging their hardware, gathered round to listen. Bottles of *raki* were going the rounds when we reached Durres and I was carted off to the barracks for a prolongation of the party.

It all ended in trouble of course — as I thought it might. An officer of military police with a warped view of life designated me as a 'people's enemy' and sent me packing. Next day at the hotel when all tourists were summoned to an assembly 'for an important announcement concerning a serious breach of discipline', I thought 'Oh Christ they're going to make it public'. But it turned out that a Swedish visitor had been caught flogging bibles round the populace and was to be publicly expelled.

All 135 miles of the railway having been negotiated I turned to another method of observing the country from an individual viewpoint. Between attendance at the official tours of mill and factory I found time to take to a hired bicycle and discovered that the sight of a middle-aged Englishman pedalling along on a heavy 1940-framed Czech-made machine turned out to be an accepted one. On the various — and more than likely illegal — excursions I made on my brakeless steed I was never stopped or approached by the law with the exception of the one time when my lack of braking power provoked a near-accident in Kavaje market square and a child ran into the front wheel. No harm was done to child or bike but the former's howls of fright drew an indignant crowd. Hostility was thick in the air when a policeman put in an appearance, but my passport produced such wonderment that, after passing it around for all to see, he forgot to charge me for dangerous riding.

Thereafter, its brakes repaired, my bike allowed me to cover quite a lot of the country and I found my way into a number of mountain villages I would have never seen otherwise. Conditions were primitive, the most primitive in Europe but, invariably, the populace, after an initial show of resentment, became warm with friendliness and curiosity.

I came to heel for the last few days of the trip and only once brought up the subject of rail travel with the guide. 'How could you or anyone *stop* me boarding one of your trains?' I asked apropos of nothing in particular. He looked at me pityingly. 'Albanian State Security is inviolate', he assured me, 'we are ever vigilant. You could never even get into the station.'

He wondered why I smiled.

My onward railway journeying commenced from Belgrade. This time I was able to see a little more of a neglected European capital.

Except for its magnificent situation at the confluence of the Sava and the Danube, Belgrade is something of a nondescript city. Much of it vanished in bomb smoke; the public squares became larger by devastation and a grandiose post-war rebuilding project never materialised. The city is no stranger to destruction and reconstruction; the trouble is that one cannot keep up with the other.

The glory of Belgrade is the Kalemegdan fortress. At the foot of the spur on which rises the highest section of the citadel is the hexagonal Nebojsa tower which served as a prison. It was here that Kara Mustafa was strangled following his receipt of a 'golden cord', the standard gift of the sultan to a general who lost a battle.

The train I caught at Belgrade Station was the Polonia Express which was to jog me through the night to Budapest. For the size of the country the Yugoslav railway's 10,000-mile network is not perhaps as comprehensive as it might be, but at least they are building while Britain is demolishing. The State of Yugoslavia, created after the end of the First World War, inherited a mixed bag of railways. There were some minor lines in Croatia and Slovenia, the lines of the former Serbian State Railways, metre gauge lines, and some even narrower ones in Bosnia, Herzogovia and Dalmatia. The initial aim of the Yugoslav Government was to establish the north-west to south-west link from Ljubljana through Belgrade to what is now Dimitrovgrad, as an international main line and things have grown steadily from there, the new Bar-Belgrade line being the latest addition to the network.

My second-class compartment was spartan but adequate for one night on the tiles. I had with me an ex-politician, a one-time supporter of Milovan Djilas, to keep me entertained for most of it. How such a man could be alive and well and travelling freely on a train in a country like Yugoslavia beat me. But it shows it can be done.

The town of Novi Sad brought the complement of our compartment to four and my politician lapsed into silence. Outside was a blaze of electric light in the darkness. Once Novi Sad was called Varadince by the Turks and, because of a cultural role it played in the nineteenth century, it has also been described as the 'Serbian Athens'. But Venice likewise has lent its name to a number of places through which a canal or two squeezes and I was right in the assumption that the Novi Sad relics could hardly match the Acropolis.

The addition to the compartment were two elderly and disagreeable German women. To give them their due their disagreeability lessened with time and acquaintance, but the initial impact sent the politician and me into the restaurant car for asylum as well as dinner.

He left the train at Subotica, close to the Hungarian border. I helped him with his bag to the station barrier and returned dubiously to my Teutonic hatchet ladies. Subotica had been occupied by Hungarian forces in World War Two, but not half so effectively as those ladies who occupied my compartment. Ignoring my presence they cackled on for the rest of the night, replenishing their strength with victuals from a giant shopping bag. At the Hungarian border station of Kelebia both fell foul of the customs authorities, who demanded a search of their hand-bags. Their stoic resistance — painfully overcome — had me full of reluctant admiration, particularly when they defended their nationality against a Hungarian bully airing caustic opinions on Germany.

Purists will be agog to tell me that Hungary is not the Balkans, and up to a point they will be right. It is difficult to define an exact border line since, geographically, it encroaches into countries that are not classed as Balkan nations. 'Balkan' means mountain, and most of the Hungarian uplands are concentrated in the north along the Austrian and Slovak frontier. Our train was now steaming contentedly across rich, flat agricultural land that was certainly not 'Balkan'.

For me Hungary was within the orbit of my happy hunting ground. I had last been there in 1955 — the year before the up-rising — ostensibly on a holiday; actually on a reconnaissance in support of the matter of getting my wife (then my fiancée), out of nearby Czechoslovakia. For a week I had stayed in Budapest and had come away with an impression of a beautiful but tragic city of half-forgotten glories.

What I was to see in the Hungarian capital during the few brief hours at my disposal on this occasion gave me a very different picture. In 1955 the influence of Stalinism lay heavily across the land and fear and torment showed clear in the eyes of its people. This torment was to erupt into the holocaust of revolution the following year, bringing further wounds to a city scarred by war. But for the grace of God and the poor organisation of a band of students with whom I had become involved, I would have been pitched into those October street battles myself. And now, fifteen years later, it was as if a new-born city had arisen to greet me. Its

109

long and painful history, its glories and its ageless beauty stood revealed, but the tragedy had gone. The people in the park of Margaret Island laughed with gay abandon. The Fisherman's Bastion, cleaned and fresh, was a fairy-tale castle and not a dungeon. The broken hulk of the Lanchid suspension bridge (built by an Englishman) was a thing of grace once more. Budapest could raise a smile again.

I caught a local train from the East Station to Komarom and its Danube bridge carrying the road across the brown waters to Slovakia on its farther bank. Here were memories for me. In those desperate days I had tried to cross that bridge by way of its girders and supports beneath the road as a yet untried method of passing through a closed frontier of Czechoslovakia. Then too I had come by train. But the effort had been in vain, my presence on the ironwork catching the eye of a vigilent citizen who had felt it his duty to inform the militia. I had retreated in haste, regained the bank just ahead of the hue and cry, and had fled into a housing estate where I lost my pursuers in a maze of flats.

I gazed at the scene, for a long time, marvelling at what one does, if pushed, for the love of a woman.

From Budapest my journey was to continue south-east. Very nearly I was doubling back on my tracks. My train was the happy-sounding Wiener Walzer and it was to live up to its name. My fellow-passengers were a real Balkan mixture: a Greek girl of diminutive but shapely proportions, a darkly handsome Romanian youth who had placed himself strategically close to her, and a middle-aged Hungarian couple who beamed at life whatever its vicissitudes.

At industrial Szolnok we became five with the addition of a plump female who developed into the wit of the party, even if few of us could understand her humour. Once she even burst into song. The dreary plains made unexciting window-gazing but, again, the train approved of it, trotting happily along at no great pace. M.A.V. — the Hungarian State Railway — is fortunate in having no great feats of engineering to endure in pushing its 8,000 miles of track about the country. In Imperial days there were three separate railways operating in Hungary, roughly one third of the system being state-owned. The privately-owned lines were the Austro-Hungarian State (despite its name) and the Austrian Southern. The Hungarian State, and the Austro-Hungarian State, were in direct competition for the traffic between Budapest and Vienna, their tracks situated on opposite sides of the River Danube. Today, although both routes exist, the northerly one — the former Austro-Hungarian — is no longer competitive; it forms the most easterly section of the main line between Budapest and Prague. The third railway entering Budapest was the Austrian Southern, from the south-west. This made a junction with the line over the Semmering Pass from Vienna, and provided a through route from Budapest to Trieste. Though modernisation on Hungary's now fully state-owned network proceeds apace her railway has actually shrunk over the years because of the changing of state boundaries after the First World War.

All the Hungarian passengers left before the border, and the representatives of Greece and Romania had reached the cuddling stage as we crossed it at Curtici. At Arad, the centre of the Romanian wine industry, was the junction for Belgrade and the line by which I would have come had I chosen to go direct to Bucharest. It would have taken me through, or at least close to, the Iron Gates, and I'm *always* missing out on the Iron Gates.

The Iron Gates proper are not, as you might expect, the mountains through which the Danube cleaves a path, but the point where the waters break clear of the rock. The lesser-known Kazan Gorge is the thing to see and far more fittingly merits the impressive title. Since the beginning of time the Danube has fought it out with the Carpathian and Balkan Mountains through which it forces its way in a seething torrent. Until 1896 navigation of this stretch of the river was impossible, but a channel has been cleared allowing passage of river traffic. The current is fierce and boats moving upstream are given a tow by locomotives on the bank.

But in spite of the omission, I was particularly pleased to be in Romania. It was the one remaining country of Europe and the Balkans I had never visited.

From the great empty plains the countryside had contracted into wooded hills and valleys with villages, each with its onion-

111

domed church, half hidden amongst the trees. The horizon had drawn in to settle close but dramatically upon castle ruins atop the more unlikely summits, reminding me of a brand of tooth-paste I used as a child. In this vein the new countryside led us romantically to the walled city of Sibiu.

Originally known as Hermannsdorf, the locality was settled by German-Saxon merchants in the twelfth century and, despite every kind of vicissitude, managed not only to hang on but to build themselves a beautiful and prosperous town. In 1241 it was destroyed by the Tartars and again by the Turks in the fifteenth century, while it had considerably more than its fair share of havoc by earthquake, fire and plague. During the seventeenth and eighteenth centuries those of its people who were suspected of witchcraft, were butchered with astonishing frequency. With so much violence, no wonder Sibiu threw up fortified walls and watch-towers and surrounded itself with moats. The town manages to retain a medieval Germanic appearance unchanged from its last disaster.

Brasov, second city of Romania, likewise was settled by Teu-tonic knights from Saxony. They came to live in the Romanian village of Brasovechi, changing the name to Kronstadt because, so legend says, a golden crown was unearthed from the roots of a tree, bringing prosperity. It's been in the rechristening business more recently, too, and was called Orasul Stalin before that worthy took a nosedive in the popularity polls. Situated on the slopes of the Transylvanian Alps, in a narrow valley, shut in on all sides except one, by mountains, it is an unlikely place to find an industrial complex. Yet the Steagul Roso (Red Banner) tractor and motor works is one of the show places of Brasnov if you like that kind of thing. The railway presumes that you do.

It was dark as we crawled into the city and dark again as we crawled out. The father of our small group was Romanian by nationality but German by birth and proved it by speaking fluently in both tongues. I had never realized how Germanic Transylvania was.

Goths, Huns and Avars were among the tribes that overran the former Roman province of Dacia. Even following the Magyar conquest, the considerable Saxon element of the new settlers was

112

strong enough to wring concessions from the new masters in the form of self-governing communities. The great Mongol invasion of 1241 checked Transylvanian development, but with the subjugation of Hungary by the ubiquitous Turks it managed a precarious independence. The defeat of the Turks at the Battle of Mohacs in 1526 brought Transylvania a period of Hapsburg rule, and in the subsequent fighting between Hungarian and the Austro-Hungarian troops both Saxons and Romanians — who had now come into the picture — took up arms against the Magyars. Parts of Transylvania have been disputed between Hungary and Romania ever since, though the present régimes of both countries are at pains to present the subject as closed. Likewise the German minority is no more, but their mark is very much to the fore.

The first railway in Romania, built in 1869, was the result of a concession granted to two Englishmen, John Barkley and John Staniforth, and connected Bucharest with the Danubian port of Giurgiu, 72 kilometres distant. But building and operating railways by private enterprise did not last long and in 1888 all railways in the country became state-owned and standardised to European gauge (except for a short length of mixed gauge, with three rails, to provide access for the Russian gauge of five feet).

With a co-operative group of people, even a full compartment can be a reasonably comfortable place. On this particular leg of the journey no overnight shake-down was necessary, but with the view outside denied us our attentions became more localised. As was so often the case, nobody would hear of me eating alone in the dining-car, and since everyone had brought their own provisions I was as usual pressed on all sides to share in the pooled resources. By unspoken consent an after-dinner nap became a natural sequel and, arranging our legs into a kind of 'cat's cradle' across the seats and sharing shoulders where arm rests were deficient, we dozed contentedly.

Sinai is known as the 'Pearl of the Carpathians', and has long been one of the most popular and fashionable of Romanian resorts. All I saw of it was the station, but my companions filled me in with an abundance of detail. One held a low opinion of King Carol II, who, according to him, spent his reign fornicating

113

in the Royal Park with Magda Lubescu. The others were more delicate, telling me of the three castles hidden among the old trees in the parklands surrounding the Palace of Peles. Naturally such a place had a legend.

A nobleman by the name of Mihail Cantacuzino was being pursued by men-at-arms belonging to an enemy, Prince Grigore Ghica, ruler of Wallachia. Mihail was not making a very good job of eluding his pursuers and when he reached the Peles Valley only a miracle could save him. To baffle the prince's men he fell from his horse and crawled along the bed of a stream, vowing, there and then that should he escape he would one day return to build a monastery on the spot. Miracle or no he did escape and he remembered his vow. Mihail's favourite design of monastery happened to be those of the mountains of Arabia and that of Sinai in particular. And so it happened that an exact counterpart of the Sinai Monastery arose in the Peles Valley, which itself came to be known as Sinai.

The Germans came back into the act shortly after when, during the second half of the nineteenth century, King Carol I, a Hohenzollen princeling who had been foisted on the Romanians by Bismark, decided to have a royal castle at Sinai. This caused a flutter amongst the aristocracy, who promptly upped and followed suit. You were absolutely the wrong side of the tracks if you had no summer villa or rustic chalet at Sinai.

Peles Castle is like a fairy-tale come true; even more so apparently than my toothpaste castle earlier. It was initially designed by a Viennese, continued by another, with final additions by a Czech. The interior is packed with the oddest collectors' pieces, with not a single item from a Romanian source.

The subject of oil in Romania invariably brings to mind the city of Ploesti (much bombed by the RAF), which is the centre of the country's considerable oil industry. The hours of darkness are the right time to see the illuminated silver cobwebs of piping that make the great refineries such a fascinating spectacle. Ploesti means 'rainy', but, though the town is the Manchester of Romania, the night remained dry. A serf by the name of Ploaie is supposed to be the first inhabitant of the original village. No doubt he lived and died in wretchedness, not knowing he was

114

sitting on a source of wealth beyond his dreams.

We drew into Bucharest about half an hour later. The Nord is a fine airy station fully capable of dealing with the capital's one-and-a-half million population. Having only one main station in a city makes life easier for a stranger.

I was to spend a number of days in the city. As well as the Romanian language having a kinship to French, the name of the French capital is invoked with Bucharest's title of 'the Paris of the Balkans'. The description would not be mine, but I could see what they mean. Everwhere there are tree-lined boulevards and beautiful parks. There is even an Arc de Triomphe half way up the wide Saseana Kisseleff. Before the last war the city had a reputation as an uninhibited spot, and seasoned travellers will tell you that by placing your umbrella in a certain position on your bed in the Athenee Palace Hotel you would be sure of a willing female bed companion!

Though politics and war have changed the face of Bucharest, it remains a lively city. It wears its communism on the back of its head and hardly a red slogan is to be seen. Its many bookshops contain works by British and West European writers, and the few compulsory Karl Marx volumes are pushed out of the way to the back. The cinemas show British and American films, the Soviet ones having long since been given the brush-off. Its restaurants and night-clubs are of a high standard.

An immediate impression of Bucharest comes from the vast area that it covers. In spite of a rash of tower blocks in the Calea Victoriei, the main street is as long as Oxford Street and Regent Street put together. It is a city which is protracted and drawn out like the hours kept by its inhabitants. No shops are open between mid-day and five o'clock, since, in summer, it is as hot as India.

Still based in Bucharest, I made a rail excursion to the north of the country. My train was the Danubius Express, that on which I had come out of Russia. In these parts the title 'express' is something of a misnomer, though I suppose they do crawl a little faster than some of the local trains.

Abruptly tired of Carpathian foothills, the countryside threat-ened to become flat and monotonous but was saved by villages made bright with onion-domed churches and the services of a paint brush. One largish town was Buzan, rich in oil and amber. Another was Foçsani, astride the Milcov river which formed the ancient frontier between Moldavia and Walachia. Wine is its stock in trade and vineyards stretch away in all directions as far as the eye can see. There is a legend here. A native of Moldavia and another of Walachia fought a dual using bowls of wine instead of swords. The Moldavian won and in honour of his victory built his house on the spot, thus founding the town.

Close up against the Soviet border the countryside became impatient again and bucked itself into a series of switchback hills covered with a snowstorm of geese. At the base of one such hill stood Nicolina, a large and obviously important town.

Nicolina. The name meant nothing to me but it seemed to to everyone else. The train was suddenly empty. Then I remembered. This was Jassy, the ancient capital of Moldavia. I had no immediate plans for continuing to Moscow so I joined the mass disembarkation.

Jassy is the town, in all Romania, which occurs most often in its history. It was a big place when Bucharest hardly existed and greatness only passed from it in the middle of the last century when the capitalship was transferred to Bucharest. It is what might be termed a wide-open town, and even from the station I could see the famous 'Trei Erarchi' Church, adorned in its coat of gilded carvings. Another oddity is a miniature of the Peace Palace at the Hague. All around are wooded hills, hidden amongst them being the monasteries of Cetatuia, Frumoasa and Galata. Here religion is still kicking.

Back in Bucharest my last evening was spent with my private accommodation hosts in whose flat I had been staying. We went to the 'Monte Carlo' restaurant in Cismigiu Park and downed several bottles of extremely drinkable white wine. Some friends joined us later, among them a woman who spoke English and turned out to be playwright Arnold Wesker's cousin. Like Cinderella I had to steal away from the party at midnight to catch a pumpkin called the Bulgaria Express.

For a relatively small country, railway construction in Bulgaria began on quite a large scale, with a main line 140 miles long from Ruschuk on the Danube to Varna on the Black Sea, in 1866. A still greater milestone was, however, the completion of the international main line across the country from Dragoman near the present Yugoslav frontier, through Sofia, to Svilengrad, and providing the all-rail route to Istanbul and Asia.

From the point of view of observing the countryside my train timings in Bulgaria were a disaster. Only as we drew sleepily into Sofia did the night relent enough to show me a capital I had seen before. But what my eyes missed was compensated for by a spate of words that poured into my ears the long night through.

The little Bulgarian lawyer had joined the train at Ruse. It was his town, the old Roman city of Sexanta Prista, or 'Sixty Vessels', now the fourth most important town in Bulgaria and I was not allowed to forget it. He was a city councillor, a member of its liberation committee, chairman of the Bulgarian-Soviet Friendship League. In fact, to me, he *was* Ruse, for he was all I saw of it. Soon the compartment became his council chamber and his fluency in the English language lent wings to his oratory.

Councillors the world over have an inflated opinion of the communities they serve, but my lawyer's enthusiasm spread easily across the length and breadth of Bulgaria. I ventured to suggest that the great Soviet Union might, even now, be milking his country dry and recieved a rap over the knuckles for my pains. Yet his vehement denials raised the eyebrows of the one other occupant of the debating chamber, who a little later found it expedient to withdraw.

'Ever growing — never old', are the words inscribed on the device of Sofia. It is a good description of the Bulgarian capital. Little shows that is very old, and the place is a patchwork of undistinguished building fads going back to the Ottoman occupation. As Serdica, after the Thracian tribe which lived there, it was considered as a possible capital of the Roman Empire, but greatness passed it by. A Roman bath standing in the courtyard of the Balkan Hotel, and the church of St Sophia, remain as souvenirs of the period. Under a new name — Sredets (Central) — it grew to importance again in the Byzantine Empire, but many of the resulting new buildings were destroyed when the Ottomans besieged it. The Turk is therefore, architecturally, the most strongly represented of Sofia builders

117

and many of his public buildings and mosques remain. At the time the Bulgarians were allowed to construct their own churches, but these had to be partly submerged so that they did not compete in height with the mosques.

My previous visit to Sofia lasted a full three days. Now I was here for less than three hours. One of them I spend parading round the city's central square, a slavish copy of Moscow's Red Square with some Stalinist architecture to match. For the Lenin Mausoleum read Dimitrov Mausoleum, but there are no queues. It is difficult to slouch or stroll in such surroundings. Goose-stepping seems more appropriate.

My Greece-bound train was not even called an express, and to rub salt into the wound, the thing left twenty minutes late. But at least my onward journey was taking place in daylight, though the smoke from five Bulgarian cigarettes obscured the view from the window. My companions eyed me curiously, came to their private conclusions and spoke not a word. It was quite a holiday.

Blagoevgrad lessened the crush and also the density of the smoke. It was even possible to read the 'no smoking' notices above the door. It was in three languages but these did not include Bulgarian. Bulgars are obviously a law unto themselves.

I was alone when we crossed into Greece at Promachon. Here is one of those borders not on the commuting routes. The train staggered about as it was pushed from one siding to another to be infested by hordes of unshaven, gun-happy soldiers. I was asked to empty my wallet but there were no Bulgarian *levs* or *stotinka* for anyone to confiscate.

Rarely does a change of country produce so dramatic a change of scenery as does this somewhat forlorn portion of the Balkans. One moment a tempestuous sea of hills rising to the stature of mountains; next everything has fallen flat on its back. It is as if someone has pulled the plug to drain away the hills. What is left becomes pleasantly monotonous allowing a doze that you know won't blot out something spectacular round the next bend. Or at least you hope it won't as you set yourself a nap of thirty minutes and wake up four hours later as the train clanks into the second city of Greece.

I had a little time to spare in Salonika, Thessaloniki — call it what you will — and wandered aimlessly into its neon-splashed heart. In the gathering dusk I became aware of a compressed jungle of demi-skyscrapers that I found difficult to reconcile with a picturesque old city struggling up the foothills of Mount Chortiatis. I sat down to a meal in a port-side restaurant whose smell offered better promise than its food. The best Greek restaurants are in Soho, I had been told, and the hash I was served went a long way to support the allegation.

A chap by the name of Cassander right back in 315 B.C. put Salonika on the map. He built a new city on the site of the older Greek Therma — so called in allusion to the hot springs of the neighbourhood — and named it Thessalonica after his wife. The port was developed by the Romans, and by A.D. 305 Salonika had reached its zenith when Galerius made it briefly capital of the empire. St Paul was there, as he was everywhere else, leaving his mark in the form of the two epistles he addressed to the community which he formed; the subsequent clash between the Christians and the Romans was inevitable. The culmination of the persecutions that followed was the massacre of 7,000 citizens in 392, the Emperor Theodosius's revenge for the lynching of his guard commander by a mob outraged at the imprisonment of a popular charioteer for making improper advances to a Gothic guardsman.

Bulgarians, Turks, Normans, Saracens and Germans have held the city at various stages of its history, the last occupiers before the Nazis being, again, Turks, who chalked up a total of 482 years of occupation, one of which saw the birth of Kemal Ataturk. The Germans in 1941 stayed four years, their legacy being the annihilation of the Jewish colony given asylum there from Spain in 1909.

My compartment on the Istanbul—Athens express was well and truly packed when I returned to the station. I was just in time to restrain an amicable little Greek from removing the bag I had placed there earlier and occupying my seat amongst a full house. Another sleepless night seemed all too likely.

In the early hours we stopped at Larissa, the capital of Thessaly, with its wide plains, distant mountains and lonely

119

towns. Larissa means 'citadel', which may be appropriate to certain British gentlemen with receding hairlines who were instrumental in its stand against the German invaders of 1941.

The train drew into Athens two hours late but still early enough for a breakfast of sorts in the small station that fails to dignify such a famous and historic capital. It is not even a terminus, since the line ends further on at the Piraeus.

The flea market cannot hold a candle to the Acropolis. I am not an archaeologist, nor can raise much enthusiasm for things archaeological, but even the layman runs out of adjectives to describe Athens' greatest landmark. But my eyes had seen Baalbek and the Taj Mahal so perhaps I was expecting too much of a ruin that, to the British, is more famous still.

For a thousand years the rock was simply a refuge for the settlers of the open plain surrounding Athens who sheltered there during the frequent invasions round the royal fortress. Following the conquest of his neighbours, Peisastratus was able to depart from the primarily defensive function, and in the pause between strife that resulted he built and dedicated a 100-foot temple to Athena, thus starting the process that was to transform the Acropolis within 150 years into an unsurpassed altar to the gods and beauty. Destruction by the Persians in 480 B.C. gave Themistocles opportunity to rebuild and remodel the ruined temples, and Athenian craftsmen realised his dream of perfect harmony, which, even in ruin, has not yet died.

The port of Athens was, at the beginning of the nineteenth century, a small fishing village known as Porto Leone. The town, now highly industrialised, is six miles from the centre of the capital, the whole heavily built up so that it is not possible to tell where one ends and the other begins. The port itself is less attractive than many large ports, the one redeeming feature being the many *caiques,* the picturesque craft engaged in coastal trade, fussing around between the big liners in the harbour.

One of the ravages of constant travel is diarrhoea and I was suffering a particularly violent attack as I returned to my wanderings in the city. These took me by a hospital so, retracing my steps, I entered the building. Health service or no health service I did not think a dose of medicine would break me financially. By dint of facial grimaces and indication of my stomach I attempted to explain my condition to a startled girl receptionist. A youth in a white coat came to the rescue. He knew a few words of English and hauled me into a waiting room.

'I can help', he announced triumphantly having interpreted my signs and dashed off to return with a potion of dark liquid. As it went down I heard him say something about the stuff being a powerful *laxative*.

I stared, wild-eyed, into the empty glass. The youth saw my horrified expression and got the message. Away he went again returning with a tumbler full of a white liquid.

'I give you double dose', he told me confident that fifty per cent of its power would cancel out the initial error.

I laughed uneasily.

The youth laughed too but not at his mistake. The girl at the reception desk had given him her own diagnosis of my ailment. How was I to know I'd blundered into a maternity hospital!

Why a 150-mile bus ride is laid on by the ferry company between Athens and Patras when there is a perfectly good train service available, is something of an enigma. I think the basic reason is prejudice. Railways have always taken a back seat in Greek transport. A long and mountainous peninsula, with many equally mountainous islands, does not lend itself to easy railway construction or running. The country has a railway that is extremely sketchy, not much more than 1,600 miles of line in fact, which is very small in relation to area and population for a European country. Much of it was destroyed in the last war, and slow reconstruction meant heavy reliance upon roads and shipping. The population has therefore become more accustomed to buses and cars on the comprehensive road network. To add to the railway authorities' headache is the fact that there are four track gauges, one of which is a rack-and-pinion operation. The Greek mainland system of standard gauge, and the metre gauge system serving the Peloponnese is now entirely state-owned, which should ensure some cohesion. Only the 25 miles of the Athens-Piraeus electric railway is under separate administration.

Until recently the international standard gauge line between Salonika and Athens was entirely single track and Athens had the unenviable distinction of being the only capital city in the world where the international main line enters as a single track almost to the platform end. This was now slowly being rectified with great inconvenience to everything.

The fastest trains in Greece are the *rapidos,* little two or three-coach diesels of unimpressive appearance. They make the journey between Salonika and Athens in a fraction over seven hours, which is good going in difficult country. This particular route forces the railway over the backbone of the Greek mainland, where it attains a height of 3,000 feet and more. Curves are legion.

No road in Greece can likewise remain even remotely straight for long, and the modest highway we picked up outside Athens soon petered out amongst the rocky undulations of a tortured land. Until near Isthmia the sea lay on our left, to disappear for a while before appearing magically on the right. If you have a mind like an atlas it is all quite clear. Steamers lay at anchor at every tiny seaside village, which is not surprising since most of them are tiny ports.

The town of Corinth, which we reached at midday, is a ramshackle place virtually devoid of anything to show for its legendary and historic past, though not so the immediate neighbourhood. Like Carthage, but in a less possessive sense, Corinth has commercial links with the Phoenician traders of Tyre and Sidon. St Paul crops up as one of its best-known residents. Other more legendary figures, once rulers of Corinth when it was more than a town, were Sysyphos, whose grandson Bellerophon captured Pegasus the winged horse, Jasan and Medea. The noblest of the local ruins is the temple of Apollo, the seven remaining columns of which I managed to glimpse.

Corinth, the city of commerce, one can discern from its proximity to the canal, the sea, and through its most famous export, the currant. But Corinth, the city of pleasure, takes a very large hunk of imagination to bring it to life. Yet was it not here that a thousand temple prostitutes, slave girls in the service of Aphrodite, made the secular sacred? The most renowned and expensive of these Corinthian ladies was Lais who entertained princes. Robert Liddell in his book *The Morea* tells of a distinguished suitor who met with a rebuff. He attributed the cause of his ill-reception to the whiteness of his hair and dyed it brown, but to no purpose. 'Fool that thou art', said the courtesan, 'to ask today what I refused yesterday to thy father'.

Our road through the big 'island' of the Peloponnese hugged the sea with such fervour that on several occasions it became a wet embrace. It was like this all the way to Patras, winding through a cavalcade of charming villages and graceful villas in luxuriant gardens. The coach driver had realized that he was behind schedule and drove with wild abandon, trusting to the size of his vehicle and the decibels of his horn to get him through.

Darkness had fallen when we reached Patras. An avenue of eucalyptus trees led us into the third town of Greece. An early king, Eumelus, it was who united three local towns, one of which was called Aroe, into a single unit. Because the ruling family, or *patrai,* lived in Aroe the new enlarged town was named Patras. Under the Romans, who loved long names, it was known as Colonia Augusta Aroe Patrensis.

Even in the uncertain light of a town by night one is aware of a distinct old-world air lent by the arcaded streets which date back to the War of Independence. They are worthy of exploration, though no doubt Patras suffers, like most ports, from being simply a place through which to come and a place through which to go.

For me it was a place through which to go. Brindisi, in southern Italy, would be my next landfall. I never saw Patras, the Peloponnese or Greece slide away into the darkness. I had treated myself to a cabin and a shower and was making the most of the luxury.

My Balkan excursion had been a history lesson — an adventure in history would be a more apt description — that had taught me much that no book could have done. History is not built by triumphs alone. Experience — the good and the bad — is the foundation of greatness and the Balkans have had more experience than most.

5
Trans-North Africa
PARIS—CAIRO

International long-distance railways, and dreams of pushing lines to and through whole continents have a disquieting habit of never being fulfilled. Yet international express conceptualists were on the brink of seeing a Paris to Cairo Express enter the world timetables when war brought the inspiring notion tumbling to the ground. Such an express is, alas, the more unlikely today with hostilities and hate in the Middle East as rampant as they were three-quarters of a century ago.

But why not, I asked myself, try the alternative route to Cairo; the one which runs via the North African coast (instead of the traditional route by way of the Levant)?

To answer my own question I set out, in 1972, on a circuit of the Mediterranean intent on using existing operational railways in an attempt to find out just why not.

Paris to Algeciras by means of the Puerta del Sol and Talgo expresses brought me to the Straits of Gibraltar, and a two-hour ferry cruise got me to Tangier.

There is a railway line across the Maghreb connecting Casablanca on the Atlantic coast with Gabés way down in the south of Tunisia, but there are no through-trains. In fact only two trains a day leave Tangier so it is not all that simple to reach even Sidi Kacem, the junction of the main line but, once on it there are less prosaic reasons for dawdling.

One of these is Fez which pulls you off the train by its exciting strangeness. William Lithgow, a Scotsman, wrote of Fez in the seventeenth century: 'There are some 12,000 allowed brothel houses in this towne, the Courtezans being neatly kept'. That was one man's observation. I had neither the time nor the inclination to confirm his statement.

To look upon Fez for the first time is a devastating experience. Clinging to the sides of a hill-ringed valley, all of it is visible as one approaches from the new town and the spectacle is strangely disturbing. There is something unnatural about those densely packed houses, jostling and crowding one another as if Fez was an island with a hostile sea lapping at its outer walls.

If its exterior is disturbing what lies inside is positively frightening. At least a day is needed to traverse the city, and another to find your way out again. Fez is actually *three* cities. Founded in A.D. 808 by Moulay Idriss, it expanded and pushed its defences outwards to such an extent that a new city was built alongside the old. It was the French who, after 1912, built New Fez, an entirely contemporary European town about a mile away.

Girding my loins I plunged recklessly into the winding residential streets, to be confronted by anonymous walls of mosques and dwellings that have turned their backs on the noisy colourful crowds that are their lifeblood. These veins of Fez defeat everything on wheels. There is no pattern. Occasionally I darted into a dark alley that breached the inhospitable walls to behold evil slums and magnificent palaces, often side by side in a contradiction of architecture and human behaviour. Near the centre of this confusion I came upon the city's oldest district where the souks break out in a rash of selling, arguing, hammering, carving, stitching; each street specializing in a product.

For me that night was to be the first of many on the tiles. There are, again, only two trains eastwards out of Fez and both selected tortuous hours between midnight and dawn to effect their departing. The Moroccan railway, like its Algerian and Tunisian counterparts, is somewhat thin on the ground. Even after twenty years of independence from the French (and from the successive international rulers of the Tangier Free Zone), the Kingdom of Morocco had not added a single mile of line to the network left by the French. It is probably true that there are still five times as many camel trains as railway trains in this quite large country. Mostly the main line steers clear of mountain and desert and follows the coast and represents the only east-west railway between Rabat and Tunis, a distance of 1,300 miles. Yet in spite of this, it is a despised railway, fit only for local travel by

125

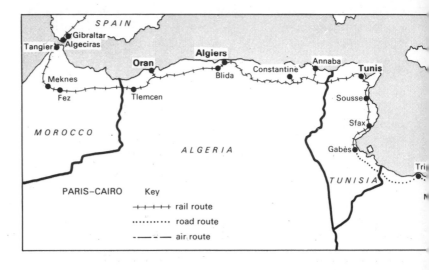

the *fellahin* I was told at the time. I was soon to learn why.

The train that drew in from Casablanca was well-loaded with spread-eagled passengers and to acquire a square inch of seat involved much manipulation of inert bodies but Arabs sleep like the dead and will accept considerable buffetting before consciousness brings growls of wrath down on your head.

The train moved at a comfortable pace. But other factors made it a very long night. The coach was cold and draughty; someone had removed my seat cushion for a pillow and the headrest protruded into the back of my neck. At intervals a dirty foot, emerging from a fragment of sock, found its way onto my knees.

Streaks of yellow showed on the black palette of the sky when we stopped at Taza. Here the Atlas massif all but meets the Rif, only a narrow corridor permitting a thoroughfare to the east. This is the 'invasion corridor' through which, first Arab, then Moorish, conquerors marched to dominate the Maghreb. On a hill commanding this crucial gap sits Taza. Today it is a somnolent backwater; gateway in one direction to the steppe and desert of inner Morocco and, in the other, the oft-troubled border with Algeria. The railway serves the new town of Taza Bas, pointedly ignoring the more inaccessible old city of Taza Haut that broods

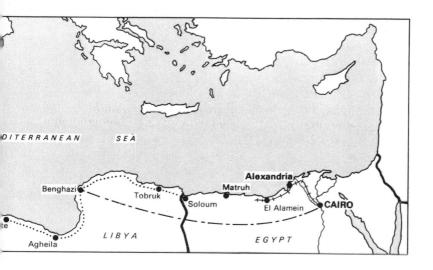

about its tightly-packed houses, mosques and citadel.

Daylight showed a bleak countryside of near desert in an unseemly shade of pink. Wadis — deep chaps in the parched earth — cut across the steppe. Only a stumpy cactus and tough clumps of desert grass could, inexplicably, hold onto life — though, as if to disprove the point, a rare stream or irrigation ditch drew a strip of green cultivation around it. Bedouin tents and little groups of mud dwellings proved that humans too could live on next to nothing. Gliding in the clear air or foraging on the sandy soil, storks and cranes were other signs of life, but in those dismal surroundings they looked to me like vultures.

To complete this picture of doom there came into sight a great mound of rock rising high and sheer above the plain. Upon it squatted the Kasbah of Taourirt. An amazing conglomeration of buildings without plan or design, it was built in feudal days to house the Glaoui family and their retainers. In an unseemly pink, like the ground on which it stands, the thing scowled at me as it does at all who pass that way.

Most of the complement of my compartment left at Taourirt, which gave me a couple of hours to iron out the creases in my neck and posterior. I made the most of it. Moroccan railways had three classes of coach: first, second and *économique,* which sounds better than third though it isn't.

The wild, scrubby country continued to Oujda, a pleasant market town bordering Algeria. It is also the starting point of a branch line southwards to Bechar and into the desert.

The border with Algeria was open though its guardians acted as if it wasn't. British nationals did not require visas but that didn't discourage the locals from trying to sell me one, and when I stood up for my rights it resulted in a savage search of my baggage.

Algerian trains are, if anything, less clean than Moroccan trains or so I found. French from 1840 to 1960, Algeria was treated as a department of France and given railways accordingly. Built to standard gauge, the trains ran with a pre-war speed and efficiency admired in many countries. However with the departure of the French conditions deteriorated. The coach of my Oran-bound 'express' contained one compartment minus a window and, in another, somebody had removed the seats. What remained was old, worn-out and dirty. Along the way train wrecks proclaimed their rusty message of a revolution many years past.

Geographically, Algeria is a country of magnificence. Five times larger than Morocco, it contains majestic mountains and is fettered to a desert that sweeps southward for 1,300 miles. Both its early history and its geography are closely bound to Morocco and Tunisia, the whole fabric of the Maghreb being the fruit of a lengthy maturing, evolved through 1,000 years of Arab-Moslem history which was itself rooted in 500 years of existence as a Roman colony. Archaeologists speak of the Maghreb as one of the earth's oldest known inhabited areas.

My attention to the passing countryside was diverted by an almighty row taking place between my neighbour, a non-commissioned officer of the Algerian navy and a potential invader of the already full compartment. It appeared that, according to the intruder's rules, two children counted as less than one adult. Both were Berbers but obviously not of the same tribe since they shouted and swore at one another in different languages, occasionally mixing in a little basic French. I'm certain they would have come to blows in the compartment had not the door been slammed between them, thus precipitating a fight in the corridor. This because the slam caught the finger of a passive onlooker in the corridor who mistook the circumstances.

We were back in alpine country amongst the Tlemcen Mountains belonging to the foothills of the coastal Atlas, the Atlas Tellien. Small patches of cultivation forced from the red soil were interspersed with desert scrub and the ubiquitous cactus. Old men, young men, and children and women with gold coins dangling round their heads watched goats and did nothing, even in the cold and the rain. A flock of cranes swooped on a plough pulled by lumbering oxen.

Between Tlemcen and Sidi-Bel-Abbes the railway enters the Atlas with a vengeance, attacking its brown crags with commendable gusto. The views were dramatic, the gradients considerable and the bends hairpin. It was all a bit much for the lady in my compartment and she made her feelings quite plain when she threw up at the closed window.

At the Foreign Legion town of Sidi-Bel-Abbes, looking Beau-Geste-like even in the rain, the mountains surrendered to both the railway's onslaught and a depressing salt plain. But a sight of the sea increased morale as we rolled into Algeria's second city and port.

I had a half a day and an evening in which to taste the delights or otherwise of Oran. It is a busy commercial centre, old and strongly fortified with massive walls, forts and kasbahs rearing upwards from an otherwise European-looking city. 'You must see the Ouled Nail girls', said a young Berber with whom I was sitting in a dockside café. I expressed interest, as any male would, and he went on to explain. Originating from a nomadic Arab tribe living in the foothills of the Atlas, the girls are brought up to be prostitutes and dancers, leaving their homes when hardly in their teens to earn their wedding dowry. Ten or twelve years later, this task accomplished, they return to their mountain villages to perform their final mission in life: the bringing of children into the world for the same profession. A mournful tale, but the dancing, he said, was exquisite and he gave me an address where I could see it.

129

Be warned if you should catch the night train out of Oran —
particularly on a Sunday. The locals, a high proportion being
servicemen, have a trick up their sleeves for ensuring seats in a
hopelessly overcrowded train. Just before the whistle blows a
rumour sweeps through the coaches that the train on the neighbouring track is the express for Algiers. In a flash, the corridor-
standers are off followed by bemused occupiers of seats in a
whirlwind of luggage. But, of course, the train opposite is going
nowhere and by the time you've learnt this you are lucky to find
a square inch of corridor for your tired feet.

For me the disaster was mitigated by my fellow sufferers. A
mixture of North African nationalities they were a delightful
bunch and I ended up with a bearded, if ever so slightly verminous, bedouin on the floor wrapped in the man's *djellabah* which
was voluminous enough for both of us.

Most foreign visitors to Algiers see the capital from the deck of
a cruise ship and it is towards the sea that the city presents its
fairest face. Coming in by train you are taken for a tour of its port
and industrial regions and are ejected a long way from the centre.
The station is a much lesser building than that of Oran and it is
plain that Algiers spurns its railway.

In need of a wash I followed the example of a cluster of soldiers
who, stripped to the waist, were making use of a locomotive
watering appliance. We scrubbed each other's backs, shared my
battery electric razor and refreshed, went our ways. Mine was
into the city.

I discovered Algiers to be a big brute of a place with some
pleasant, elegant and even spectacular corners. Its face is a
sequence of white steps and terraces rising from the water's edge
and backed by splendid buildings. Behind this rises the vivid
green of the Sahel Hills. But Algiers is two-faced. The Arabs
may call it a diamond set in a frame of emeralds, but it is a pretty
rough diamond. I had no time to venture far into the kasbah but
what I saw gave a foretaste. Narrow streets, slippery with
garbage, loud with aggressive vendors and high with offensive
smells led into a rabbit warren of squalor.

The modern city is a complete contrast. Broad streets built by
the French, fine public buildings, luxury hotels and chic shops of

130

not quite Boulevard Hausmann. Somewhere in between is the real Algiers.

My onward journey took me out of this urban pot-pourri to a far more enticing edifice; a violent eruption of the Atlas called the Massif du Djurdjura. All around was a weird country of rocks weathered into preposterous shapes which led us towards Constantine.

With me in the compartment was a young Algerian, native of that city and full of the marvels of the place. We pooled our provisions and told each other of our respective home towns. My Sussex resort could raise a hill, but Constantine lay across a gorge. If the train was on time we should see the impressive Rhummel gorges and the delicate bridge that spanned them.

Of course, the train was late and it was nearly midnight when we reached Constantine. But a thoughtful moon obliged with illumination more effective than sunlight and there, in stark relief, was the gorge. With this giant cleft cutting the town in two, Constantine is a most impressive place. It is very old and has withstood eighty sieges — which is not so surprising when one notices that the town is guarded on three sides by ravines. From the train my friend pointed out the new university, but my eyes were for the palace of the Beys that, for me, had come to life with his description of the harem guarded by oft-replaced negresses. These, and the older girls, were disposed of by being tied in bags and thrown into the gorge. Sometimes, in a fit of do-it-yourself enthusiasm the Bey pushed them over — bagless — with his own hands.

Annaba received me in the middle of the night with a series of closed hotels. Annaba. A large sprawling city but why hadn't I heard of it? Ah, yes. This was Bône, an agriculturally industrial city that is also a fine resort.

To stretch my legs I went for a walk. I was striding purpose-fully down the main street when I was stopped by a posse of suspicious and heavily-armed police. 'Where are you going?', they asked. 'Nowhere in particular', I replied. But nobody apparently goes nowhere at 3 am in Bône and I was briskly returned by jeep to the station. But in the meantime, to keep out the strays, the gates had been thoughtfully locked, so for the rest of the night, I had to doss down with the strays on the pavement outside.

The most dilapidated train of all rescued me from Annaba as dawn broke, and I was rattled through the majestic territory of Kabylia, to Souk-Ahras and the border with Tunisia at a fast pace. There, my fellow-band of weary travellers and I were squeezed into the passport office of the station and before long an obnoxious policeman appeared. He insisted on filling in our exit forms himself to show, presumably, what a bright boy he was. 'Occupation?' he spat at me, (having already misspelt my name), 'Pirate', I replied with indifference and watched as the word 'pilot' went down on the form.

A big hunchbacked berber took me into his confidence 'They're all the same,' he whispered, 'jumped up little thugs with uniforms and guns.' He was referring to the policemen. 'We were better off under the French', he went on, 'at least they didn't come snooping about looking for trouble.'

The train crept into Tunisia and with red-hot eyes I looked upon a new country without great enthusiasm. One experience I'd missed in Algeria was that of an Algerian bed. .

Even the Tunisians, with their knowledgeable handling of a considerable tourist industry, accepted no currency from their neighbouring state. Tourists were obviously not expected to arrive by rail; an oversight that was to the benefit of a band of ruffians who with a great sense of the dramatic, changed my Algerian dinars into Tunisian dinars — at a price.

The 118 miles of line between Ghardimaou and Tunis is narrow (metre) gauge, hence the reason for no direct connection between Algeria and Tunisia. Although a fraction of the size of its massive neighbour, Tunisia can boast almost as much track mileage: 2,200 miles against 2,570. Both countries are handicapped by two or more gauges, the ratio, as far as Tunisia is concerned, being about fifty-fifty. For a change our train was clean and fast. Darkness overtook us for the second half of the journey, but before Beja I gained an impression of a gentle rolling landscape with abruptly prosperous villages not afraid to come down from the hills.

The capital, was slick, gay and civilised. And in Tunis I got my bed.

The coastal run, again by rail, was by way of Hammamet, Sousse and Sfax all geared to the whims and desires of the tourist. The train to Sfax was a joke. A jet-black locomotive producing balloons of smoke to match led us cheerfully along the coast, across the edge of the Bled and into the olive forest of Sfax. Our coaches were spartan, badly sprung and communal. With me in my enclave were four men and a woman, though since everybody in the coach knew everybody else it was like one big noisy family. Solemnly I was led from seat to seat to be introduced, hear a digest of the family fortunes and offer a version of my own. At least one fact registered in both directions. My name became Mister Porty; theirs, with individual variations, was Muhammad.

The man sitting opposite me had a transistor radio. Stations Tunis, Tripoli and possibly Baghdad poured out their wailing songs into that unlovely coach in a cacophony of competition. Injected into this came another sound at irregular intervals. My neighbour, an unattractive little man in a badly-torn suit, had either 'got' religion or was an off-duty muezzin. Triggered by a particular musical note from the transistor he would let go a prolonged and blood-curdling howl of such volume as to drown the combined efforts of Tunis, Tripoli and Baghdad. Nobody took the slightest notice.

Between the howls there was an issue of cake. Arab cakes are sweet, syrupy and delicate. They do not travel well particularly when lumped together in old newspapers and stuffed into over-loaded baggage. What went the rounds was a gluey wreckage that still managed to retain its delicious flavour. The noisiest eater was, of course, our religious friend and his expression of thanks must have deafened Allah.

The lone woman across from me said not a word during the whole five-hour journey. She was ignored by all. Just once she gave me a fleeting smile, a sort of near apology for the odd behaviour of her menfolk.

Sfax is a commercial city. I don't mean it has belching chimneys or rows of factories. It is, in fact, one of the most beautiful places in Tunisia, but it is an industrial city all the same. The fruits of its labour are visible long before you get there. Olives by the million acres and then a belt of almonds, pomegranates and aromatic plants and flowers, all of which Sfax puts to use. The air is heavy with the powerful smell of exaggerated growth.

The town holds nothing that is soft or seductive. Its great walls, spiky with merlons and pierced at intervals with embrasures for cannon, are workmanlike in themselves and provide frame and shade for a great variety of handicrafts going on at their base. Inside the walls the streets are heavy with sculptured doors and ornamental embellishment on gate and mosque. Sfax is a handsome city and its blatant prosperity a reward for centuries of unbroken toil.

From Sfax there are only two trains a day to Gabès. That I was nearing the end of the line was patently obvious. The railway authority of Tunisia virtually gave it up at Sfax and what continued to Gabès was simply an expensive toy. Some bright spirit had built a track decades ago and industrious Sfax was not going to be the one to terminate a labour of love, so, since two trains a day kept the rails clear of sand, the service continues.

The Sahara invades Tunisia from the west, coming in like a tide via the great salt lakes or *chotts* that almost cut the country in two. It clogs the valleys near Gafsa, brushes the foothills of the high steppes, and around Gabès rivulets of sand dribble to the sea. Huge herds of camels dot a landscape that doesn't know if it is desert or steppe, but civilisation continued to be represented, if only by Arab children spending their days looking after camels and making obscene gestures at our toy train. The two coaches were nearly empty and the loneliness of the desert reached out to touch me.

I don't know where I got the idea that Gabès was a town. It looks a big place on the map and gives a bay its name. And it *could* look a bigger place if you rolled all its bits and pieces together. As it is there is simply a collection of untidy villages, a cinema standing incongruously in the middle of nowhere and a rash of petrol stations. Probably for the traveller from the south Gabès, with its tufts of date palms, offers the first faint promise of a greener land. Rank thickets of apricots, pomegranates, tobacco, henna and bananas cuddle the inland springs defending this last oasis from the drying action of the sun. Once Gabès was the northern limit of Tripolitania and, as Roman Tacapae, the terminus and wholesale market of the Saharan slave trade. Bits of history form part of the living of today and the market place sports a grandiose portico of Roman columns entirely out of place and proportion. But the heart of Gabès is dust, boredom and the end of the line.

One of the finest institutions in North Africa and the Middle East is the *servis*. Far cheaper than a taxi, more personal than a bus, the *servis* taxi runs between two points 5 or maybe 500 miles part, touting for customers at its point of departure or along the way. The favourite vehicle of the *servis* driver is the Mercedes and its maximum complement is usually seven. The subsequent 1,500 miles of my journey I was to travel by this means.

I picked up my first *servis* in a back street in Gabès. Perhaps it would be more accurate to say it picked up me. A string of place names was eagerly flung at me: Tunis, Sfax, Gafsa, Nefta, Pisida Ben Gardane, but no one was for Tripoli. Go to Pisida, said the agent, it is the border.

Squeezed between two bearded Arabs, I was whirled out of Gabès in a cloud of dust. At the check-point at Ben Gardane we picked up a policeman. He sat on my knee and solemnly told me that, even with a visa, the Libyans would not let me over the border. I began to fear for my onward progress. 'But the English is coming with *me*', announced one of my companions. 'He will accompany us to Tripoli on my lorry.' It was news to me.

In a region of *ghorfas* and empty horizons the Libyan border station makes almost as much impact as does the El Djem amphi-theatre out on the Tunisian plain. Suddenly a palace of chromium-plate and marble is before you, rising like a genie from the dust. However its promising appearance is deceptive. Inside is a chaos of confusion — which was probably the reason I got by. Nobody was exactly rude or unpleasant, though the officials went through their little pantomimes of officialdom with heavy-handed precision. Everyone wanted to know my father's name.

Outside it had begun to rain. Also outside was the lorry. It was a dilapidated boneshaker of great antiquity with a Morris Cowley bonnet. The buck was piled high with crates of live chickens. A driver in the cab grinned a welcome. The question of where we were all going to sit assailed me — as if I didn't know.

Tripoli was all of 125 miles away. The rain was of the solid North African variety. Though the surface of the road was smooth tarmac and noticeably superior to what had gone before, the lorry contrived to move with a most peculiar gait that had the four of us rolling about on top of the heaving crates. I clung to a handhold as far from the edge as possible and wished I were a chicken. It was one hell of a ride.

Somewhere along the way, out in the wet darkness, was Sabratha. Sabratha was an ancient city of Africa founded in the sixth century B.C. by Tyrian settlers and flourished under the Phoenicians. Though but a satellite of Carthage, its excavated remains are the more magnificent. But, with water dripping down my neck, my interest was, to say the least, lukewarm.

We lurched into Tripoli about midnight. Close to the site of the trade fair I was dropped off outside what was alleged to be a new hotel but it was so new that it hadn't yet opened. I wandered miserably down the road puzzling over a scintillating array of neon signs that spoke only Arabic. I forced open the door of what looked like a factory to enquire the whereabouts of a completed hotel. 'This *is* a hotel', came the reply.

I was to see much of Tripoli over the next two days. Ancient Oea to the archaeologist, Tarablus-al-Gharb to the Arabs, Tripoli is the only city in what the Phoenicians called the 'Land of the Three Cities' to have survived and prospered. The other two — Sabratha, and Leptis Magna — have died and, in their dying, they settled permanence upon a town that has become capital of Libya.

More western now than Arab, the city has grown up around a lush oasis situated on a promontory extending into the sea. The residential area is spread along a broad palm-shaded boulevard facing a ship-infested port, while the inevitable old quarter, with its narrow streets of trades and approached by way of the castle and the Arch of Marcus Aurelius, is the cleanest and most un-North African I have seen. The port was once the haven of fierce

136

Libyan pirates, the scourge of the merchant sailors on passage through the Mediterranean. In the centre of new Tripoli lies the king's palace — now no longer a palace and, since a revolutionary colonel could hardly have the nerve to live there, it is something of a white elephant.

Tripoli to Benghazi is about 650 miles. Yet these *servis* drivers make the journey nearly every day or night of their lives. Admittedly the roads are good and traffic not heavy, but it is still quite a performance bearing in mind that a lot of the way is across open desert with special hazards of its own.

There is no railway in Libya, but this is not to say that it has always been a trainless nation. Once there were four independent sections of line, totalling some 230 miles. Fragments are left but now the Libyans put their faith entirely in roads, many built for them by Mussolini's Fascist Italians.

And for me it was the road again and a heavy dose of it at that. By the time my *servis* driver had got himself two more clients — a minimum long-distance load — it was dusk. With nightfall we stopped at Homs, close to the remains of Leptis Magna, and ate a hearty meal in a simple little stone restaurant that might have been part of the celebrated ruins. The driver was a close friend of the family so we ate in style in their cosy kitchen-living room seated round an ancient stove, while outside rain beat upon the tin roof. I asked about the nearby ruins and elicited two more facts about the defunct city; it was the birthplace of the Emperor Septimus Severve, whoever he was; and it contains a W.C. with a marble seat.

The rain gave way to wind, a hot searing torrent of air called the *ghibli*, which stirs up the vast sandy wastes. In compensation, the moon rolled out from behind departing clouds to illuminate the desert in all its awful desolation. We bowled through palm-fringed Misurata to enter the Syrtic Desert, an arid crescent lacking in fresh water but immeasurably rich in crude oil. Beyond Sirte (famous for its saffron cultivation), our progress was made slow and painful by the appearance on the tarmac of hard-packed wedges of sand blown across by the howling wind. Each had to be circumvented or driven over in bottom gear (they were capable of breaking an axle), while all the time a fog of sand

137

crept into the car and stung our eyes. For one who had never seen an angry desert before, it was an alarming hour made palatable only by the balm of human companionship.

At intervals we came upon lone transport cafés, little concrete structures, hugging petrol stations, welcoming and brightly lit in the frightful solitude. Here we drank beakers of mint tea in the company of other travellers of the night while flying sand lashed the walls and turned strangers into friends.

Coming in from the desert is not the most flattering approach to the second city of Libya. This is again reserved for the sea and the air, the latter ending in an impressive dual carriageway sweeping into the centre from Benina Airport. We entered by the back door through a smelly suburb of mean streets muddied by recent rain.

Most towns are built on or by a hill, astride a river or at the head of a valley. Benghazi's only claim to a geographical reason for existence is that it is by the sea. Dead-flat desert and salt marshes stretch away on its other three sides. It suffered cruelly during the fighting of the Second World War, changing hands five times in all before the British and Allied forces finally drove out the combined Italian and German armies in November 1942. The scars have healed, leaving it a surprisingly attractive town overlooking its harbour across the sweep of a majestic promenade.

I left Benghazi oblivious of the fact that I would be seeing it again within very few days. My vehicle was once more the *servis;* my destination, Tobruk. There were six of us tucked inside an old Packard and the driver said he could do the 310 miles in five hours including stops. I didn't believe him but he did.

When I mention to any Eighth Army man that I spent a couple of days in Tobruk recently he invariably asks what the hell I want to do that for. I see what they mean. I arrived in a sandstorm but the short streets and small shops were strangely peaceful, as if the siege had been lifted but yesterday. A friendly taxi driver, asking no fee, insisted upon driving me to the military cemetery outside the town. Maybe my blonde sand-caked hair deceived him, for it was to the German cemetery I was taken. Inside the gaunt fortress that encloses the tomb are black walls inscribed with thousands of fading names.

Tobruk boasts a small port, an oil terminal, a royal palace and one largish hotel. The suburbs peter out into a rash of shacks and encroaching sand. My taxi-man ran me to earth the second day, full of apologies for taking me to what he considered to be the wrong cemetery. To make amends he took me to the beautifully-kept 8,000 British graves back along the Derna road and would, I think, have thrown in the French ones as well given half a chance. If nothing else Tobruk has its sombre memories.

The farthest east anyone wanted to go was Bardia. The town's *servis* agent eventually managed to persuade four lost souls that in Bardia lay their destiny and inveigled them into the car. He squeezed another half a Libyan pound out of me for the extra 12 miles to the Egyptian border and off we went.

The main road bypasses Bardia, but we had to go into the small town to drop off clients. A slap-happy, dusty place, it put me in mind of a film setting for *High Noon*. At Um Sa'ad, in a slight dip of land that likes to think of itself as a pass — the famous Halfaya Pass — a Libyan policeman checked my passport and pronounced it good.

The border station between Libya and Egypt is not quite so grandiose as that between Libya and Tunisia but is adequate enough. Libyan emigration searched my bag, counted my money and cancelled my visa. A little farther on the Egyptians searched my bag, counted my money and then discovered I was British. 'The land borders of the U.A.R. are closed to foreigners,' I was told by an officer with great firmness, and his statement went a long way to confirming a notion that I'd tried to put to the back of my mind for some time. 'The Libyan authorities should not have let you pass. You'll have to go back.'

But the Libyans had done things to my passport and processed me out of the country. Without another visa from their embassy in Cairo or London or somewhere equally inaccessible I could not go back. I was a non-person. Nobody wanted to know me.

The Egyptians were adamant that I couldn't go on either. 'There's a war on,' they said.

'Yes, but that's on the next border.'

'It doesn't matter. All border zones are forbidden to non-Arabs.'

139

'What's to be done then? I'm here now, might as well let me continue.'

But it was not to be. My first sojourn in Egypt lasted four hours. This was the time it took Egyptian authority to coerce Libyan authority into taking me back. And it well could have been longer had I not been making such enthusiastic inroads into Egyptian police rations and their stocks of beer.

With some difficulty — for there was a marked lack of *servis* vehicles going west from the border — I got back to Benghazi from whence a jet whisked me to Cairo. This section of the trip was a bit of a bore for I had been looking forward to some train-riding again, if not from Soloum then at least from Mersa Matruh. There and then I decided to back-track once in Cairo and cover, by rail, the territory denied me by my enforced about-turn.

That the Egyptian capital has deteriorated over the years was very clear. There is howling poverty and a hopelessness of dust that cries aloud. The wealthy have been robbed but this has not enriched the poor which for me, detracted considerably from a city that is large, impressive and historic.

The first night I lost myself in the Mouski. At first it was amusing. Everywhere in the evil little streets men were earnest in the pursuit of money. There was little friendliness, no hostility. A man without legs tried to entice me into his shop by pulling at me from a table top. A dumb child, for the price of a cigarette, led me in the direction of what he thought would be Ataba Square but succeeded only in losing himself too. A policeman shrugged at my attempts to elicit information and a soldier confided to me, with much expressive drawing in the air, where the most voluptuous girls were to be hired. I walked many miles that night.

My second morning I returned to the trains.

A weird method of acquiring tickets greeted me at Cairo Main Station. It appeared that entry to an Egyptian train was only possible with a ticket *and* a reservation. There were three sets of ticket booths in different parts of the station, each dealing with its own class of travel, and, having pre-selected your status, you then had the choice of an air-conditioned or non-air-conditioned train.

Though Cairo itself, unlike Libya, is not averse to diluting its Arabic with a seasoning of English and French, the station sticks firmly to the mother tongue. Hence I joined wrong queues and ended up at windows selling tickets to destinations that were not mine. Porters and touts were quick to smell a lost foreigner and I was directed from pillar to post by a retinue of little men all clamouring for reward. One had an original line in rackets. 'Foreigners need a special permit to travel', he told me, 'I will get it for you,' and away he ran. But I followed him to a crowded Railway Transport Office where I watched him pause, draw a piece of paper out of his pocket and return. I looked the man in the eye and smiled grimly. He had the grace to smile back sheepishly and I gave him three cigarettes for his initiative.

My train was the 08.00 Air-conditioned for Alexandria. It was occupied by businessmen, and businessmen are the same all over the world. The 129-mile journey, normally of two and a half hours, took three and was dull. Dull, that is, except for the panoply of the green, cultivated Nile Delta with its palms, palmettos and exaggerated lushness through which the silver-coached express, headed by its heavily-armoured diesel unit, sped importantly. As well as air conditioning there were sun visors and smoky-blue windows and uniformed waiters who dispensed refreshment at the flick of two fingers. I began to yearn for my broken carriages and verminous Bedouins.

The Nile came into sight between Tanta and Damanhur when the train rolled across a big bridge spanning the wide main stream. Thereafter a system of canals criss-crossed the flat country and high-masted sailing barges (feluccas), glided disconcertingly across the fields.

Alexandria is something of a sham. The sea front is modern, impressive and European. Graceful stone buildings and the slender mosques please the eye. The old city was long ago destroyed and buried by desert sand, which, like Cairo, lap at its doorstep. In its place has appeared the standard Egyptian phenomenon: mean streets of unsavoury smells.

My request for a ticket to Mersa Matruh was greeted with patient resignation. The man behind the grill indicated a notice in Arabic and English above my head 'Special permission has to

141

be granted by the government to go to or beyond Mersa Matruh,' repeated the man in case I couldn't read.

I asked how far I *could* go.

There was a brief consultation in the ticket office. It was clear that not many Britons used the Western Desert line. A consortium of officials decided I could go as far as El-Daba. I wasn't sure where El-Daba was but decided it would do.

My train was pure Arab. No businessman's special this and no pretences of being an express either. Instead it was a happy little train of village elders and merchants who could afford the run into Alex at regular intervals. After an initial show of distrust I was accepted into the brotherhood and invited to tea.

Out in the desert there was a sudden cleansing. The stone walls of Amriya and Hamman were bleached white by the sun, while nomad tents dotted across the sand, lent a romantic air. One small station name held more impact than the others; an impact quite lost upon my chattering companions. But why should they bother themselves about a place called Alamein? To them it was just another hamlet in which to live. To me, as a soldier not in the famed 1942 battle or even the campaign, there arose a feeling of trespass...

I did not alight at Alamein since its dunes and depressions would have meant nothing to me. Instead I continued to El-Daba, another hamlet that could have been Alamein, Amriya or Hamman. I walked its dusty, uneven street and drew curious stares for not even old soldiers come to El-Daba. Thereafter the road and railway passes through territory of a dying fame. Names like Fouka, Mersa Matruh and Sidi Barrani are its stepping stones.

But for me El-Daba was the end of the ride. About 180 miles of desert separated me from Soloum and the point of my broken journey. Perhaps I could have wangled my way through. In fact I'm sure I could, for regulations in the desert get worn by sand. Instead I called it a day and overnight I returned to Cairo. I must have had indigestion for all at once I was eager for a new country.

With Cairo attained and my honour satisfied by personal coverage of most of the Western Desert line I resolved to return home by way of the traditional route of the much-vaunted Paris to Cairo rail route thus, in effect, completing a circuit of the Mediterranean. In this endeavour I was baulked by the then un- resolved Egyptian-Israeli conflict which firmly denied me entry to the land of Israel though I did manage to reach the Suez Canal on a local train where my onward progress fizzled out at the hands of a slightly ruffled colonel of military transportation who wanted to know how I had got that far in the first place.

Thus I was forced into the air once more, this time to Jordan.

After teeming Egypt, little Jordan was an oasis of peace. Actually, the kingdom is not so little, but its cosiness gives that impression. At Amman Airport policemen dressed as British bobbies took me in hand and fixed me up with accommodation.

Jordan contains the sandy beaches of Aqaba, the rose-red Petra, the Dead Sea and divided Jerusalem but the big attraction for me was the Hedjaz Jordan Railway. I was now too far south of the Cairo-Paris line but the new country into which I had been deflected promised some interesting trains. And the promise was not in vain as I was to discover when I received my invitation to take over the whole train and its operation for a day. Word had got around that I was an acquaintance of Princess Muna, the British then-wife of King Hussein — though the true facts were that my father had once met her father when the latter lived at Ipswich. But who was I to quibble over misunderstandings when breakfast at the royal palace and a ride on a gigantic Japanese oil- burning locomotive heading a twenty-wagon train were in the offing.

Thus, in the delightful company of a Jordanian engine-driver, his fireman, guard and a character brandishing a Lee Enfield rifle — designated as our anti-aircraft and anti-guerrilla defence — I took my appointed place in the cab for the drive across the Jordan Desert to Ma'an, southwards towards the Saudi-Arabian border. We performed various loading and unloading tasks en route but much of the journey was taken up with tea and chat with the garrulous railway staff along the line.

Forty-eight hours later I was back in Amman, my conscience demanding that I cease playing trains and resume my prescribed route. The northern section of the Hedjaz Railway into Syria was, of course, closed by one of the frequent disputes arising

143

between the two nations so it had to be a *servis* again that conveyed me to the border. But this border (at Dera'a) was closed
too. However I was learning the ropes and when one official
denied me entry I simply hung around until another came on
duty who approved of my face and let me through.

My *servis* driver on the Syrian side was a jovial Palestinian who
claimed to be the father of sixteen children but was outshone by a
passenger boasting of eighteen. The road accompanied the track
of the Hedjaz Syrian Railway with trains conspicuous by their
absence.

Damascus, the guide books say, is the oldest continuously
inhabited city in the world as they do for half a dozen others in
the Middle East but it matters very little. The city is alive with
biblical reminders and old Damascus is a step backwards into a
school divinity class. The most wonderful building is probably
the Omayyad Mosque, but it was the way to it that fascinated
me. In the bazaar of the old city you have mankind — and
womankind — as you may never hope to see it again. Within the
hubbub of the souks are white-turbaned Druses from the mountains, Bedouin women jangling with necklaces and coin earings
yet flowing in smoky black robes, and the true desert Arab in his
kaffiyah headgear with the colour of his tribe woven into the
cords. Over the narrow passageways of the souks are roofs of
corrugated-iron sheets offering strange contrast to the abrupt
appearance of the great mosque itself, a classical vision of Greco-
Roman architecture formed from the Temple of Jupiter that
stood upon the site.

I suppose it was inevitable that I should end up at Damascus
railway station. I went there at the instigation of a friendly airline
clerk in Pan-Am's booking office who claimed close acquaintanceship with the deputy station-master. And it was only
through this tenuous connection that I could hope to catch a
train to Beirut.

A narrow-gauge railway links the Syrian and Lebanese capitals.
It is a goods-only line and I had seen its Lebanese end three years
previously. Occasional goods trains plied its single track through
the mountains and it was upon one of these that I pinned my
hopes. Alas, I could rustle up no relation of the Syrian president

whose name I could brandish, but even so the deputy station-master was impressed with my enthusiasm for trains and promised to do something about it next morning.

I duly reported in next day, but no train to Beirut of any sort put in an appearance. Neither did the deputy station-master. I gave it up as a bad job and made tracks for the *servis* station.

The road to Beirut is a fine undertaking, splendidly engineered and equipped with magnificent scenery. But it does not satisfy the speed craving of either Syrian or Lebanese. On that Friday afternoon the road was full of drivers released from offices and the pile-ups were legion, some of agonising proportions. A huge cement plant thrust its ugliness into the beauty of mountain and forest, while a rash of little restaurants lined the hairpin road out of Damascus.

On the crest of the Lebanese mountains the panorama of the Bekaa Valley holds one breathless. The horizon is full of the long rampart of the Anti-Lebanon with snow-capped Mount Herman to the south, while, at your feet lies a corrugated trough of waving grass. Orchards, villages and rich cereal fields extend to the limits of vision.

The frontier barriers between the two countries were some 5 miles apart. Again the great Arab unity seemed to have come unstuck as Syrian and Lebanese machine and anti-tank gunners aimed convincingly into each other's territory. Since my visit of course the whole region has erupted into open war.

Traffic jams are as bad in Beirut as in London. Taxi and *servis* drivers have a strange addiction to courting death, and it is a startling sensation to be driven at speed by a young Levantine (there are no old or even middle-aged taxi drivers in Beirut) in his shirt-sleeves, one hand on the wheel, while he gestures with the other out of the window.

From Beirut I attempted to do what I had done in Egypt and back-track along a rail route denied me. This involved a *servis* drive to beyond Tyre where I dodged two checkpoints and nearly got into Israel. But a miss is as good as a mile and I ended up, as you would expect, being ever so slightly arrested and returned to whence I had come. If nothing else, however, I had followed closely for 60 miles the one-time coastal line constructed by

British engineers between Beirut and Cairo, its broken sections still visible half-buried in sand.

It was hardly surprising that nobody had heard of St Michael's Station. It turned out to be a wayside halt sort of place; yet it was the Grand Central of Beirut. But for all this it was pleasing to board a train back on course once more, even if the little red two-coach diesel was hardly an inspiration. The seat reservation rule did little to eliminate the confusion that preceded departure, and how was I to know the Arabic symbols for 12? We left the Lebanese capital by the tradesman's entrance, the train slinking out through a jungle of dilapidated tenements divided by mean refuge-choked streets and, on the sea-shore, filthy black beaches.

The working railway north of Beirut takes a back seat in Lebanese economic circles, but is a fine vehicle — and safer than the roads — for viewing its sensational coastline. Together with the *corniche* road it takes hairpin bends, ploughs through tunnels in the rock headlands and only strays inland to avoid the seaside towns.

Banana palms growing on the shores of the tideless sea herald ancient Byblos. A paradise for the excavator with its pre-historic, Phoenician, Roman and medieval sites in muddled array, it is the sea and the land that steals the show; particularly perhaps the rocky gorge down which the Dog River scampers. Near Tripoli — another Tripoli, this one the second city of Lebanon — we trundled past the terraced salt-pans that turn the countryside into a chessboard with little iron windmills as its pawns.

We were back into Syria with classical *Emesa* which is now Homs and it still remains a gloomy city. Far older than its Libyan namesake, the modern blocks of flats compare no more favourably with its unimaginative minarets, "square black towers of basalt" as someone called them. The market place was full of Bedouins on a shopping spree from the desert.

If Homs is a washout the next city along the line makes up for it. Hama sits astride the Orontes in a valley of blood red soil sprouting great bursts of blossom. But what makes Hama unique is its water-wheels. The creaking of the *norias,* as they are called, is something one becomes aware of the moment of entry into the town. The biggest is 120 feet across and it creaks and groans in a

never-ending tortuous racket as it lifts water into ancient aque-
ducts. Smaller ones dot the Orontes valley around the town, each
one groaning miserably. I asked a native of the town how he
could stand the eternal racket. "You're an islander", he said,
"how would you like it if the waves of the sea stopped sluicing
the shore?" I saw what he meant.

Across the great plains we stumbled; the granary — and stable
too — of Syria, for here are reared some of the finest Arab horses.
Then in the midst of boredom came the unique sight of the
northern beehive villages. At first they were diluted with mud
houses of standard pattern but soon complete communities of
windowless beehives — each hive housing one family — dotted
the plain.

The train ended its run at Aleppo. I was back once more on the
Baghdad to Istanbul line. On the northbound Taurus Express
the familiar stop at Adana in Turkey was like coming home.

6

Trans-Asia

PARIS—DELHI

If the Paris—Cairo Express nearly came into being, the concept of a Paris—Delhi service has been a project on the drawing board for equally as long. A lesser dream, perhaps, but one of considerable significance and potential is the credibility of a direct service to India. Yet, with the exception of a single gap, the basic ingredients of such an accomplishment exist.

There are actually two routes available. That of the mooted trans-Asian line takes in the main line between Haydarpasa (Istanbul) and Teheran via the Lake Van ferry in eastern Turkey after which, at Qum Junction, it proceeds on the existing line to Kerman in southern Iran. The gap of some 200 miles of flatish, open country lies between Kerman and Zahedan but this is steadily narrowing. The tracks start again at Zahedan, and a desert line runs (when not closed for strategic reasons), to Quetta in Pakistan from whence there are good rail services abounding to Lahore and Delhi.

As with the Paris—Cairo route there is an alternative and the map shows the overall picture today. A second route as far as Teheran could take in Istanbul, Baghdad and Basra. At Basra lie several checks: thirty miles of sand dunes, a river (the Euphrates and Tigris combining to form the wide Shatt al Arab), and, currently, conflict. At Khorramshah in south-western Iran the tracks recommence to carry regular services to Teheran.

A more direct onward route to India would, of course, be via Afghanistan but since she is a railwayless nation the lines end at Mashhad before the Afghan border, and do not resume until Lindikotal at the head of the Khyber Pass in Pakistan. From Peshawar, at the bottom of the pass, are regular trains once more to Lahore and Delhi.

Thus there is a network available for development but, in

148

addition to economic problems, there are those of a human nature which manifest themselves in the form of political strife: war and hate between Iraq and Iran, a Soviet occupation in Afghanistan, frosty relations between Pakistan and India.

On my 1973 journey of investigation into what might have been and could transpire I travelled out via the traditional 'India route' to Teheran continuing on the railwayless section across Afghanistan, then returning on the more southerly route including the Baghdad 'detour'. In 1973 Afghanistan was still a free nation while between Iran and Iraq there existed a hate that had not yet ignited into war. But given even these more optimistic conditions the journey was to offer little hope for a Paris—Delhi Express in my lifetime.

I saw little of Lake Van on my long slow ride across Turkey because the train was late and it was dark when we arrived at Tatvan pier to catch the ferry across. My entire experience of Turkish train travel has been on slow 'picturesque' trains with the exception of a dull spasm on the Bogazici Express from Istanbul to Ankara, a route that is also covered by her crack Anatola Express which is more luxurious than fast. Yet Turkey, as well as Iran, *is* seeing an increase of international traffic which bodes well for a future Trans-Asian Railway, at least as far as her territory is concerned.

As well as for its cathedral of a station, Tabriz is famous for Persian carpets. Capital of the province of Azerbaijan the bazaars of the city ring with the offer of 'bargain prices' for the provincial specialities, many of strikingly beautiful design. I remained in the city a few days which was the length of time it took me to obtain a second-class seat reservation on a subsequent Istanbul—Teheran express; the only train that ran between Tabriz and the capital. It took me almost my entire last day to collect all the pieces of paper deemed necessary to ride the train, which was one of just two or three that use the station each day.

My compartment on the Vangölü Express was occupied by an assortment of Persians, an Australian, a roll of carpets and two live turkeys. The turkeys were roosting on my reserved seat but were persuaded to perch aloft on the luggage rack to make room

149

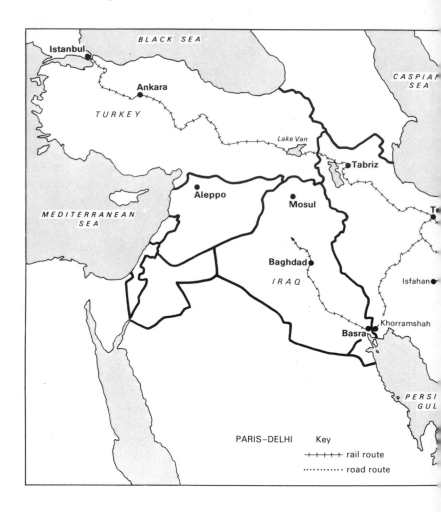

for me. The train ran for miles parallel to the snowy rampart of the Elburz Mountains and over the desolate landscape of stones and sand. Most of the way the black tarmac road huddled close to the railway as if reluctant to lose contact in a land of no flowers and no birds. One town en route was Qazvin, once the Persian capital — as were Isfahan, Shiraz, Suleimanieh, Ardabil, Nishapur and Mashhad. Qazvin had its fling in the sixteenth

150

century under the great Shah Abbas and its blue-tiled domes and shrines offer a touch of capitalship to an otherwise nondescript town. The Australian in my compartment was a talkative Queenslander from Toowoomba, on his way home after an itinerant year in Asia. When not talking to me he spent his time in conflict with the Persian owner of the carpet roll which kept digging into him.

151

Tehran, the present capital of Iran is the creation of Reza Shah and is a recent accomplishment. 'An opera house, a stock exchange and no camels', he ordained, basing his ideas on Ankara which was the only other capital he had seen. But the opera house, faultily conceived by an Iranian architect, could not be completed and the stock exchange never got further than the drawing board. The camels, however, vanished. Its twelve tiled gates and the ramparts were erected chiefly with money sent from Europe for the Persian Famine Relief Fund. The railway station into which I emerged sprinkled with turkey droppings hardly deserved the publicity it generated when first opened. Rome yes, Helsinki up to a point but Teheran has no right to laud its railway station, particularly as it serves so few trains.

Even after several days there I could raise little enthusiasm for this city that, by heritage is eastern and by ambition western. It is a traffic-snarled jumble of a place containing a lot of hideous art nouveau with the occasional truly beautiful building like the white and grey marble National Bank in the Avenue Ferdaysi.

There are currently two slow trains daily to Mashhad and an express on Mondays, Wednesdays and Saturdays. I chose to leave Teheran on a Tuesday so got lumbered with an overnight slow train. Before 1939 Iran had no railway but World War Two brought British and American railway builders in strength who laid a line from the Persian Gulf through Teheran to the Russian frontier and the Caspian Sea which was to carry enormous freight loads supplying the Soviet Union with munitions. After the war things sprouted from there and the line across the edge of the Great Salt Desert towards Afghanistan was one such to blossom.

From the corridor where, by mutual consent, the males among us chose to sleep, I watched Mount Demavend slide by, its snowy peak brilliant white in the fierce moonlight. The valley of the Karaj river is beautiful: extravagantly sweeping lines of plain and mountain are exhilarating stuff to an islander. The whitened surface of the plain was startling; it looked like snow but was in fact salt. My European clothes made a poor substitute for the *chapan,* a garment so practical for train corridor travel, and I was, once more, to envy the Asian's ability to find sleep in the most uncomfortable of positions. An indefatigable ticket inspector made periodic hikes up and down the body-filled corridor adding to my discomfort when he did so. And then suddenly, during a dawn stop at a remote station, there was a commotion and the corridor emptied. The next moment my companions lay prostrate on the platform facing Mecca.

With devotions brought to an abrupt end by a blast from the locomotive I was pressed to accept various breakfast offerings by my now garrulous fellow travellers who enquired after the size of my family. My disclosure of a brother and two offspring produced only sympathy and strange looks as if something was wrong with me. In Persia a large family is important and socially desirable. A long delay at Nishapur gave opportunity for a leg-stretch beneath a warm morning sun. Small and insignificant, today Nishapur is nevertheless a lovely town with cascades of weeping willows and beds of carnations, roses and geraniums around and about the mud walls. I took my turn at the communal tap but the water was lukewarm. With the exception of Afghanistan public water is safe to drink all the way to India though only ice can make it palatable. A few miles ahead a stir of interest in the coach indicated a modern abomination that is the tomb of Omar Khayyam, revered by Persians young and old.

Mashhad is the holiest city in Iran; even holier than Qum. The tomb of the Iman Reza is the equivalent of Mecca for the Shi'ites and to go with such distinction are buildings of sublime magnificence. The place owes its foundation to the burial there of Harun-er-Rashid, of *Arabian Night*'s fame, who died nearby. Its glory, however, stems from the bones of Reza, the eighth Imam who died after eating a bunch of poisoned grapes a year or two later and was buried in the same tomb chamber.

The holy city, less than 50 miles from the Afghan border, is the end of the line. In fact it is the end of the line for the best part of 500 miles. I remained in the city some days exploring its mixture of glory and shame. The bird-soiled golden dome of the mosque housing the tomb is the strongest magnet to a visitor and I was straightway drawn towards it. Though entry is forbidden to infidels I managed to sneak into the inner courtyard wearing a *djellabah* but was ejected with some vigour. A few years earlier I

153

would have had my throat cut. Mashhad is that sort of place. 'Colourful' the guide books call it.

For the overlander the route east is by road or nothing. There is a regular bus service to Taibar, the border town, and the road runs straight across a broad plain with blue and white mountains barring the horizon. By the roadside, as we left Mashhad, were yellow irises, scarlet tulips and a dead camel. Flies had been my most devoted companions in the city and my strictly-no-star hotel, behind a butcher's shop, was their favourite haunt. 'If you get lost', the hotel manager told me, 'just follow the flies'. At Fariman two ludicrous plaster lions guard the approaches to a model rural community that never was. Another Reza Shah dream of Western innovation that died with him. What was built has long since decayed or has been looted. The lions, not being of combustible material, remain, guarding a forgotten dream of Utopian paradise.

Taibar is not the border but is the border town. If you know the dodges you can reach Herat from Mashhad the same day. The secret is to reach the Afghan bus which leaves from a different terminus at the same time as the Mashhad bus arrives in the dirty little square. The Afghan bus will be full of people stranded from the night before. Assuredly both Afghan and Persian drivers are getting a cut from the Taibar hotel people for every traveller left there overnight.

The hotel is not to be recommended. When I was there it was composed of shacks around a central yard knee-deep in mud. Most of the shacks were without beds though some held ledges artfully titled 'thrones of sleep'. Should you have to use the beds, thrones or floor let it be a last resort.

So try to catch the other bus. You'll recognize it because it's like no other vehicle on earth. Tall and ungainly, made almost entirely of packing crates, the whole contraption is painted with unveiled cherubic-looking women, camels and aeroplanes. Every inch is packed with people.

Strangely enough the thing moved and moved fast. Bits fell off here and there but nobody worried. Halfway along a straight stretch of road a sign shouted 'Afghanistan' but there are another ten miles of Persian territory before the actual border at Islam Kala. A soldier propped up the sign that said so.

154

Herat, Kandahar, Kabul, Jelalabad. These are the semi-urban stepping stones across the barren wastes of Afghanistan where time appears to have come to a standstill three centuries ago. At first our 'blacktop' road was American-made but later the tarmac became of Russian origin. Four tall chimneys mark Herat; four minarets against a horizon of desert. Once called Hairova, and then Alexandria-in-Asia, Herat is situated where two trade routes meet, a situation made for constant destruction and resurrection. The crossroads are the town centre and nearby can be found the minaret and tomb of Gaudhar Shad, that great lady of Herat renaissance who also gave to Mashhad its famous dome. Her buildings and those of Baigara, clustered at the same end of town, were levelled on the advice of a British military adviser in 1866 to make a field of fire against a Russian attack that never came. Four minarets remain, crooked fingers scarred and pitted, that will one day fall to join the brown earth. My hotel, the Behzad, cost me 40 pence a day and there were others charging only 20.

Kandahar, along a concrete road that takes in Ghazni with its delicious minarets only slightly less graceful than their famous counterparts at Djem, is a community of bazaars. Here the best skull-caps, waistcoats and fine silk shirts are made and sold for a pittance. Cradled in rock, its situation is softened by patches of light green water and dark green pines. I was accommodated at the Marjur Hotel in a room shared by an Indian snake-charmer who had lost his bag of cobras, and a Peruvian hippy. The toilet was outside upon a flat roof and if it *had* to be used there was a three to one chance of falling into the restaurant below. I slept badly, worrying about where the cobras might be.

Twenty years ago there was not a modern building in the Afghan capital. Now adventurous modernity pushes out among the booths and dried brown mud as the untidy sprawling city struggles for form among the hills. Several luxury hotels have appeared but they were not for me. All Asia can be seen thronging the streets and bazaars of Kabul. Tall Pathans, black-bearded and turbaned, flat-faced Mongols, long Tajik profiles, Indo-Iranians, Uzbeks from the upper Oxus, and the bright eyes and uncombed heads of the pagan hillmen of Nuristan. Only the women present a uniform picture, though their fragile silk

155

chadari offers mysterious and colourful anonymity.

While at Kabul I made an excursion by local bus to Istalif, an impressive village atop the Khair Khana Pass in the snow-dappled Paghman Mountains. The return journey amongst the baggage on the roof of the bus, my favourite position on most of the Afghan bus journeys I made, took place in early evening and was a lesson to me on what not to wear in Afghanistan. As it had been a hot day I was wearing shorts and straightway my legs attracted the unwelcome attentions of a set of ruffians who were accompanying me. One by one they sidled up to me and, grinning inanely, began fondling my knees and thighs. Slowly I backed away from the growing threat of a fate worse than death until I came to rest hard against the guard rail at the front end of the roof. In the nick of time the conductor appeared up the iron ladder at the rear and I beckoned wildly to him. Over he came with one swift leap in spite of the wildly swaying chassis and without so much as a 'good evening' or 'what's your name?' joined the mêlée, his hand halfway up my calves! A passing lorry had me on my feet in preparation for a James Bond-type leap from one fast moving vehicle to another but I was forcibly restrained by my amorous assailants, the conductor remarking that since I had paid for a ticket to Kabul then to Kabul I should go and on *his* bus. Fortunately we drew into the suburbs of the capital before my self-respect was entirely despoiled.

My loss next day was of a more material nature. Passing through a bazaar (my legs now completely hidden by trousers), my wallet was stolen. The loss was more inconvenient than disastrous since my passport and main cash reserves remained securely if sweatily next to my skin but, nevertheless, a sizeable amount of local currency and personal papers were involved. I reported the incident to the nearest police station not with any hope of regaining the wallet or its contents but simply with a view to obtaining a certificate for my insurance company stating that the theft had occurred.

But this in Afghanistan is easier said than done. I spent the best part of two days closeted in various police offices going over the theft again and again, to get absolutely nowhere. I made out a crisply-worded report but no way could I get the police authorities to stamp and sign it. 'You'll have to go to the Prime-Minister's office', they said and out of desperation and stubborness I did precisely that. In a smart office block near the palace I passed before a series of increasingly senior clerks until I reached the prime-minister's secretary. 'First you'll have to obtain a certificate of who you are from your embassy', he said and lost further interest. So to the British Embassy I repaired by taxi and following two return journeys into town, first to extract my passport lodged with my hotel and again to obtain a photostat of the embassy certificate — which was simply my original report stamped and signed by a third secretary — I suspended operations and, thankfully, turned my back upon Kabul.

Again atop a local bus I travelled the zig-zag road down the breathtaking Tanghi Ghuru, the Kabul Gorge, into a heat that proved India was near. I was to spend the night in Jalalabad. I have read descriptions of the town as being the nearest one can get to paradise and indeed the cypress trees and lake at the approaches tend to encourage optimism. But any optimism is short lived; the town sweats in its own humidity, disease and filth. My 'hotel' was the Majestic which, I should explain, is a doss-house where a bed cost me the equivalent of 5 pence. I slept on a bed frame in a kind of sleeping hall, where my neighbours were bearded, leering tribesmen who sported tattered robes and exuded powerful smells. They went to bed not only with their baggy trousers on but also with their daggers, swords, assorted rifles and AK47's. Trapped in the middle of this snoring mob I could feel the rats running over me and, in the early hours was forced to watch the awful sight of the biggest, most bulbous spider I had ever seen slowly descending on me from a bug-infested ceiling. The 5 pence was sheer robbery.

Another bus took me to the Pakistan border and a jeep taxi to Lindikotal at the head of the Khyber Pass. Lindikotal is another den of thieves with everyone armed to the teeth as the Pushtu tribesmen demonstrate to the Pakistan government who is boss of the region. But, for me Lindikotal had one priceless attraction: a railway station. I chanced lucky too, for I arrived just in time to catch the once-a-week no-charge train that was then running between Lindikotal and Peshawar (more as a counter-demonstration by the Pakistan government to show that *they* controlled the

Khyber than a social service).

There was, however, not an inch of space to spare on the three-coach train that waited at the platform so I took up residence on the left-hand front buffer of the Vulcan foundry-made 1923 steam locomotive sharing it with a jovial Pakistani. The Khyber Pass is not a patch on the Kabul Gorge for grandeur but that 40-mile ride was, to me, a high-spot of many years of train travel. We travelled at no great pace through a series of short tunnels which failed to deter those hanging on to the coach sides. Empty forts made a walnut topping to every hill and a jutting rock proclaimed the names of regiments — British, Pathan and Indian — carved in stone where years and blood lie eaten by the sun. The Khyber is the steepest non rack-and-pinion stretch of track in the world and, even with two engines (there was a 1936 German oil-burner at the rear), it was heavy going. The route takes the form of a letter Z, the train changing direction at each apex and the locomotives taking it in turn to lead. On the steepest sections, safety tracks have been installed so that runaway trains can be diverted up into the hills.

I took a *tonga* (two-wheeled taxi) into Peshawar town from a station that, like those everywhere in the Indian sub continent, hold fast to the traditions of the British Raj with their strictly segregated classes of waiting room, toilets and restaurants. A hundred things to see, a thousand faces to absorb in a single glance in this city which lies at the foot of the pass and is a halting place for caravans. If the Mall remains vitally English in conception, the centre of the town is equally as vitally Indian with its maze of mean streets of trades. A bus ride to Kolhat, a village that gives itself entirely over to the manufacture by hand of guns of every description, offered another slant to this rebellious region.

The train I caught from Peshawar next day was the express to Rawalpindi. Back on the main line it differed from my 'Khyber Special' in age, length and stature but not in carrying capacity. Travelling second class (there wasn't a third class) I was not alone and, by dint of giving as good as I got, won myself a few square inches of corridor. Pakistan Railway notices intimated that it was dangerous to travel on the outside of coaches — and

158

our diesel-powered locomotive would not tolerate a necklace of humans round its belly.

I remember Rawalpindi chiefly for the tea and cakes its station produced before my Lahore-bound train came in. It was not crowded by Pakistani standards and I managed a seat as we dawdled unconcernedly across a lush countryside mainly populated by buffalos.

A city of faintly decaying beauty is Lahore and I was to spend four days immersed in its offerings. Moghul history with a dash of Kipling is one way of describing the city's past but my strongest impressions were of the turmoil in its streets where the people fought, lived, slept and died; it was all so visible in Lahore.

I crossed the border into India by taxi and found myself in Amritsar, stronghold of the Sikhs. After the flat, dull terrain of the Punjab this city of the Golden Temple is exciting. The temple is set like a jewel in its polluted 'Pool of Immortality' surrounded by some of the meanest streets and most dreadful human squalor imaginable. What Mecca is to the Moslem, or Benares is to the Hindu, the Golden Temple of Amritsar is to the Sikh. Destroyed and desecrated again and again by the Moghuls, the Sikhs never gave up in the face of blood-curdling torture and persecution. I lived for a day or two in a run-down establishment recovering from an attack of the 'runs' and also in the shelters offered to Sikh pilgrims to the temple. Though I had to keep a tight hold of my belongings I received from my fellow transitees nothing but kindness.

More or less fit again I caught the Delhi Mail. Indian Railways have the largest railway system in Asia and it is one of the most heavily used in the world; it is also still expanding. The magnificent network was probably the most valuable bequest the British administration made to India. Handed over as a cluster of private companies in 1947, names that have a similar ring to our own companies of a generation ago, became absorbed into a nationalised system. Household names in transport and engineering circles like Great Indian Peninsula, Bombay, Baroda and Central India, Madras and Southern Mahratta, and 'His Exalted Highness the Nizam's Guaranteed State Railway' are now worked under centralised control divided into nine territorial sections.

In bottom class again I spent a sickening fourteen hours standing with three dozen others in a compressed gel of sweaty, unclean humanity in a compartment meant for eight. In the morning, at New Delhi station, I watched them sweep out a corpse with the rubbish from my coach. I can't say, in all honesty, I felt very much better myself.

Delhi is the only one of India's larger cities — and it is not the largest — to offer more than a millennium of history in its stones. When Bombay and Madras were but trading posts and Calcutta a village of mud-flats, Delhi had already been the capital of an empire for 500 years. Various Hindu and Moslem dynasties, the Moghuls and, finally the British, established their seat of government with the British realizing their dream capital of New Delhi just in time to turn it over to the new independent nation it had spawned. To this day the city wears its British-made capitalship with style and pride, the stately buildings and cool spacious avenues contrasting oddly with the labyrinth of small crowded streets studded with mosques, temples, monuments and bazaars. The teeming street called Chandni Chowk, leading from the Red Fort, is a far cry from the almost deserted Rajpath between the dignified India Gate and Parliament House. Contrast. It is a word that crops up again and again in any narrative about India. Alas, it is not just a contrast of architectural styles but, more starkly, that between the people who have and those who have not. While in the capital I varied my pad between a cockroach-prone 'hotel' in Connaught Place and the luxurious apartment of a prosperous acquaintaince living in a well-to-do suburb.

The route I had set myself for the homeward journey followed that of the long-designated Trans-Asian Railway at least as far as the junction at Qum, in western Iran. Thereafter my railway wanderings would take me south to the Persian Gulf, then northwest into Iraq and Syria and back into Turkey along a line frail and broken in parts that provides for an exciting alternative route. After a week or two nosing around India, and Delhi in particular, I was ready for the run home. Not that my explorations precluded rail travel — my period of random train rides culminated in a trip in the air-conditioned class of the crack Taj Express which took me to Agra and the Taj Mahal to see how the other half lived.

I left New Delhi Station on another mail 'express' bound for Amritsar. Even with an open border between the two countries there is only one rail crossing point, at Atari between Amritsar and Lahore so it is necessary to return by the same route in spite of the fact that, in Pakistan, I would be travelling south towards Karachi. My train was packed. Even before it had pulled up at the station the coaches were assaulted by a crowd of would-be passengers using their baggage as battering rams to struggle through windows against intense resistance from those who had already got into compartments. The mood was ugly. As for me, I was simply washed aboard by a sea of people that deposited me next to an enormous and unfriendly Sikh. My interval of high living came to an abrupt end at this point.

I counted more than forty in my compartment. Even the luggage racks were two deep. After a few miles the crush lessened slightly when the contents settled. Later I was to win a 'seat' when I shared a step at the open door with an amiable Afghan, our feet dangling out of the train.

This was another leg of a journey I could have cheerfully missed. And yet . . . surely it is part of the experience of India and Indian Railways. Born 130 years ago it could hardly be imagined that the first steam 'boneshaker' that ran out Bombay's Bori Bunder Station to nearby Thana would expand into the fourth largest railway system in the world.

Pakistan Railways have been overtaken by history. Its eastern section, once the pride of the then East Pakistan, has been lost to Bangladesh. Like Indian Railways it carries three classes of passenger accommodation: air-conditioned, first class and second class. In addition some trains, provide an air-conditioned chair class which, like first class, can be converted into a sleeping compartment.

From Lahore my next train was to be the Quetta Mail. Again arose the problem of boarding the second-class coaches but I was learning. Selecting the toughest-looking of the many red-jacketed porters on the platform I offered him a rupee if he got me a seat; two if it was a window seat. The train arrived late from Rawalpindi and before it stopped my man took a header through the window into a second-class coach. He earned his two rupees.

161

My new companions were a strange bunch. All were Pakistanis but of very assorted breeds. One was busy carrying out his devotions up on the luggage rack, a tricky business on a swaying train. Another lay on the floor oblivious of his compatriots' feet on him. The others squatted, cross-legged, on the wooden seats watching me and smiling every time they caught my gaze. If I took out my notebook to scribble an observation all would crowd round to look.

The line ran straight as a die for a hundred miles over flat, uninspiring territory with our electric locomotive coping effortlessly. We were travelling the old Indus Valley State line which formed part of an undertaking, started in 1853, to link Karachi with Calcutta as a step in the larger concept of a fast transport complex to improve transit between Britain and Calcutta. The first planned route was via Egypt and later by way of the navigable waters of the Euphrates, Mesopotamia, the Persian Gulf and the Indus river. But the opening of the Suez Canal and such matters as the differing gauges between European and Asian track ensured that it never materialised.

Yet the Indus was in use for years as a watery artery before the Indus Valley State Railway came into being, the final link in the chain of railways giving through connections right across the sub-continent to Calcutta. The only break was the crossing of the great river at Sukkur where a ferry conveying wagons and passengers sufficed until the opening of the Lansdown Bridge in 1889, then the largest cantilever bridge in the world.

On through Multan and Sukkur, and a dull roar in the night coupled with stabs of light showed we were passing over the great bridge. If I found the flat terrain of the Punjab dull I was in for a surprise as we penetrated Baluchistan. Soon after the Indus crossing the dawn illuminated a brown plain of desolation supporting no more than an occasional mud village and the beseeching arms of stunted trees. The Quetta Mail's defection northwards from the Karachi line had allowed it to escape the worst of the Sind Desert's excesses, a flat expanse of sand and scrub winnowed by hot winds and scoured by limitless horizons. But dust there was, even here, and it piled up against the doors and window ledges while tiny avalanches slithered to the floor with every halt. With the change of scenery came a change in the composition of my companions. The Punjabis had become swarthy-faced Balochis flaunting fierce bushy eyebrows and beards. They stared at me with a prolonged and disconcerting intensity and when they spoke their questions were sharp and to the point. Why had I come to Baluchistan they asked as if my invasion of their ancient and terrible land was a grotesque anachronism.

Sibi town sits on another junction of the line. Its scattering of houses, cowering beneath a merciless heat, serves a railway that was as grotesque an anachronism in this territory as myself. A friendly Balochi came and sat by me to put me wise about the reasons for the unrest that grips his land. Pakistan was the source of all evil, or so his version went and his spit was one of hate rather than habit. The lack of water and food was the government's fault, he complained, and I was a mite mystified as to what Pakistan could do that God couldn't. But it seemed an old story of broken promises concerning sundry irrigation schemes and food distribution projects which left his fellow villagers and their animals to die. Thus the friction and the feuding in which the odd military patrol gets itself wiped out among the rocky defiles.

At intervals along the track were white-painted markers carefully framed in painted stones that showed a devotion to duty inherited from a past generation of railway staff. Long before Partition in 1947 the then Pakistan Western Railway had been the Kandahar State Railway. The story of its construction has no parallel in all the history of the railways of the sub-continent. It is a tale of appalling muddle in the beginning, of extreme privations in the face of frightful heat and bitter cold, and of success achieved through sheer determination to force a route through some of the most forbidding territory on earth. Much of the line was built in record time in spite of destruction by flood, landslide and earthquake and the very fact that the line is kept open today in the face of the additional handicap of Balochi hostility is evidence of a quality of endeavour unsurpassed anywhere.

During the second half of the nineteenth century, the politics of north-west India were dominated by the fear of Russian invasion through Afghanistan. So when, for purely strategic reasons, the

163

government in 1876 determined to take all measures to keep open at all times and seasons at least one route from India into Afghanistan, orders were issued for the immediate construction of a railway to Quetta and, beyond, to the Afghan border. Today, of course, their worst fears have been realized and thus the carefully-laid white stones mark a railway line, though slender and bearing but half a dozen trains a day in both directions, that is of vital importance to the free world.

Through the historic Bolan Pass where General Roberts bade farewell to his troops after his epic march from Kabul to Kandahar, and onto the Dozan Gorge. This is the third line to have been constructed here since the original was laid along the stony bed and, when not in tunnels, it crosses the ravine nine times within four miles. Once through the storm of rock we emerged into the calm of avenues of Chinar trees that grace the former capital of Baluchistan, Quetta.

It is quite a small town with little of the concentrated bustle of other Pakistan cities and none of their grandeur. The buildings that were once the Residency and the Commissioner's Secretariat remain, exuding still an air of English upper class life. At the further end of town stands the memorial to the British victims of the 1935 earthquake. Fifteen thousand died but only Christians are commemorated.

I met my first hotel problem in Quetta, eventually solving it with the help of a cheerful American hippy couple. 'Come to our pad, man', they said, 'It's a snake-pit but if we frighten some of the bugs out there'll be room for the three of us'. The accommodation was one of a row of cabins surrounding a muddy square and when the door was shut it was pitch dark because of the lack of any window. The three of us shared the same bed but because of the amorous activities of the couple it was hardly a peaceful night.

The next leg of the journey was that to Zahedan in south-eastern Iran. I purchased a second-class ticket for 25 rupees and a knowing porter established me in a first-class coach together with instructions as to how to dodge the ticket inspector. The train was a mobile oven and was headed by a dilapidated steam locomotive. It stopped for the slighest excuse and on one occasion long enough for the playing of a football match: locals versus a team of captive opponents. Being a single track line the delays were necessary, it appeared, to allow approaching trains to pass, though I'm convinced the signal system was geared to the football schedules.

This lonely line was once known as the Nushki Extension though it runs hundreds of miles past Nushki and fifty miles into Iranian territory. It bifurcates from the Quetta line at Spezand, homeground of the first football match of the series, to run parallel with the Afghan frontier. The railway was built during World War One when the British and Russians were policing the territory between the Caspian Sea and the Persian Gulf.

Between Dalbandin and Nok Kundi, a distance of 104 miles, the landscape is wholly without habitation, virtually devoid of vegetation and can only be described as a hell upon earth. The tracks cross stretches of ground covered with sharp black stones broken only by patches of coarse sand. For eight months of the year the heat is intense and the '120-day wind' lashes the sand so that it lacerates the skin of anyone caught out in it. The whole desert is coated with sulphur dust, and water, when it is obtainable, is a concentrated mixture of common and Epsom salts. When there is any rain the year's fall may occur within an hour. The river beds, bone dry for ninety-nine out of a hundred days, then hurl a mixture of water and stones it has picked up on its way at the exposed railway. To overcome this disconcerting obstacle the engineers constructed Irish bridges or 'dips', and the train drivers using them were expected to rely on their discretion as to whether or not they could get through without the water putting the fire out.

This is not all. There are also the *do-regs,* or 'marching sandhills' to contend with. These are crescent-shaped sandhills formed by the wind and they are constantly on the move. Again the line is the target, this time for the wind and, from time to time, diversionary tracks have to be laid down to take trains round the back of the *do-regs* to avoid having to remove several thousand tons of sand. The sandhills move in parallel lines for many miles across the *dasht,* as the mixture of sand and rock is called. Their speed is between 500 and 600 yards a year so the duplicated tracks are simply left in position and trains switch to the one that is clear of sand at the particular time.

These, then, were just some of the vicissitudes of my trans-Baluchistan Desert journey. Another was to come. Having dodged the ticket collector for a whole day I was caught out during a doze and banished to second class. With every seat occupied I took refuge, during a station stop, in the locomotive. An Englishman was a rare client it seemed and I was welcomed aboard but the transfer was akin to jumping from the frying pan into the fire. The locomotive was an American oil-burner of 1930 vintage, and the heat of its roaring boiler easily matched that of the sun. By sticking my head out of the cab I caught the pitiful remnants of a breeze while, periodically, tumblers of oily tea went the rounds of the crew to lubricate parched throats. I felt it expedient to earn my keep so, as well as taking over the duties of look-out, I fussed around undertaking odd jobs whenever we stopped to take on water.

My fellow crew were a couple of friendly ruffians who took full advantage of a source of free cigarettes. In return they shared with me their meat-stuffed chapattis thus creating a friendship of sorts between us. We moved at near walking pace with male passengers in the coaches jumping out to urinate and jumping back again. The scenery, shimmering in the savage heat, was of austere desert backed by a long low range of lifeless mountains where nothing moved except for the occasional camel train plodding to some nameless destination. I stripped down to my underpants and suffered an endless day in a lather of sweat, oil and dirt. Evening brought a delicious coolness; the horizon joined forces with the dying sun in a great suffusion of vermilion and gold. Then darkness.

It was early next morning, while on look-out duty — a useful ploy for catching the breeze — that I spotted the bent rail. I'm sure if I hadn't seen it nobody else would. We slammed on the brakes and, together with a number of passengers, walked over to examine the damage. The blistering heat had caused excessive expansion and it was obvious that the rail would have to be replaced. No-one seemed the slightest bit concerned however and it occurred to me that this was probably a regular hazard.

166

Now, the lengths of spare rail that I had noticed lying at intervals by the track made sense. From a potential workforce of hundreds a dozen passengers were despatched to bring up a replacement rail from the nearest dump whilst, under the supervision of the driver, others crowded onto the track to remove the bent section.

Having done my stint I wandered off into the desert intent on investigating a tiny mud-walled village I had noticed in the distance. I was to pay for my nosiness. About a hundred yards short I was intercepted by a gun-toting bandit of bearded magnificence who stuck his musket into my ribs and, with his other hand, rubbed the tips of his fingers together. He wasn't joking, so I hunted about for loose change (carefully avoiding my money-belt), and flung a handful of rupees into the sand. I had a vague notion of belting him when he bent down to pick them up but a commotion in the village sent him into retreat, and I thought it prudent not to push my luck, so retreated likewise but in the opposite direction, back to the train.

We limped into Mirjaveh, the Iranian border village, many hours late the following evening where, to our intense irritation, we were made to attend a customs inspection. This was followed by the building up of a long queue for the ticket to take us the 50 miles across Iranian territory. Tired and short-tempered, the complement of the train were in no mood for such frivolities and when a power cut plunged the station into darkness it was the last straw. Collectively we left the queue and returned, ticketless, to the train and when a ticket collector escorted by two soldiers attempted to regain authority they were shouted off.

The faint outlines of a live volcano, the sometimes smoking Koh-i-Taftan, stood out in an otherwise empty landscape and in the grey shrouds of another dawn, we finally drew into Zahedan. The Nushki Extension was, in the beginning, a purely strategic line. Looking to the future it will need a great deal of redevelopment to turn it into a worthwhile section of the Trans-Asian Railway. In the meantime it remains, surely, the world's slowest, hottest railway journey.

For a town on the edge of eternity Zahedan is not really a bad little place. It is an oasis in the midst of purgatory and its simple amenities are the more remarkable for it. But the one amenity I wanted was unattainable: having reached Zahedan I wanted nothing more than to find a bus and get out of it. There were four bus companies in the town, all under siege by hundreds of intending travellers with the same goal. 'You'll have to wait at least three days for a seat', I was told by harassed booking clerks. Joined by two antagonistic Australians I first attempted hiring a taxi and then, at a strategically-placed petrol station, tried begging a lift from the few cars that appeared — but all to no avail. Then I had a brainwave.

As a frontier district, Zahedan possessed a sizeable barracks so, around midday, having left the Australians at the garage, I presented myself at the main entrance demanding to see the duty officer. Gradually I worked my way through the ranks until I found myself in front of a full colonel of infantry. The gist of my argument was that since I was an ex-British soldier and he was an Iranian soldier, we were all soldiers together so how about helping me with a little transportation? By elevating my rank a little I finally got the message through. I was invited to a snack in the guardroom and eventually an armoured car of Russian origin was put at my disposal, together with a driver.

Off we went out of Zahedan and, with a drive of 200 miles to Kerman ahead, I felt rather pleased with myself. I was just settling down comfortably when two miles out of Zahedan I was brought down to earth by my sergeant-driver, 'This is as far as we go but I'll fix you up', he announced and proceeded to block the road junction with his vehicle. His victim was a high-sided lorry with three Baluchis jammed in the cab. I said goodbye to my military taxi rather reluctantly and clambered up the sides of the lorry into the buck. Too late, I discovered it to be full of extremely smelly sheep and goats, a wild-eyed tribesman and an English youth from Leamington Spa.

I shall never forget that lorry ride. The road led into the satanic hills which we crossed in a series of zig-zags, at never less than 70mph, in a cloud of choking dust. On the straight the speed and density of the dust increased and whenever the driver braked, (which was often and violently), all sixty-odd manure-caked beasts would be catapulted into me. All the while a number of sheep stood or relieved themselves on my feet which wasn't funny since I was wearing open sandals. Whenever the three of us attempted to sit on a heap of sacks it caused a roar of fury from the inmates of the cab, although none of us could understand why. The lorry stopped briefly at some villages and scores of amused peasants clambered aboard to stare and prod at the funny 'Ingleesh'. But twice we were offered tea and yoghurt from these folk who seemed kindly in spite of their aggressive curiosity.

The unfriendly driver and his mates threw us out at Bam, a town 125 miles short of Kerman. At an all-night transport café I teamed up with a Good Soldier Schweik-like character, cross-eyed and unbuttoned who kept urinating in the most public of places. Together we caught a bus in the early morning. The bus was luxurious after the lorry but the driver, quite plainly, was another of those who fancied me to the point of embarrassment (mine) and at Kerman I was inveigled into being his guest for the day. I accepted because his bus was going westwards to Yazd that night, in the direction I wanted to go. Once I had made the limits of our friendship clear, I enjoyed his hospitality which included a substantial lunch and the ecstasy of a Persian bath.

Settled in the reserve-driver's seat next to Momeny — we were on christian name terms by now — I looked forward to reaching the railhead at Yazd (there were no trains running from Kerman to Yazd at that time). Repeatedly I fell asleep only to be awoken by the affectionate Momeny.

Both Yazd and Kerman are famed for their shawls which rival in quality those of Kashmir. But whilst Kerman is a very medi-ocre, if sizeable, town of bazaars, Yazd can raise a skyline reputed to be the most picturesque in all Iran containing, as it does, the highest minarets in the country. Many of its citizens are descendants of the Zoroastrians whose custom was to lay out their dead for the vultures on their flat-topped Towers of Silence though, these days, they have to be content with more conventional rites. Again I arrived in the middle of the night but what I missed in the darkness I saw bleary-eyed, in the cold light of dawn.

My train towards Qum dropped me off at another junction, where with a little bribery I was allowed on the goods-only train for Isfahan. I dallied a whole twenty-four hours in this fabulous

169

city but, with a small but luxurious hotel as my base, and weary with the hours of rough travelling I had endured, I spent most of them in bed. A night train now leaves Isfahan daily for Qum and Teheran but it was a postal van that provided me with my transport to Iran's second holiest city. Qum looked its age and, since Fatima, sister of the Imam Reze is buried there, it is consequently full of pilgrims and infidels, the latter being no more popular than in Mashhad.

Through a misunderstanding I caught a bus to Kermanshah instead of Khorramshah which in my tired and confused state had sounded the same. The trouble is that the two places are 250 miles apart so my ride to the borders of Kurdistan was something of an exhausting mistake. Back at Qum I purchased a rail ticket for Khorramshah and, once bitten, made the ticket office spell it out to me, to make sure it was the right place.

I was seeing too many dawns to be good for me and yet another was to present itself at Ahvaz. The train had been excruciatingly slow, stopping at stations and between stations along the way. We were being hauled by a scruffy specimen of steam locomotion and on this particular train the compartment floor had been my bed. Ahvaz, at dawn, was the prayer stop. Approaching Khorramshah the terrain flattened out to display a dreary covering of burnt grass lapsing into bald patches of sand as if a flame-thrower had been at work. I began to smell the sea and oil of the Persian Gulf.

Passenger trains on the Trans-Iranian line have their southern terminus at Khorramshah though the tracks go through to Banda Shapur. Technically an island, Abadan, seat of the great oil pipe-line terminus and refinery, is a few miles further on. Khorram-shah was a pleasant surprise: it was something of a garden city with mimosa and luxurious flowering growth hanging from many a wall. Demolished by the Turks at the beginning of the nineteenth century on the grounds that its commercialism was detrimental to nearby Basra, the British and Russian governments stepped in to keep the peace by allocating territory to both sides. But they had reckoned without the Karun River, a tributary of the Shatt-al-Arab, which promptly upped and changed its course inserting a damp spanner into the works. As recent history has shown with a vengeance, nobody was happy with the result.

170

Basra, once in Iran, is now, of course, firmly Iraqi but the hate continues to boil. War hadn't broken out when I was there; only the border was closed which was inconvenient enough for me. I tried half a dozen taxi drivers before I could persuade one, with the help of an exorbitant bribe, to take me to the frontier. His vehicle was an antique Packard and on the way out of town he picked up three labourers and a soldier. They all got out at a place called Shalamcheh, and since none of them paid I perceived I was subsidising the trip. Shalamcheh turned out to be a hamlet of five houses all taken over by the military. I detected an air of the front line with barbed wire coils ineffectively laid, clusters of khaki lorries and a lot of rubbish. At one of the five houses my taxi left me. Inside, a civilian stamped my passport and gave me a glass of tea but, in the next house, the customs officer was in bed. He eyed me without enthusiasm, rose from the blankets and carefully strapped on his revolver belt over his flame-coloured pyjamas. Dressed for duty as it were he enquired as to whether I was carrying hashish, firearms or precious metals and when I said 'No' to all three, he let me go with the parting shot: 'You'll be back you know. They won't let you in there', as he jerked his head towards Iraq.

A dog yapping at my heels, I commenced the four-mile walk across the desert towards a dot in the far distance. I was alone in a hushed and threatening world and thankful that my baggage wasn't a couple of trunks. I felt like an actor walking into the sunset at the end of a film. Except that it was sunrise.

I held, as I have already made clear, pre-conceived and not very flattering ideas about Iraq and my first encounter seemed to bear them out. The guard at the Iraqi border was festooned with Russian hardware and suffered from five o'clock shadow. The duty officer was a grumpy individual who was all for sending me back and it was only my portable electric shaver that saved the day. The instrument was discovered in a baggage search and promptly went the rounds of the detachment who, having exhausted its battery, felt obliged to pass me through.

Possessed of no Iraqi currency I had to tempt the one and only non-military driver of a non-military car with pound notes before he would take me the 13 miles to Basra — and then he only did it

171

because he was an incurable romantic and liked the look of the Queen on the banknotes. Within sight of Basra I met two further hurdles. One was the wide Shatt-al-Arab river that separated me from the city and the other was the fact that my arrival coincided with a Friday when, as in all Moslem lands, the banks and change offices were closed. The ferryman, no fan of a British queen, adamantly refused to accept sterling. 'Go to the Shatt-al-Arab Hotel', he said, 'You can always change money there'. 'Where is it?' I enquired. 'Across the river', came the not-too helpful reply. But further enquiries elicited the information that the hotel was eight miles up river and all seemed settled when I found a boatman to take me there. The subsequent trip past lines of Soviet freighters and date palm-choked inlets was pleasant but spoilt at the end by the hotel refusing to accept my Barclay's Bank travel cheques. 'Lackeys of Israel', a swarthy young man explained darkly. So I changed the last of my sterling which, back at the ferry point, just about covered the cost of the voyage to the west bank.

Wondering how to continue I walked the two miles to the railway station escorted by a bevy of friendly Iraqis. Basra I found to be more Arab than most of the towns I'd seen in Iran and, as I was discovering, its people were pleasantly disposed to helping a lone stranger in their midst. The town is a hotch-potch of other people's development: Carmathian, Mongol, Turkish and European with a thin veneer of Moslem construction. At the railway station, searching for the ticket office, I blundered into the domain of the stationmaster and was, again, invited to tea. He was an educated man, spoke English quite well and, on learning of my interest in railways, aired his progressive ideas of a Trans-Asian Railway passing, of course, through Basra. Hearing of my financial predicament the good man promptly contributed a first-class ticket valid for the air-conditioned de-luxe overnight express to Baghdad.

Basra to Baghdad is 380 miles and we covered the distance in nine hours which is good for a Middle Eastern train. For some of the way we followed the Euphrates river and passed within two miles of Ur, of the Chaldees fame. We also flashed by a short platform designated 'Babylon Halt' which even local trains pass with a derisive whistle. And in the morning we drew into West Station, the Grand Central of the Iraqi capital.

I have already charted the course of the railway between Iraq and Europe to close the circuit of a mystical Trans-Asian Railway so let the combined impediments I found speak for themselves. A Paris to Delhi Express may not run yet awhile but, in the meantime, its local predecessors make an incident-packed ride for those who hanker after adventure on the iron road.

7

The East African Railway

MOMBASA—NAIROBI—KAMPALA

I had, for a long time, nurtured a desire to ride the one-time East African Railway. Not only for the universally-acclaimed purpose of being able to observe big game from a moving train but also by reason of the very evocativeness of its history. My chance came in April 1976 when I was invited to participate in the Tana River Expedition, a military-supported, scientific investigation of the remote environment of eastern Kenya that was to involve three months of paddling down the country's longest river. My timing was both lucky and unfortunate. The year 1976 was the last before the complete break-up of the confederation of railways of Kenya, Tanzania and Uganda (Tanzania had virtually withdrawn before I got there) so I was fortunate to be able to ride a considerable portion of the famous network while it still *was* the East African Railway. My misfortune was that the despotic ruler of Uganda, Idi Amin, was at the zenith of his power and this was to result in my dream ride into that most delectable country turning into something of a nightmare.

When construction of the railway began in 1898 it became known in Britain as the 'Lunatic Line' by virtue of the fact that it was seemingly going from 'nowhere through nowhere to nowhere'. In spite of the fact that its creation was a very considerable feat of engineering few could raise great enthusiasm for the project even though one of the declared purposes of the railway through unknown East Africa to the remote landlocked country of Uganda was to put down the Arab slave trade. But the builders and promoters maintained their faith and the line took shape, snaking its way through the uplands, meeting but overcoming obstacles such as hundreds of miles of sponge-like quagmire, hostile tribes, waterless desert, man-eating lions, tsetse flies and malaria. The route brought the workforce over the mile-deep

174

volcanic Rift Valley escarpment down which trains were lowered on an inclined plane assisted by ropes. It continued across the Highlands and over the fierce Mau Summit and on to the shores of Lake Victoria.

At first the line was known as the Kenya & Uganda Railway, and British indifference to its conception and construction is illustrated by the fact that its metre gauge was a direct result of being supplied with cheap, secondhand rolling stock and equipment from India. The Tanzanian section was originally metre gauge anyway from the time of its construction by the Germans when the country was known as Tanganyika. The two railways merged in 1948. Under British influence the union was effective but political and economic differences since independence have gradually wrenched the three systems apart.

Looked upon in the early days as no more than an imperialistic manoeuvre aimed at enabling Britain to control the upper Nile and thus maintain her hold on Egypt and the Suez Canal, the outcome was surprising. As well as being vitally instrumental in putting down the slave trade the railway opened up Uganda, created the country of Kenya and developed what has become East Africa's major metropolis, Nairobi. Nowhere else in the world, and at no time in history, has a journey been so dramatically shortened from a six-month walk fraught with danger, to a four-day ride in comparative comfort and safety. Freight movement gained spectacularly — no longer restricted to what a black human head could carry.

As the years went by the line was improved by elimination of the inclined plane of the Rift Valley and a new route up and over Timbaroa into the Highlands which made possible through-train services to Kampala. In spite of the recent truncation of the complex, the Night Mail still covers the 308 miles between Nairobi and Mombasa but the famous and luxurious Uganda Mail has fallen victim to man's folly. I was lucky, very lucky, to have ridden from Mombasa in what turned out to be the last express that ran between the two countries.

I began my journey from Nairobi as soon as I could escape the razamataz of press conferences and commercial sponsor-wheedling that are a vital adjunct to any expedition, but not

175

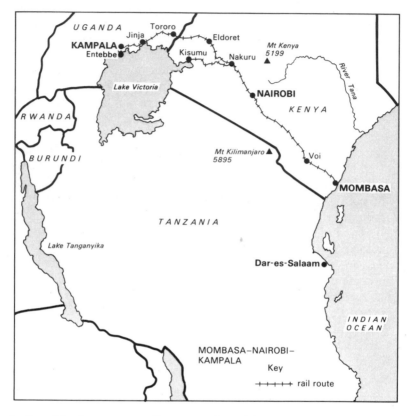

before I had put some of my new-found knowledge to use on my own behalf and gained a press-facility ticket valid for the whole passenger network in Kenya and Uganda. Few Africans themselves could raise the vestige of a crocodile tear over the death throes of the E.A.R. Hard-headed Kenyans with realistic views on life simply exclaimed 'so what?' in response to my expressions of regret, but then I was not a Kenyan taxpayer on whose shoulders fell most of the burden of financing the running of the tri-country network. Alone with my regret I set off on the Night Mail to Mombasa.

Against the endless Athai Plain fading into dusk I contempla-ted East Africa's premier city. For anyone coming to Africa for the first time, Nairobi serves as the perfect decompression chamber. The steel and glass shopping centre, parking meters, red postboxes, Wimpy's, Woolworth's, fish and chip shops, and traffic that circles roundabouts clockwise in the British manner are homely touches. A metropolis, now, of dazzling white skyscrapers rising from avenues adorned with statues and lined with Bougainvillaea that fail to hide a suburb or two of disease and poverty. Even in my father's lifetime Nairobi has grown from a malarious swamp to a city of well over a million. In 1902 this one-time railway construction camp called 'The Cold Well' — or Nai'robi — held but one small shop and a tin shanty that served as a hotel. It is noticeable that, even today, the main streets are wide enough in which to turn a wagon and team of oxen.

I began to wonder if Kenya's other big city bore a grudge against Nairobi. The fact that Mombasa was a thriving urban community back in the eleventh century while Nairobi only received its city charter in 1950 must have rankled when the former lost its capitalship to the new upstart. Mombasa's *raison d'être* was that its site was opposite a break in the coral reef that stretches along the Kenyan coast. Ships were able to enter Kilindi — 'The Place of Deep Water' as the port is called — and landlocked Uganda could scarcely have survived without the Mombasa road and railway.

My dinner in the dining car was adequate and afterwards, when I was back in my compartment a steward brought me my bedding. He had been with the E.A.R. ten years and expressed relief that he would soon be working for just Kenya Railways. 'Might get paid more promptly', he observed. I gave him ten shillings which was the cost of *reserving* bedding rather than for the loan of it, and he bade me a good night promising to wake me early next morning to see Africa. I turned out the light and lay looking out of the window at the train's flickering reflection.

I awoke at Voi, the junction for Dar es Salaam and Tanzania. Somewhere back down the line was Tsavo where the famous man-eating lions had so effectively depleted the railway construction workers and their master, Superintendent Ryall, who was dragged from his sleeping car and likewise devoured. There have since been enthralling stories of lions and other wild animals resenting the passage of trains and hurling themselves against the coaches, while a heavy Garrett locomotive was reputed to have been derailed by a charging rhino. But over the last decade the four-footed inhabitants of the plains have come to terms with the railway and there are no more such interesting stories to record.

Reaching Kilindi meant we were approaching the outskirts of Mombasa and we were in the city proper as soon as our train had clanked across the bridge to pull into the one-time eastern terminus. A row of cubicles attracted my attention: '1st Class Ladies & Gentlemen's Toilet', pronounced one. '2nd Class Ladies & Gents', read another, '3rd Class Male & Female' was the notice on the last door. Shades of India.

And assuredly Mombasa is a slice of not only India but all Asia. It is a town reflecting, in both character and architecture, mixed cultures that have joined together in true unison. Arabs and Asians, Africans and Europeans live contentedly together in a blatantly humid oriental sprawl that could be ten thousand miles from Africa. I spent the day feeling uncomfortably sticky and walking the narrow streets of the Old Town in the shadow of tall houses of elaborately-carved ornamental balconies and slender mosques. Itinerant Arabs sold coffee from traditional long-beaked copper pots, while oriental music drifted from the shops of goldsmiths, money-lenders, tailors and tinsmiths. On a massive hill, Fort Jesus and its silent guns covered the harbour, looking out beyond English Point to the line of shipwrecks that have become as permanent as islands.

I returned to the station in the evening in good time to catch the Uganda Mail. Given the wrong sleeper number I came face to face with two formidable English matrons who held very definite ideas as to how first-class travellers should be attired and made it plain to me that I failed to measure up to their exacting standards. 'Sir', they observed in stern reproach, 'You appear to be in the wrong class'.

An English Electric diesel hauled us through rich dark palm groves into the gathering dusk and a land of endless thorn trees. These waterless wastes and the red dust of the Taru Desert ensured East Africa's isolation from the world until the end of the nineteenth century. For me it was a first sight of the African bush and, with the dawn, my first living perception of the size of Africa. Tall grass, as far as the eye could reach, swayed like a vast field of ripening corn in a perpetual summer wind.

In the grey light the plains of the Masai presented me with its fruit: water buck, gazelle, wildebeest, zebra and giraffe steadfastly ignored the train, continuing with their grazing as if we were no more than some insignificant caterpillar. I felt a surge of excitement at the prospect of soon being among even more dramatic animals of the wild. In the meantime I revelled in the luxury and satisfaction of observing East Africa from the comfort of a train.

It was not my intention to continue straight on to Kampala from Nairobi but to catch a later Kisumu-bound train. This entailed travelling the same line as far as Nakuru and then branching north-west towards Lake Victoria. The railway, which had created Kenya simply as a by-product of its construction, was, in the late 1920s, to open up new and empty territory for development. The high wastelands through which it passed on the way to Lake Victoria had been settled and found lucrative. Farms had spread all over the green highlands to the west of the great Rift Valley, near Eldoret and around the Uasin Gishu country. A new main line started to crawl towards them, branching off from the Kisumu line at Nakuru, itself a growing town, and climbing to a height of over 9,000 feet, the highest point ever reached by a British Commonwealth railway. Since that time the Kisumu line has become subordinate to the Kampala route by virtue of the fact that the Ugandan capital was later linked by rail instead of the original ferry service from the Kisumu railhead. But for me the old Uganda Railway route was one I had to see.

Hardly had we left behind the suburbs of Nairobi when the track started climbing. It rose through green pastures towards the summit of the eastern wall of the Rift Valley. The first sight of this phenomenon is indelibly marked on my memory. Abruptly the forest thins and there, 2,000 feet below, at the base of a sheer escarpment, is the Rift, quite certainly the most gigantic valley in the world. Thirty miles away the opposite wall rose, dark purple against the sky, a procession of clouds drifting across

179

the peaks. This colossal fault in the earth's surface is as though some immense thermo-nuclear plough had dug a furrow striking right across Africa from Lake Baikal in Siberia to the Red Sea. The geological disturbance must have convulsed half the world in some prehistoric age to become an inland ocean from which the waters have receded leaving a succession of lakes to this day. Dozens of volcanoes have erupted in the Rift, the greatest being Kilimanjaro, and their threat still hangs in the air like the curl of smoke I could see rising from a herdsman's fire.

The town of Nakuru lies on the floor of the valley and at the foot of the Menengai Mountain the top of which is reputed to have subsided into some subterranean vacuum. To the south of the town is Lake Nakuru, a large expanse of shallow, saline water, the shores of which are the sacred nesting ground of ten thousand flamingoes. An acrid smell of soda rose from the lake to increase the allure of this mysterious region while great flurries of pink-white feathers made a fairy-tale snow-storm that was reflected in the water.

Nakuru, not an unpleasant urban centre by any means, makes no use of its lake which is a mile or two away. But what it lacks in a lakeside scenic backdrop it makes up for in friendliness. Simply through asking directions I was invited by two African ladies home to tea. The tea expanded into a double scotch and, subsequently, the biggest mixed grill I have ever consumed in my life. I was also pressed to have a bath — perhaps because I looked as if I needed one. The good ladies were all for me staying the night but I had a train to catch. I suppose my interest lay as much with the railway as it did with Africa, for continuing towards Kisumu and Lake Victoria I found myself pondering the fact that it was not the steep climb to Fort Ternan but the easy terrain to the lake that had troubled the line's builders. Americans in 1903 built the tunnels and dozens of bridges within a section of fifty miles but found problems with the soft littoral which caused an uncanny number of derailments. And the locals *would* keep pinching material like telegraph wire for their womenfolk's decoration and tools for adaption into weapons. But Kisumu entered history with the Uganda Railway which terminated at the then Port Florence.

180

Kisumu aspires to bigger things than Nakuru and makes better use of its lake — as it should since Victoria is the second biggest in the world. Like Mombasa, Kisumu is a mixture of Africa and Asia and, additionally, is something of a garden city. In the main square a conglomeration of Christian religions were militantly competing for custom and recognition amongst a Sunday crowd of onlookers with nothing to do. Even the Salvation Army, beaming black faces under stiff bonnets and peaked caps, was represented, although the band was composed entirely of percussion. The weather turned from warm to sweltering and, together with a gang of African boys, I managed a quick dip in the lake in spite of dire warnings of crocodiles and other deterrents. Back at the station I obtained permission to visit and photograph the engine sheds full of greasy old steam locos but not before a fracas with an obstinate member of the railway police. This ended in a draw when he agreed I could have the run of the sheds so long as he was included in every picture I took.

Back at Nakuru a new emotion assailed me. Ever since I had decided to cover what I could of the E.A.R. network, the situation at its western end had been a nagging worry that I had pushed to the back of my mind. World newspapers had been screaming about the tension on the border for weeks as the then Ugandan dictator, Idi Amin's crack troops stood poised to invade Kenya. For weeks too Uganda had been pouring invective at Kenya, Britain, Israel and anybody else who had failed to support his monstrous edicts. Just ten days previously the Israelis had scored their triumph against Amin with the successful raid on Entebbe Airport so the hate across the border was fresh and vitriolic. Everybody said I was a bloody fool to stick my nose into certain trouble including the Defence Secretary at the British High Commission in Nairobi who vouchsafed the opinion I'd never get into Uganda anyway. That Amin and his régime were bad the world was learning fast; just how bad it had still to discover. But, in the meantime, the border was still open though there were long delays and those who crossed it were mostly refugees fleeing into Kenya.

I had a number of hours to kill at Nakuru so spent them exploring this quite large and prosperous town. Its railway

181

station is the smartest in East Africa, I was told, and certainly its locomotive sheds held offerings that deflected my morbid thoughts from the gathering crisis up the line. I had arrived at the paragon of stations at 3.30 in the morning having spent a night on the tiles. However my Uganda Mail, when it drew in soon after three in the afternoon, was resplendent with sleepers, one of which was mine.

Nakuru vanished and, out of the window, I caught more glimpses of the Rift Valley, only now it was becoming more fertile as the red soil deepened and lush foliage folded round the line.

Eldoret, they will tell you, is where the bank was built around a safe. Again, it was the railway that made the town though it was through an accident that the big safe fell from a wagon. Found to be too heavy to move they simply constructed a building over it and things grew from there. Unconcerned by its unscheduled beginnings Eldoret flourishes as a busy market town, the last sizeable community before Uganda.

I had several companions in the compartment who drew me into animated conversation and pressed me to edible delicacies from an assortment of newspaper packages. One of the men was a Ugandan law student from Nairobi University who was returning to Kampala to see his parents. He thought he could do it, stay a couple of days, and make it back to Kenya before the border closed. This cheered me up a little since my plans were to remain in the Ugandan capital just one day, returning, in fact, the same day as my arrival. The schedules offered a nine-hour stay which was quite long enough for a glimpse of the city. The aluminium coach in which we were travelling provided very adequate comfort with our compartment making up into four beds at night. I was secretly pleased that I had not been given an individual 'cabin' as I had between Nairobi and Mombasa for, as we drew nearer and nearer the border, I became increasingly in need of human companionship.

It was, however, nothing less than human bloody mindedness that kept the train standing at the border station of Malaba for all of five hours that night. Neither the law student nor myself, were able to sleep with the rumours and counter-rumours that were floating about as money-exchange touts and Kenyan border police stamped up and down the corridor. Cold daybreak saw us mooching along the side of the stranded train, so that when the Ugandan authorities finally let the train go we almost missed it. Rolling across a wide brook I saw a notice reading 'You are entering the Republic of Uganda' which evoked in me a similar sense of depression to that of crossing the east-west German border into the totalitarian East.

Ten minutes later we drew into Tororo and the train filled up again. An immigration official examined my passport and made me an icily polite speech of welcome pointing out, with acid sarcasm, that, since I was a British subject, I had no need of the visa I had obtained from the Ugandan High Commission in London. He then afforded me two days on Ugandan soil and stamped the deadline date against the visa.

The train did its best to make up for lost time but, with many scheduled halts en route, it was a forlorn hope that I would get my full nine hours in Kampala. Every station was a hive of activity, the colourful crowds having little to do with the train's arrival, but grouping there simply because they represented the local community centre; the place where the action was, and where they would be most likely to sell their goods. Even though I had no Ugandan currency I nevertheless became the recipient of a bunch of thirty bananas because, it was explained, 'I looked hungry'. They were right — I was — the restaurant car had been detached at Nakuru.

As we crossed the Nile over the great bridge at Jinja — Uganda's Sheffield — I sensed an air of crisis at its station. The crowds were less exuberant here and uniformed police more in evidence; indeed even while the train stood at the platform I watched two of them arresting a man.

This region of Uganda is a green and pleasant land, well watered and fertile. Exotic blossoms and bloated leaves pressed against the track and my student friend was considerate enough to treat me to a running commentary on their botanical names and details.

It was raining when we reached Kampala and the grey clouds did nothing to enhance a city full of near-empty dual carriage-

183

ways, tall buildings in need of renovation and beautiful homes run to seed. I estimated that my planned nine-hour sojourn had been cut to four which worried me not at all. My friend escorted me up the stairs to the station concourse.

An officious-looking civilian stood behind a desk close to the ticket barrier surveying the happy jostling crowd with distaste. His gaze fell on me. 'You. Here', he barked.

'You talking to me?' I asked with scarcely-veiled sarcasm.

The obnoxious individual demanded my passport and that of the student and thumbed through the pages. To me he asked, 'Why have you and your friend come here?'

I sensed the start of something more ominous than mere immigration control, and noticed too that the unease of my companion was profound. 'We only met on the train', I explained hurriedly, 'I've only come to spend a few hours in Kampala'. The student gabbled his own reasons for coming.

'Wait here'. The man moved away, taking our passports. We watched him arrogantly pushing through the crowd, knocking a woman almost to the ground as he went.

He returned a while later to take us to a bare office where a colleague sat, smiling sardonically, at a table. We were not invited to sit down.

The new man started to question me. 'Why have you come?' 'How long are you staying?' 'What is the purpose of your visit?' I answered as best I could though aware my reasons sounded inadequate to an African unappreciative of his railway. The student was steadfastly ignored though I saw his mounting fear out of the corner of my eye. 'What is your connection with this man?' came the question I had been expecting.

I repeated that we had been no more than travelling companions and that, once out of Kampala station, we would be going our different ways. He was obviously not impressed by my answers and a few minutes later the two of us were taken outside and pushed into the back of an antiquated black saloon car. As we were driven through the town the rain fell in buckets and I almost managed to convince myself that this was the best way of seeing Kampala anyway.

Rarely have I witnessed a more depressing town. The shops

were no more than eye-sockets in a face of empty streets where only policemen hung around the intersections. Halfway up a hill the car engine began to cough and the driver to moan loudly about the shortage of fuel coupons even for official vehicles. I now understood the reason for the lack of other traffic. When the engine finally gave up the ghost we had to abandon its dry interior and push it in the wet, all the way to the Kampala Police Headquarters. Despite the seriousness of the situation, I could still appreciate the irony of it.

Inside, a stench of stale sweat, rancid tobacco and an unidentifiable sweet odour permeated the bare-walled corridors. Handcuffed prisoners, wild-eyed and perspiring, passed by in the charge of young policemen. The student's face had gone deathly pale and I guessed he knew more about Ugandan security police methods than I did. In an office almost as bare as the corridors we found ourselves before yet another inquisitor, this one in civilian clothes and nameless. The only furnishings were a cheap desk, a hard-backed chair or two, a filing cabinet, a telephone and a lop-sided photograph (unframed) of Idi Amin. Previous interrogation scenarios went through my mind. Such sparse furnishings fitted the Gestapo, the Czech STB and the Soviet KGB though nobody in Nazi and post-war Communism days would dream of displaying a lop-sided Führer or an unframed Stalin.

Ugandan interrogation was different too. Not unpleasantly did the new man repeat the same questions though he added a new emphasis. Now it wasn't so much 'Why have you come?' but 'Why have you come for so brief a spell?' He also wanted to know why I was in a railway carriage with a Ugandan exile returning to his country (when everyone else was leaving) and why we had exchanged addresses (they had found them during their search of our wallets and pockets). It had been the student's idea and a very harmless one but, abruptly, I was aware how small inconsistencies could be blown up into a balloon of suspicion.

Then came a new hurdle. 'How is it your passport indicates you are a company director and this card pronounces you a journalist?' To explain that I was once a company director and had retained the title in my passport in preference to the sometimes provocative 'journalist' would only have complicated matters —

185

even though here was an example of just such a provocation. So I offered the white lie that I was still a company director and that I was a journalist only in my spare time. To two fresh interrogators in another room the repeated explanation sounded even less plausible. And, you know, there comes a moment when you actually begin to believe that you *are* a spy or whatever it is they are trying to suggest you might be. It creeps up on you when they catch you out on some harmless answer to a question. I felt the symptoms and resolved to keep my answers *simple* and to stick to them the second time round.

For instance: 'What school did you attend?' I was asked. I gave the one I was at the longest. There was no need to bring up the other two.

My regimental association membership came up for scrutiny. 'What rank did you hold?' they enquired.

'Corporal', I replied, giving the lowest rank I had held. Pride alone stopped me from saying 'private'. 'Which army?', came the startling enquiry. I had to admit that it was British.

My camera was the centre of attention. I was asked what photographs I had taken on Ugandan soil and truthfully reported that I had taken none. They made sure I was telling the truth by exposing the film.

Every now and again I would point out that I had a train to catch — more to establish a cornerstone of normality than having any expectation of catching it. And there comes too, a point in all interrogations when there is a lull in proceedings during which one can mount a counter-attack of the 'Why-the-hell-am-I-here? What-crime-am-I-supposed-to-have-committed? or I-want-to-see-my-consul' sort which, at least, raises morale if not the roof.

I was taken before a further set of interrogators in another room and, this time, the student was not with me. I was never to see him again. The new room was a carbon copy of the previous one even, I could swear, to the number of fly droppings on Amin's photograph. My new tormentors, also attired in civilian clothes, had the same depressing air of a black Gestapo.

The same old questions were trotted out and I was careful to stick to the same answers. I added that not only had I train to catch but an expedition to join.

'What expedition?' asked one of the black faces before me.

Aware that I had broken my own rule and given them some potentially complicated information, I had no alternative but to offer a rundown of the Tana River Expedition, its aims and role, its sponsors and its personalities. All harmless stuff though I saw no reason to mention support by the army, British or otherwise.

Solicitously I was asked if I was hungry. I said I was. 'What would you like?' they enquired.

Optimistic to the bitter end I suggested steak and chips.

'Do you want some tea?'

'That too please'.

Neither the steak nor the tea put in an appearance, of course, but I felt grateful for the enquiry.

Then followed a period for my statements to be taken down at dictation speed by a typist who couldn't type. It got bogged down in such a muddle that I suspect it was another ruse to trip me up. If so I won hands down. My answers continued to match even if I did feel like a parrot.

Back in the second office the whole rigmarole commenced again like some macabre game of verbal musical chairs. One muffed answer; one forfeit. Outside the barred window the rain still fell. A church clock struck four.

'I really shall miss my train', I began again to the new face that wore an air of more senior authority. 'It's due out now'.

'It was late coming in so it'll be late going out' I was told, and I took this to mean that I might yet be on it if I played my cards right.

Some endless telephoning punctuated by wrong connections took up another fifteen minutes. Surreptitiously I packed some of my belongings strewn about the desk into my bag. The action raised no objections.

Then suddenly and without any warning they told me I could go. A moment of disbelief kept me rooted to the floor and then I was out. My sense of urgency to get to the railway station must have communicated itself to my two guards because they broke out into a run to get to the car. Suddenly the couple were no longer my guards but the means of catching my train — almost certainly the last train. Ensconsed in the car I impatiently listened to some excited chatter about authorisation and fuel coupons but I told them it didn't matter. In spite of the sparse traffic every red light was against us and we had to stop each time. Even before the car had pulled in at the station building I was bounding through the crowded concourse. Down the stairs and, Glory-be, the train was still there. It was packed solid inside and out, with the overflow hanging onto the outside of the coaches. I joined a trio of anxious youths on the steps of a second-class coach. The rain splashed down on me but I was too relieved to care.

For fifteen minutes nothing happened and then without any warning the train abruptly upped and left. I never felt so pleased to see the back of any city as I did that one.

But my good fortune was short lived, for as we approached the gradient to Seta, the grossly over loaded English Electric diesel ground to a halt. A wave of panic washed through the train. Up front a crowd gathered round the green locomotive with its distinctive yellow stripe. Everybody yelled advice and instructions to the driver and such was our desperation to get the train on its way again that we, the passengers, began *pushing* it. In a different situation it would have been funny, but there was no laughter here. The atmosphere was tense as the men strained to push the wagons and the women stood in silence by the track, in the rain, with their babies and small children. Even the children were quiet. At our third attempt the wheels gripped the track and we were away. In a flash I was inside the coach and settled into a corner seat.

Back at Tororo they grabbed me again. I couldn't believe it. A posse of uniformed, armed police made straight for my compartment, and after a cursory glance at my passport, bundled me off the train. In a police office that formed part of the station I was grilled once more, this time by uniformed interrogators. I complained that I had already answered all their questions back at Kampala but they said that they weren't satisfied with the reasons for my presence in Uganda and that I was not to answer back. With a sinking heart I watched the departure of my train. So near and yet so far. .

Dusk had fallen when I was consigned to a draughty waiting

room to await return to Kampala on a morning train. It had been a long day and prospects were gloomy: by the time I had been through these further police attentions my Ugandan sojourn permit would have run out and they would have me on a technicality. No doubt it was all an elaborate scheme cooked up by the security and immigration authorities between them.

The room into which I was put was, to all intents and purposes, a prison cell. It held no more than a wooden bench on which previous inmates had carved their names, and one window, high in the wall, which was too small to use as an exit. The door was locked but the key remained in the lock. The one impediment to a voluntary departure was an elderly guard with a Lee Enfield rifle of World War One vintage. Beyond an occasional grunt he never spoke a word. We sat in stoic silence through the night, the darkness of the room confounded by a low wattage bulb suspended from the high ceiling. Around midnight the guard nodded off and I began to perceive a way out of my predicament. The border was no more than six miles distant and though the Ugandan army was massed enthusiastically along it I presumed they would be looking the other way. Furthermore I was unable to believe that the Amin régime had caught up with the finesse practised by Nazi Germans, Communist Germans, Czechs and Hungarians in their methods of discouraging illegal emigration.

I debated this during the night, even managing a brief doze or two, until in the morning, with the guard still snoring regularly, I let myself out. It was so easy, I even had a pang of conscience about doing it and hoped that his punishment for losing a prisoner would not be too severe.

Nobody was about the station and the trees behind it offered good cover. I made straight for the border, keeping the railway to my right and in sight so as not to lose direction in the thick undergrowth. I crossed the track in a clearing where the rails began a circuit that I had noticed on the inward journey and fastened my eyes upon a distant hill which I thought might be in Kenya. Foliage dripped incessantly as if it were raining again.

I bumped into the army a moment before I became aware that I had company; a bunch of soldiers trying to get their radio to

189

work made a not-so-frightening apparition. As a one-time military man myself how could I forget my own frustrations with radio sets that never worked when you wanted them to? Feeling an affinity with their predicament I offered them my help.

The group of men seemed more concerned with the state of their equipment than with me though I felt obliged to explain that I had missed my train and was therefore walking to the border. After all, an Englishman walking into a war zone at dawn plainly needed *some* explanation.

The radio squad could not have been friendlier and one of their number presented me with a bottle of lager. 'Breakfast' he explained. Rashly I enquired whether one of their lorries and a driver could be presumed upon to give me a lift to the border. When the corporal said he'd have to ask his officer I wondered if I was pushing my luck too far.

But not so. A lieutenant came over, and showing not the slightest surprise at my being there, apologised for not being able to take me to Malaba but said that his driver would drop me close by.

And so it came about that, in the warm, petrol-reeking cab of a 15 cwt Bedford van I made the border about six miles away. The driver was all for taking me to the Ugandan checkpoint but I gently persuaded him to drop me just short of it.

With the truck out of sight I left the road and struck out across pleasant rolling country in front of the conical hill for which Tororo is known — and also the landmark I had wrongly gauged to be in Kenya. And there was the railway again. Parallel with it I turned eastwards and came to the brook that is the physical demarcation line between Uganda and Kenya. I got my feet wet by failing to jump the obstacle by a yard.

In Malaba I boarded a bus to Eldoret. And at Eldoret, believe it or not, I caught up with my train again. It had been delayed, again, at the border but it was only later that I learnt that it *was*, in fact, the last train out of Uganda.

Relaxing in my compartment on the journey back to Nairobi I prepared myself for transition from traveller to explorer. My new beard was thickening nicely and I no longer felt such a novice so far as East Africa was concerned. On a more practical

190

level I was able to treat myself to a substantial three-course lunch, my first meal for over seventy-two hours.

There was still plenty of East African Railway track I had not covered and I wistfully thought of the line beyond Kampala to Kasese on the Congo border and, eastwards, across another closed frontier into Tanzania. The Kasese extension is lightly laid making for anything but a smooth ride but the Buganda townships, through which the line passes, are reputed to be prime examples of African life. In normal times the journey from Mombasa, far away on the Indian Ocean, to Kasese and the Ruwenzori Mountains would take 62 hours though, alas, even this very modest achievement is no more.

Kenya's line to Nanyuki, in the shadow of Mount Kenya, is open only to freight traffic. Though I was unable to travel it from the junction at Nairobi I was frequently to see the hefty Beyer-Garrett steam locomotives hauling long trains of wagons between Sagana and Nanyuki. They made a brave sight.

But with the advent of the Tana River Expedition I was on the threshold of new adventures in which railways played no part.

8

Trans-North America

NEW YORK—LOS ANGELES
VANCOUVER—FAIRBANKS

An invitation from Amtrak, the United States National Railroad passenger Corporation, to travel its air-conditioned services, coinciding with one from Canadian Pacific Rail to ride the cab of their trans-Canada train across a country I had barely seen, sent me to the North American continent with no qualms except the lesser one of an expected dullness. For here were two railway systems slowly dying on their feet and crying out to be travelled before *rigor mortis* on its more romantic lines could set in.

This was in 1973, shortly after the formation of Amtrak which made it an interesting year to sample the new brainchild of the American government and those denizens of the transportation world who could no longer stand the plummeting standards of the various passenger-carrying railroad companies.

Before 1970 those passenger services had declined to a point when they could hardly be described as a 'service' at all. In the increasing scramble for the more lucrative freight transportation, human cargo went by the board. If a company was unable to ditch its travelling clientele by fair means it resorted to methods bordering upon the foul. Overcrowding, inconvenient hours of departure and arrival, ill-timing of schedules, soaring fares; anything, in fact, to prove to the Inter-state Commerce Commission that passenger services were running at an ever-increasing loss and so were fit for abandonment.

One company, the Chicago, Burlington & Quincy (since merged into the Burlington Northern) on learning that the commission had upheld its application for abandonment, allowed one of its trains, the Humming Bird, to stop in mid-journey and dump its complement of passengers at a remote hamlet before an appeal could reverse the decision. It was in this climate of bitterness that, by government decree, Amtrak was born.

For a start, out of the score of passenger-serving companies, Amtrak merged thirteen to give the United States its first nation-wide rail passenger system. By 1973 it was operating more than 200 passenger trains daily over 27,000 miles of track connecting 440 cities and towns plus Montreal and Vancouver in neighbour-ing Canada. Though in 1973 there were still a number of short-comings, the improvements were remarkable.

Americans are not at all railway-minded. In the land of the automobile, multi-lane interstate highways and shuttle-service internal airlines, the train ranks with the lowly bus services of Greyhound and Trailways, and even then cannot compete in convenience and speed. For although Amtrak continues to improve in efficiency, its trains are, on most routes, slow by European standards and, with many lines still single track, infre-quent. That they are luxurious by comparison to European trains is a bonus for the pleasure traveller though this is not enough for the business commuter. This is a sad state of affairs when you remember that American history is threaded through and through by its famous railroads.

With the introduction of the Tom Thumb locomotive and its counterpart 'Best Friend of Charleston' in the early 1830s, passenger rail service came into being in the United States. The building of various railway lines progressed at a fairly rapid pace culminating in America's first transcontinental railroad in 1869. There was a great celebration at Promontory, Utah, that year when the line from San Francisco by way of the High Sierra, Nevada, met the one from Nebraska. By 1883 Portland, Oregon, was joined by the Mid-West and San Francisco was connected by rail to New Orleans. By 1909 the last of the six main trans-continental rail routes in North America was completed.

I started and ended my 1973 sampling of the railroads of North America at Montreal. The Washingtonian, I think my train to New York was called though I see it is now the Montrealer. It wasn't the fastest of trains. Leaving Montreal in the early evening it deposited me at Penn Station, New York, 444 miles away in time for breakfast next day. I have made the same overnight jour-ney by Greyhound coach in far less time though New York's Port Authority bus terminal is a place to avoid at four in the morning.

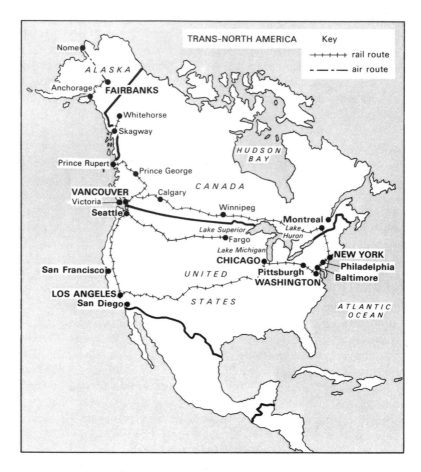

New York is one of those places you love or you hate. There's no in-between. Personally I detest its brash discourtesy and cubic architecture that is no longer a novelty. To encourage grey hairs try riding the subway system which, like our London Underground, is a misnomer because a lot of it is above ground. Even before you start you have a gobbledy-gook of IRT, BMT, IND, 6th AVE, 7th AVE, BROADWAY, 8th AVE, LEX to decipher and choose from, and where these infuriatingly independent lines all go to I've yet to discover. Give me the refreshingly straightforward Montreal Metro with its quiet efficiency and trains bouncing along on rubber tyres any day.

From New York I caught a Metroliner to the United States capital and, by so doing, rode one of the then fastest trains in the world with more than a dozen departures daily in both directions between New York and Washington DC. Travellers on the Metroliner are elevated to the calibre of superior beings, qualifying as patrons of a special coffee lounge — with free coffee — at Penn Station while waiting for departure. The train was electrically powered and covered the 225 miles in about three hours inclusive of brief stops at Trenton, Philadelphia, Wilmington and Baltimore. It consisted of four sleek coaches with accommodation offering a choice of comfortable armchairs, a jazzy snack and cocktail bar and the exclusive cosiness of what is described as a club car.

The architecture of Washington goes outward instead of upwards which may account for the more peaceful way of life compared to most American cities. Being there on a cold November day I might have picked up a false impression but it cannot be denied that the capital's imposing real estate, its wide lawn-surrounded boulevards and majestic statuary provide a certain calming influence.

With Chicago as the clearing house there are four main rail routes across the United States from coast to coast, most of them serving just one train a day: the San Francisco Zephyr runs from Chicago to its namesake city; the Empire Builder, and North Coast Hiawatha run to Seattle; the Inter American to the Mexican border, and the train I settled for, the Super Chief, goes to Los Angeles. I joined it at Chicago from the Broadway Limited, 907 miles out of Washington. There is a fifth coast to coast route that ignores Chicago and covers the southerly route via New Orleans and so to Los Angeles.

Each of these superbly-named trains is an eye-opener to those accustomed to the comparatively shorthaul services of Britain and the Continent. My roomette contained an adjustable armchair, washbasin, toilet, wardrobe, radio, a selection of reading lights and various temperature and air-conditioning controls. By pulling a lever it all turned into a well-sprung bed. Just down the corridor was a cocktail bar, reading room, upstairs observation lounge and a very-moderately-priced restaurant. In the reading room up-to-date feature films are shown and pretty girls in red blazers come round to inveigle you into party games and bingo. For those not needing a bed the 'sitting up' coaches provide very adequate relaxation facilities with reclining seats, adjustable foot-rests and paper-covered pillows. At the top end of the scale a bedroom provides a full suite of rooms for two.

My route from Chicago to Los Angeles was as magnificent as the train itself. In forty hours it crossed seven states, a distance of 2,222 miles of flat farmland, high mountains, forests and the semi-desert of the legendary Wild West. With two, sometimes three, giant 3,000hp diesel locomotives leading the silver train the sense of event was strong indeed.

Los Angeles Union Passenger Terminal — the main station — is the best thing in Los Angeles and about the only edifice of any historic significance. The city is a nightmare given over entirely to the automobile. To the first-time visitor it is a frightening place. Its urban sprawl goes on and on into suffocating eternity with parts of it labelled Pasedena, Hollywood, Long Beach, Glendale, though it is all Los Angeles. Criss-crossing this mega-lopolis is a system of urban motorways that is concrete madness. Six one-way lane carriageways spew traffic in all directions over, above and under six one-way lanes going in the opposite direc-tion. I found myself with a Ford of vast proportions equipped with an automatic gearbox, to which I am unaccustomed, faced with the proposition of getting from Hollywood-Burbank Airport to Pasadena in the rush hour. The gearbox had a fault that changed gear when I didn't want to change gear. I still sweat at the recollection of that drive.

Once a useful subway system existed but the concrete tide swept it away. There is a bus service of sorts but in LA it is the ubiquitous automobile that rules the way. The best way to escape the endless suburbs is by train.

I did so by courtesy of the Coast Starlight, a fine train that begins its run at San Diego on the Mexican border, travels to Los Angeles (where I joined it) and then to San Francisco and Seattle. At Seattle the Pacific International takes over for the remaining journey to Vancouver. For much of the 1,500-mile route between San Diego and Vancouver the train sticks close to the Pacific coast and offers fine views. Of all the cities it serves, the most spectacular is, without doubt, San Francisco, midway between Los Angeles and Seattle.

Every American, it is said, has two home-towns — his own and San Francisco. It is enchantingly beautiful with a humorous, rakish, slightly zany air. Railways and freeways stay clear of San Francisco and its internal public transportation is vested in buses, trolleybuses, the famous old cable-cars, and BART. And in BART (Bay Area Rapid Transit) you have the ultimate in sub-way systems. Smoothly, silently, effortlessly, its silver trains accelerate to nearly 100 miles an hour between stations. The system was still suffering from teething troubles when I tried it out and, somewhat disconcertingly, the doors kept automatically opening in the tunnels and refusing to budge upon arrival at stations.

Amtrak took me right into Vancouver, Canada's third and perhaps loveliest city that is full of gardens and beaches backed by the great barrier of the Rockies. If I had to live anywhere outside my own country I think it would be here.

After a few days of exploration I returned to Vancouver station to begin my trip across Canada to Montreal.

The two principal railway operating concerns in Canada today are the state-owned Canadian National and the company-owned Canadian Pacific which had kindly given me my ticket.

Canada is the second largest country in the world, its area of almost four million square miles is exceeded only by that of the USSR. Its enormous size can best be appreciated from the fact that the distance from Halifax on the Atlantic coast to Victoria on the Pacific is 300 miles further than that by air from Halifax across the Atlantic to Preswick in Scotland.

In so vast a land transportation has always been, and will always be, the key to its development. The canoe journeys of the Canadian pioneers were often of epic proportions, distances of 100 miles a day being not uncommon, but they carried only a few hundreds along the waterways. Distances were such that early roads were merely links between water routes, and it was not until the coming of the railways that any major settlement could proceed other than on the banks of rivers and lakes.

The story of transportation to the west coast of Canada perhaps started with the great canoe journey of Alexander MacKenzie who, on 22 July 1793, first reached the Pacific coast. Other great travellers of the fur trade followed MacKenzie's lead so that by the early years of the nineteenth century links were already being forged between the fur settlers in the west and the well-established colonies in the east.

Gradually the idea of a transcontinental railway took hold and obsessed the dreamers of railway conception. Surveys were made, money raised, companies formed until finally, on 16 February 1881, the construction of the Canadian Pacific Railway Company received the green light to go ahead. It was anticipated that completion would take ten years.

So began one of the great railway-building epics of all time. Distance was just one of the problems ahead; the great mountain barrier of the far west presented another, and the climate provided a third with its extreme temperatures ranging from 20 degrees below zero Centigrade to 40 degrees above. As though these problems weren't enough, the company faced continuous financial difficulties with sustained opposition not only in Canada but also in Britain, and the start in 1882 was delayed by one of the worst spring floods on the Red River at that time.

Men, supplies and horses were poured in to keep the work going at top speed. Winnipeg was the main supply point, receiving rails from England that were shipped to New Orleans and up the Mississippi River, lumber from Minnesota and ties from eastern Canada. By the end of the first year 417 miles of main line track was completed, a truly phenomenal achievement. Over 5,000 men were now directly involved, night shifts were put on bridge construction, and with the summer of 1883 the line from the east reached the summit of the Rockies at Kicking Horse Pass.

Meanwhile, work on the difficult section west of Lake Superior started and here some 12,000 men and 5,000 horses were employed. As during the construction of the Trans-Siberian

198

Railway, strife interfered with the project and the uncompleted line became a weapon. The second Riel Rebellion broke out in the prairies and for its suppression troops were transported to Fort Qu'Appelle over the unfinished track, a most uncomfortable ride for the soldiers who had to repeatedly disembark at railless sections and untested bridges.

In 1885 a regular passenger service was inaugurated between Winnipeg and Moose Jaw, followed by that of the lower Northwest Territories, now the province of Saskatchewan. In the mountains, track-laying had proceeded up and over Roger's Pass, then down the spectacular valley of the Illecillawget River, past Revelstroke, crossing the Columbia River towards Eagle Pass. Construction was also proceeding apace eastwards from the coast and at Craigellachie the meeting of the rails took place on 7 November 1885, just four and a half years after building began.

Completion of the unbroken rail link of 2,893 miles between Montreal and the Pacific coast was far more than merely the end of a stupendous construction job. In a very real way it gave life to the concept of the Dominion. Almost immediately, settlement along the track began spreading out on both sides. British Columbia at last began to feel that it was part of Canada.

The success of the Canadian Pacific in developing the prairie regions led to the building of competitive lines. Its two rivals from Winnipeg to the Pacific went through the Yellowhead Pass instead of the Kicking Horse, the Canadian Northern to come abreast of the Canadian Pacific in the canyons west of Kamloops there to eventually reach Vancouver, and the Grand Trunk Pacific to continue north-westwards through virgin country to Prince Rupert. Both these railways, and the lines connecting with them from the east at Winnipeg, were to combine to form Canadian National Railways, publicly-owned, and working alongside the privately-owned Canadian Pacific.

My train was CP's Canadian. In the early 1900s it had been the Imperial Limited that made its stately way across the great continent. This gave way to the Dominion which, together with another Canadian, became the fastest train in the world in 1931. My Canadian, however, was diesel-hauled and with me ensconsed in the cab, we left Vancouver at 17.45. Ahead lay 2,893 miles of slender track that breasted the mountain barriers of the Coast Range, the Monashees, the Selkirks, the towering Rockies and the long, steady slopes eastwards across the Great Plains, all of which took three days and nights to negotiate.

The two drivers in the cab of the front locomotive were salt-of-the-earth CPR men. Their lives were wrapped up in their railway and the big diesel unit was more nursed than driven. The fact that Canadians were deserting their trains for their cars was, to them, a crying shame that bordered upon treachery. Their bitterness was something you could feel.

Canada has been described as a country 3,000 miles long and two railroads wide. Her railways — and especially the CPR — have not only helped enormously in welding the far-scattered provinces of Canada into a single, strong and united nation but the route by which the latter went through the great mountain ranges of British Columbia befits, in every respect, its role in what has been so aptly called the 'National Dream'. It was over the section between Calgary and the canyons of the Fraser River, that Van Horne, the original general manager and architect of the line, astounded earlier councils which had 'decided' the route must go much further north through the Yellowhead Pass. In the well-nigh incredible adventures that the pioneers had in finding any sort of a route at all through this maelstrom of mountain peaks, densely forested slopes, and swift flowing rivers; in the magnificent engineering embodied in building the line; and in the never-ceasing challenge its curves, gradients and tunnels make to the locomotive men of today, it must remain a route without parallel on the world's railways.

For me the most fascinating portion of the line both from a geographical and construction sense was that of the 'Big Hill' on the descent to Field after Kicking Horse Pass. Dangerous in descent, the 'Big Hill' was a major operating problem for the east-bound trains that had to climb it and each train had to be split and taken up in sections by the small locomotives of the day working to the limit of their capacity. The problem was solved by the construction of the two spiral tunnels, now world-famous. The first, under Cathedral Mountain, is 3,206 feet long and

200

turns through 234 degrees in its descent of 48 feet between portals. The second tunnel correspondingly drops 45 feet in its length of 2,890 feet and turns through 232 degrees. Emerging from the second tunnel it is an odd sight to see one's train travelling in the opposite direction to its main journey in the short level stretch between the adjacent portals of the two tunnels.

An equally important improvement is the Connaught Tunnel. Sixty miles west of Field the line turned south and commenced another great climb up the west side of the valley of the Beaver River in order to reach Roger's Pass, climbing 1,900 feet in 17 miles with gradients of 2.2% most of the way. The route through the pass had many curves, and from the start of operations it was plagued during the winter months by avalanches. The Connaught Tunnel, built to take a double track, is just over five miles long. Trains still have the long haul up from Beavermouth to the eastern portal of the tunnel but the summit elevation is 552 feet lower than the summit of the pass; 4⅓ miles are saved in distance travelled, and no less than the equivalent of seven complete circles of curvature were eliminated.

The route of the Canadian across the country varies in its scenic and historical interest; but apart from the tremendous spectacle of the Rockies one of the most beautiful stretches occurs when the train is making its way along the northern shores of Lake Superior. It was a terrible section to build, since it was necessary to cut a ledge in the towering walls of rock that rise sheer from the waters of the lake. After this I found the Great Plains, though dramatic made monotonous window-gazing for the last day of my ride on the CPR.

We drew into Montreal almost on time having made up for time lost caused, for the most part, by my endearing locomotive crew dawdling in the particularly scenic bits to give me better opportunity to take photographs!

Four years later, in 1977, an Amtrak-type operation was mounted to revitalize the country's lagging rail passenger business and reduce the financial burden carried by the government to maintain these services. Thus VIA Rail came into being which, in June 1977, took over the passenger marketing function for

201

both railways. It is, perhaps, an enforced climax and a sad reflection to the history of Canadian railways.

With my return to North America in 1979 I had become not only six years older but, perhaps, wiser. My brief, mostly flying, visits to the United States in the meantime had taught me that within her vast territories was ample scope for my adventurous yearnings and wilderness wanderings. The concrete jungles of New York, Chicago and Los Angeles are a far cry from the rural outback of the Middle West and arctic Alaska as I was to learn most forcibly the summer of that year.

My kudos as a travel writer had risen to the point when the world, or parts of it, were my oyster. The man from the US Travel Service said, 'We want you to take an adventurer's look at America. Go and see what you can find'. So I studied the map for a while and resolved to follow old trails by horseback and wagon in the Dakotas and go to the far north of Alaska to see if Eskimos really *did* rub noses in greeting. Between these two assignments lay Canada and her wealth of railways which were to get me from one project to another.

Why I had to fly to Anchorage, Alaska, by way of Chicago beat me but TWA's first class service offered me no cause to complain. Anchorage did, however, for it turned out to be a modern metropolis with a street system as characterless as a grid. Where had I dreamed up the notion of quaint wooden houses between which the good citizens padded contentedly in snowshoes? With some trepidation I took a train going further north.

Anchorage is not, as one might expect, the terminus of the Alaska Railroad for it disdainfully continues south to the smaller town of Whittier on the coast, to connect with the state ferry system. Northbound, the train winds through the farmsteads of the Matanvska Valley passing historic gold towns like Talkeetna, over the Susitna River, across Hurricane Gulch and along the eastern edge of Denali State Park (for Mount Mackinley) to Fairbanks.

One travels in an air-conditioned coach called 'AuRoRa' (after the northland's aurora borealis) which is a dashing blue and gold streamlined vehicle offering Amtrak-style comfort and observation facilities. The restricted service and the clientele make it plain that the passenger side of the Alaska Railroad is predominantly dependant upon tourists. But it is North America's northernmost railway and it notched up another milestone for me.

But, in spite of Anchorage, there *is* much of the frontier about the far north of North America and this includes Canada's Yukon and North-west Territories. It is a land of airstrips, of cold lakes bordered by seaplanes, and flat vistas merging into the mists. It is also a land of startling beauty. Alaska throws up unique obstacles to Man, and he in turn invariably finds novel ways of surmounting them. Farmers and builders must compress their year's work into the brief summers, nearly all provisions must be shipped in from the United States and Alaskans live with the threat of earthquakes such as the one that struck on Good Friday 1964. They also fly over roadless terrain; take to their boats despite bone-chilling water and rugged coastlines, and exist in temperatures that we in luke-warm Britain can hardly imagine. It is, above all, a land of challenge holding beneath the surface of its permafrost and waters the vast wealth which first attracted the scruffy hot-eyed miners in 1896.

Alaska's northernmost town is Nome on the west coast facing the Bering Sea, not many miles from the arctic circle. I flew there in a 707 of Wien Alaska Airways for there are no roads or rails to it. Spawned by the discovery of gold on the beaches in 1898 it boomed into a gold rush camp of tents and frame buildings. Once the community numbered 40,000. Today it is about 4,000 but growing once more. The gold rush has passed and mining is on the decline but an aura of those glamorous days lingers on. Touring the ramshackle town is like sight-seeing in a junkyard with most of the tottering houses surrounded by a collection of pipes, boilers, tin cans, old cars and discarded ice-boxes which form a treasure chest of valuable spares. Telegraph poles and television aerials lean at drunken angles for nothing holds up for long on the shifting permafrost.

Based upon Nome I visited the outback of arctic Alaska in a gritty little British-made Norman Britton Islander aircraft of Munz Northern Airlines, for the few local urban roads lead nowhere. My 'bush pilots' were Eskimos and for a week, I flew

203

in the co-pilot's seat sampling the daily flights to and from a
number of tiny communities amidst an awe-inspiring desolation.
Our destinations included Little Diomede Island, just 22 miles
from Siberia and in sight of its equally desolate landscape where,
across the international date line, today is tomorrow. Another
flight was to Shishmaref where I watched local ladies making the
mukluks and parkas which is *de rigueur* wear in such climes, and
another was to Wales, the westernmost point on the North
American continent, where we flew low over the vast jig-saw
puzzle of fractured ice-floes still covering the ocean. The arctic
scenery here is one of the unsung wonders of the world. If we
could ride some mythical trans-arctic express in the winter we
would stop thinking of this region in shades of blue and see it in
hues of red, orange and subtle pink. The wild-life too is spectacular. Witness the overwhelming impact of thousands of majestic
snow geese sweeping across the horizon and you will appreciate
the magnitude of God. Alaska is a refuge for many endangered
species, such as the trumpeter swan and the bald eagle. One
million caribou range across Canada and Alaska, and a train
would not disturb them. Once the Bering Sea is reached it is only
a short hop to Gambell Island. I flew there too and watched the
Siberian mountains appear to go down into the frozen water and
come out again. Such wonders are available to our generation if
only it had the imagination to attain them.

There's no myth at all about the White Pass and Yukon Railway. Travelling this down-to-earth line is one of northern
Canada's experiences and its history is an integral part of the
story of this exciting land, just as much as that of the great
Canadian Pacific. From Nome, Fairbanks and Anchorage I
travelled south into Canada and came to roost at Whitehorse,
capital of Yukon, a pleasant friendly town of 6,000 souls. It sits
astride another artery of land transportation, the Alaska Highway, paved at this point for some 80 miles.

The 110-mile narrow gauge railway connects Whitehorse to
the Alaskan port of Skagway and the coastal ferries that call
there. In so doing the line passes through the territory of Yukon,
British Columbia and Alaska. It was constructed to transport the
thousands of gold seekers and their supplies from Skagway

through the coast mountains to the beginning of the river route to the Klondike gold fields. Started in May 1898, the railway's last spike was driven at Carcross on 29 July 1900, the conclusion of 26 months of the blasting, chipping, shovelling and hardships of construction crews whose number fluctuated from 700 to 2,000. They were the stampeders who, en route to the Klondike, stopped off to work as construction crew long enough to make a grubstake, then left to follow the 'Trail of '98' to Dawson City, almost 600 miles north.

A narrow, moss-filled ledge beside the railway track, marked by a stone inscription, is a mute reminder of the trudging steps of the thousands of men and women who believed in the rainbow's end and the streams filled with gold.

The gold rush died away, the Yukon population dwindled, and during the dark days of the 1930s, the trains operated only once a week, but the steam locomotives and the rotary ploughs kept the line open. Today it is used only by tourists, and for them the journey is truly spectacular. Some of the parlour cars in which I travelled were built as early as 1883 but their ancient silhouette and interiors made strange bedfellows with the heavy steel mineral wagons and multiple diesel electric locomotives that formed the rest of the train when I was there.

Probably no tunnel in the world was built under greater difficulties than the one which penetrated a perpendicular barrier of rock which juts out of the mountainside like a giant flying buttress some ten miles north of Skagway. A short distance from the summit of the pass, a deep canyon is spanned by a steel cantilever bridge, 215 feet from the creek's bed. Below, in Dead Horse Gulch, winds the old White Pass Trail, worn into the native rock by thousands of sourdoughs. To improve the grade and curvature of the railway, both bridge and tunnel were replaced in 1969 but the originals still stand. From sea level at Skagway, the line climbs to the summit of the pass, 2,885 feet in 21 miles. The highest point is Log Cabin, British Columbia, which is at an altitude of 2,916 feet.

In 1979 the White Horse Pass and Yukon carried 75,000 passengers. From terminal to terminal the trip takes about eight hours and the views of mountains and lakes are fine indeed. Just

40 miles from Skagway is a rambling frame building called 'Bennet Eating House' where trains from both directions meet and passengers descend to sit down to hearty prospectors lunch (included in the fare) of stew, beans, sourdough bread and some tasty apple pie.

I rode the line in both directions, spending the intervening night at a Skagway hostel as there was no other accommodation available in the little town hardly changed since the days of '78. Snow was falling as we crawled back into Bennet the next day adding to the hazards of a rickety line that is all heart and not over-endowed with safety features. But then the White Pass and Yukon Railway is not state-owned or financially secure and its continued existence is a battle for survival.

Southwards again and it was the Alaska Highway that was to carry me since no further iron road exists northwest of Fort Nelson. I was now in a part of the world where motor roads have a more evocative image than the railways, with the Alaska Highway predominating, and, since I have returned to travel the wilderness highways of the north — which are, in part, fed by the sparse railways — another short digression can be excused.

Few roads in the world have a more adventurous image, especially to us crowded, restricted and overtaxed drivers on the traffic-snarled, bottle-necked trunk routes of Britain, than that of the Alaska Highway. Yet the allure of this 1,523-mile artery to the top of the world will surely decline as the black-top (North Americanese for tarmac) spreads along its unpredictable surface. Already there are long tarmacked stretches on either side of Whitehorse and the other principal townships while all 300 miles of the American portion is hard-top — though the permafrost ensures that even here it remains well-blessed with horrific pot-holes. No longer is this once-named Alcan Highway classed as a wilderness road in Canadian or United States motoring circles, though with petrol-filling stations and facilities sometimes a hundred miles apart, we pampered Britons might not agree.

If there's an elusive pot of gold at the end of the rainbow then surely there must be reward at the end of the Alaska Highway, or so the notion came to me as I gazed at Milepost 0 in the centre of

Dawson Creek. It took me four days of hard, pothole-dodging driving to find out that a sense of achievement is the only prize.

The road was built by agreement between the government of Canada and the United States as an overland lifeline to relieve Alaska from the wartime risks to shipping and to supply a land route for war material and equipment. The pioneer road was then turned over to civilian contractors for widening and gravelling and the replacement of primitive log bridges with permanent structures. Built by the United States Army from the 'end of the steel' — the railway — at the then remote frontier village of Dawson Creek, the Alaska Highway has become a legend in the annals of road-building. Officially opened in November 1942 when a ribbon stretched across it at Soldiers Summit (Milepost 1061) was cut, the highway climaxed a road-building achievement begun only eight months before.

If the Alaska Highway is no longer classed as a wilderness road there are still plenty of Canadian and Alaskan routes that are. From 'the end of the steel' I was to spend weeks driving roads of unimaginable loneliness and trekking a 'ghost highway' through the multiple barrier of the Mackenzie Mountains in Canada's remote Northwest Territories with grizzly bears breathing down my neck. Adventure indeed.

At Fort Nelson I took to the tracks once more. They belonged to the British Columbia Railway and ensured that my further southward journeying in Canada was by train. Many railways in the world contend for the title of the most scenic, the most beautiful, the most thrilling, but I have no doubt at all that the line which holds the most sustained enjoyment for the passenger from a visual point of view is that of the B.C. Railway.

Fort Nelson to Vancouver by train means a ride of some 1,000 miles though, at the time I was there, regular passenger services were in operation only between Prince George and North Vancouver. On this, the most spectacular portion of the route, my train was the Caribou Dayliner.

The B.C. Railway was formerly the Pacific Great Eastern Railway, a title that is more nostalgic than geographical. When construction began in 1911 it was by men recruited from the

207

Great Eastern Railway of England who came to Canada to build a line intended to open up the rugged, remote Caribou country beyond Squamish, 40 miles north of Vancouver. After immense difficulties and major engineering problems the Pacific Great Eastern was pushed 580 miles up-country to expire at the little township of Quesnel on the Fraser River, where the stream was navigable. This rugged section was opened to traffic in 1921 but it was not until 1949 that work commenced on the 80-mile extension, northwards to Prince George, completed early in 1953. At the southern end of the line the eagerly-awaited extension to Vancouver was opened only as recently as 1956. Two years later the line had reached the Peace River in the north and, by 1971, the link to Fort Nelson and Fort St John provided rail connections from British Columbia's capital to its northern border.

The Fraser River provides travellers by both the Canadian Pacific and Canadian National routes to Vancouver with some grand spectacles. But these are less astonishing than the first sight of the Fraser River when descending from Williams Lake to Lillooet. This is a route of amazing scenic variety, ranging from an almost pastoral Scottish-strath quality between Prince George and Williams Lake, and finishing alongside Howe Sound, in fjord-like surroundings, from Squamish into Vancouver. This last section now has the compelling attraction of a vintage steam-run, regularly-scheduled and worked by one of the magnificent Royal Hudson 4-6-4 locomotives.

I was back with Amtrak the moment I boarded the early morning Pacific International out of Vancouver's CN station and on a route I had covered before. But the Chicago-bound North Coast Hiawatha out of Seattle broke new territory for me. Working an alternate daily service with the Empire Builder on a partly differing but parallel route, the 2,300-mile, 50-hour journey is a fine way of reconnoitring that country's rural Montanan north-west prior to more prolonged investigation at a later date. Many of my fellow-passengers were making their first train ride of their lives and were enchanted with the experience. The lines had for long been threatened with closure in the hard-fought battle between the railways and the automobile and, alas, when I returned to Montana a year or two later it was to find that the southernmost line had been closed to passenger traffic.

I broke my journey for more than a month at Fargo, to commence a new one of 400 miles by yet another mode of transportation, that of horseback and by covered wagon. Thus motivated I followed an old stagecoach trail between Medora and Deadwood in the Dakotas, across the rattlesnake-infested Badlands and Butte country with horizons shimmering in temperatures of 106 degrees and more, to the cool loveliness of the Black Hills before joining the annual trek out of Jamestown of the Fort Seward wagon train; both, of course, forerunners of the railway.

Robert Louis Stevenson wrote that he preferred to 'travel not to go anywhere'. With the interstates and freeways of America choked with speeding cars, their drivers hell-bent on the single objective of putting distance behind them, those who linger along the byways of history and saunter by the wonders of nature aboard a train, turn travel into a rich experience — with adventure available along the way . . .

9

Trans-Andes

LIMA—CUZCO—GUAYAQUIL— QUITO—SAN LORENZO

Whilst it was an expedition that brought me to East Africa in 1976 it was another that took me to South America a year later. Back in the fifteenth century a Spaniard by the name of Francisco Pizarro conquered the Inca armies, sweeping southwards through what are now the Andean countries along roads the only twentieth century counterparts of which are, perhaps, the interstate highways of the United States. It was the royal road of the Incas, the remarkable fourteenth-century artery along the spine of the Andes between Cuzco, in southern Peru, and Quito, the capital of Ecuador, that drew me to Lima in April 1977. For three and a half months I was to trudge the route of this historic highway in the opposite direction to that of Pizarro and his little Spanish army. It may have been the lure of a road that brought me to South America but I managed, nevertheless, to take time off to sample the entire network of railways in Peru and Ecuador and observe something of those in Bolivia and Colombia too. But first let us look at the state of the railways generally in South America.

The densest and most effective network belongs to Argentina with 27,000 miles of railway. The British built most of it — as they did in Brazil and elsewhere — and because of the flat 'pampas' the lines were easy to lay. Chile too has a sound rail system. Here there are only 5,200 miles of track but they are adequate for a country 2,600 miles long and less than 100 miles wide. One of the major railways in Chile is the *Antofagasta*, which is still owned by a British private company.

Brazil has many different railways but little money to spend on them so they are in poor condition. Here there are 23,000 miles of railway made up of five different gauges covering, in the main, only the southern portion of this immense country. But Venezuela,which is also vast and the richest nation in South America,

210

has almost no railways at all at the present time.

The most evocative railways in South America are, surely, those of the trans-Andine lines. Two connect Chile and Argentina, three give landlocked Bolivia access to the Pacific, one links Lima with the mountain valleys and mineral region of central Peru, and the most northerly connects Guayaquil and Quito in Ecuador. These railways were built between 1870 and 1914, to a variety of gauges: standard gauge in Peru and metre gauge in Bolivia, and 3'6" gauge in Ecuador. At the time of their construction they helped to bring some political unity to the scattered and diverse population of the countries they served but their main function was economic and their chief interest freight traffic. They were, and still are, vitally important to the mining industries of Peru, Bolivia and Chile. Passenger traffic has never been more than a troublesome obligation.

Crossing the Andes meant constructing the highest railway in the world. The highest of all is the Peruvian Central Railway which I was to ride during my stay in that country. Railway construction in such circumstances presented civil engineers with major problems for they had, in a confined space and short distance, to build railways over passes which exceeded Mont Blanc in altitude. The solutions they adopted were tight curves, zigzags and rack sections. Operating the lines created further difficulties: steep gradients, lack of local sources of fuel, heavy wear and tear on locomotives and rolling stock, and frequent landslides and washouts. Changing from steam to diesel was, initially, a step backwards because diesel units were prone to losing power in the rare air and there were many cases of trains being unable to take the gradients.

My first experience of riding a trans-Andine railway was on the Southern Railway of Peru. Three lines serve the *altiplano,* a grassy windswept plain 12,800 feet above sea level, and one of them is the Southern. Of standard gauge, it runs from Mollendo on the Peruvian coast through the country's second city, Arequipa, to the town of Juliaca on the *altiplano.* Here it divides. A short section continues to Lake Titicaca and around its shores to the port of Puno while a 211-mile line from Juliaca runs north to Cuzco, the ancient Inca capital, crossing a summit of 14,154

211

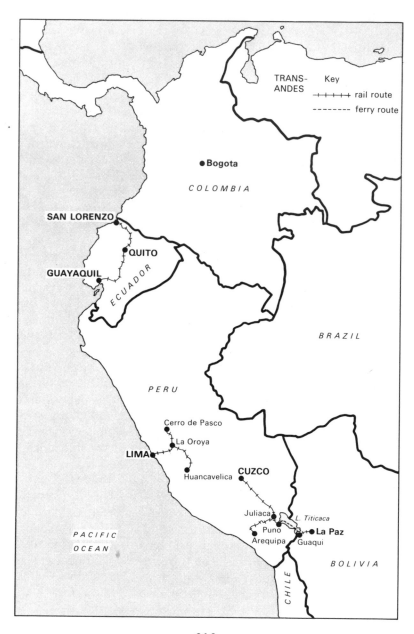

feet at La Raya. I planned to ride both. Access to Bolivia is maintained by a steamer service between Puno and the Bolivian port of Guaqui, and another short railway line to link with the capital, La Paz. The Southern Railway of Peru is not a major trans-Andine route but is, nevertheless, a very worthwhile ride. The line is single track throughout, and on the Arequipa to Mollendo section, the passenger trains have succumbed to road competition. This necessitated my having to travel from Lima to Arequipa by an overcrowded, smelly abomination of a bus that was delayed four hours during the intense heat of the midday sun by a nationwide bicycle race.

The city is full of old Spanish buildings and churches made of *sillar,* a pearly white volcanic material used almost exclusively for the construction of Arequipa. Though an Inca city it differs in many ways from Cuzco with few buildings taller than one storey. Earthquakes are the scourge here, the last being in 1960 when much damage was done. Travelling on a tight budget I knew my urban nights would have to be spent in the most basic of accommodations and the pension-cum-dosshouse I located at Arequipa set the standard.

The Puno train was supposed to leave at 0815 and, in the event, left at 0915 which is not bad at all in a land where *manana* doesn't just mean 'tomorrow' but can also mean 'never'. It was impressed upon me that tickets had to be purchased two hours in advance but there were no problems when I rolled up at the station ten minutes before the scheduled time of departure.

The early morning scene as the train wound up the valley towards Juliaca was enchanting. All around were fields of alfalfa and corn and, behind Arequipa, the volcanic peaks of Misti and Chachani. After Crucero Alto, the highest point on the line, the first mountain lakes appeared: Laguunillas and Saracocha, each on either side of the train. My guide book, ever practical, told me that all water east of Crucero Alta flowed into the Atlantic thousands of miles away.

I was travelling second — lowest — class and though the seats were hard my journey was not uncomfortable. The coaches were British-made, sturdy and ancient, their windows either jammed shut or jammed open. The train was full, but not overcrowded,

213

with cheerful people. I was soon to learn that there is no need to go short of food on an Andean train ride for there are vendors both on the trains and at every stop. And Andean trains do a lot of stopping. All sorts of edible oddities were thrust under my nose by large peasant women wearing bowler hats and voluminous skirts of many colours inflated by layers of petticoats. There was no restaurant car on my train but that a kitchen existed was plain from the huge roast chicken dishes that none-too-clean waiters brought round to those that ordered them. With the chicken went generous measures of *Pisco* brandy which kept everyone in high spirits.

Except for some girls who, to my pleasurable but uncomprehending surprise, all bore a remarkable resemblance to Sophia Loren, my fellow travellers were of Indian extraction. The older womenfolk in their absurd hats and skirts wore their hair in standard greasy black plaits joined together at the nape of the neck. For most of the day-long journey everyone gorged themselves silly on huge chunks of semi-raw meat cut from an obscure joint of an equally obscure animal which was hawked by vendors from bundles of filthy rags. I stuck to the *Pisco* which possibly accounted for my being on a coach so liberally inhabited by Sophia Lorens. The train was diesel-hauled but so much black smoke issued from the locomotive it could have been a steam engine at our head.

Descending to fertile pampa I saw my first llama, alpaca or vicuna — I don't know which because the bowler-hatted brigade were each telling me something different, interspersed with great guffaws of laughter and display of nicotine-stained teeth. Juliaca, the junction, involved an interminable delay before the shores of Lake Titicaca came into sight and were slavishly followed by the train for the 30 miles to Puno. Weighed down by a heavy rucksack I fought my way off the seething platform.

Another hostel-type hotel — a kind description — became my home and in the morning I had a whole day for investigating Puno and Titicaca. Neither added up to anything very much in my estimation and though the lake was beautiful from a distance, closer inspection revealed a shore line befouled with scum, excrement and dead dogs amongst which the locals were happily drawing water. Comment from a fellow traveller on the train who had also noticed Sophia Loren's doubles: 'The titi's OK but I don't go much for the caca'.

Puno boasts a fine square, a coldly austere cathedral and a lively market full of local colour. But around the small port there is ugly poverty that cannot be hidden by the description 'quaint', an adjective which my guide book was fond of using for everything that differed from the British middle-class way of life.

I developed a touch of altitude sickness — no more than a head-ache — while in Puno, so was glad of the restful voyage on the good Newcastle-built ship *Inca* across the huge lake into Bolivian territory. The *Inca* may have been elderly but she was far from senile and was spotlessly clean. Brought overland from Lima in pieces, the steamer was put together in Puno and has been work-ing ever since. It was an eleven-hour crossing and, on the outward trip, I managed a bunk bed. At Guaqui, which my guide book described as 'nondescript' — not being able to find anything remotely 'quaint' about the place — we were herded into an equally unquaint train for the run to La Paz.

The train was no more than a railcar and was capable of contain-ing only about half the passengers from the boat, the rest having to go by bus. First off the steamer got the choice. The little diesel stopped for half an hour at Tiahuanaco to give a glimpse of the pre-Inca ruins standing on a flat, draughty plateau.

My days in La Paz and beyond were mostly occupied with last-minute investigatory matters into things Inca but these activities offered me opportunity to see something of the highest capital city in the world. The Spaniards chose this site to build their city, sunk in a natural canyon, in 1548, both to avoid the chill winds of the plateau and because they had found gold in the River Choqueyapu which runs through the canyon. Mount Illimani, with snow-covered peaks, towers over the city. In this topsy-turvy capital the strata of society runs downwards: the poorer Indians live in the higher terraces below which are the business quarter, government offices, main hotels, restaurants and the university. The wealthy live lower still, reaching down to the bed of the valley. Much of La Paz is modern so that numerous skyscrapers often break the traditional patchwork of red tiles and corrugated iron.

Bolivia is the fifth largest country in South America but possesses a mere 1400 miles of railway, most built by her very many victorious enemies. In the beginning each of the three main routes serving the country encountered snags, still not entirely overcome. On the Peruvian line there was — and is — Lake Titicaca where freight as well as passengers have to be transhipped twice. On the Arica line the rack section caused — and still causes — delays. And until 1928, when the Bolivian Railway Board changed the gauge of its Chilian section, all freight on that route had to be transhipped at Uyuni as none of the ports, until the construction of Matarani in southern Peru in 1948, had adequate facilities. The major engineering problem, though, was not the crossing of the Andes, but the descent into the city of La Paz. Many lines on varying routes were constructed, none being a great success. Currently financial problems are the vogue, particularly since nationalization in 1972 and, as a result, many steam engines that were once put out to graze have been reharnessed. I was even to see a couple of Henschells pushing wagons around in the La Paz yards.

The planned direction of my travels being northward I made haste to return to Peruvian soil and, within a week, was back at Puno ready for the railway journey to Cuzco. An added satisfaction for me was that the line roughly followed the route of the southern extension of the old royal road to the Inca capital.

Departure of the train was in the hands of fate. 'No trains today' vouchsafed the station staff. 'Yes there is a train today' was the opinion of the bulk of the potential clients. Fate was kind and the clients correct. Again I travelled second class being low in *soles* (the Peruvian currency) but the run along Titicaca's contaminated shore offered splendid views of a Titicacan sunrise as a backdrop to the fishermen in tiny reed boats.

Back at Juliaca vendors came aboard selling alpaca fur hats that could have fetched a fortune in London. Thereafter the northbound line climbed gradually, reaching its climax at La Raya. The countryside was pure magic with astonishing panoramas of snow-capped peaks, tall mountains, green pastures and woods. With La Raya behind, the train picked up speed and pounded down the straight to Sicuani, near which the ruins of the Inca

216

temple of Viracocha, grandiose and lonely, stand. North of Sicuani the fields were gorgeous with Californian poppies and lupins before they gave way to the River Vilcanota which the line accompanies. More stops with strangely alien names, and we came to Cusipata, Rumicola, and Huambutio. Dusk saw us in the rugged sierra surrounded by mountain rocks of purple and red, cacti with long fingers and grey moss hanging like a tattered veil from cliffs and shrubs. Scotch broom trees added a more cheerful note of bright yellow as we emerged out into the valley head with its gnarled pepper trees. And all this to music thanks to the guitar and mouth organ talents of a blind family and their sweet rendering of a well-known Quechua love song. A golden sunset was to climax our entry into Cuzco.

All who go to Peru today find their way eventually to Cuzco. It breathes its Inca history as can no other place throughout the Andean countries. Over the years it has become a shrine to the Incas, the place where the visitor can do the rounds of its museums and memorials, themselves part of the Inca heritage. Assuredly there is much to see in this remarkable city that lies in the hollow of a valley at 11,000 feet with, on three sides, the mountains rising precipitously and, in the south-east, the valley stretching away to distant peaks. Sacsahuaman, the massive fortress which guards Cuzco, is the hub of all pilgrimages. This amazing structure, standing high on the plains of Chita beyond the northern suburbs of the city, is a third of a mile long with 60-foot high terraced walls of monolithic blocks. Some of them weigh up to a hundred tons and measure seventeen feet by ten. And, remember, the Inca never possessed the wheel yet those blocks have been fitted together so perfectly and without the aid of mortar that the blade of a penknife could never pass between them.

During my stay in Cuzco I caught the early morning train to Chaullay which dropped me (and a thousand others) at the legendary Machu-Picchu — the 'lost city of the Incas' — which Hiram Bingham stumbled upon in 1911. There are no roads to Machu-Picchu so the train is the only vehicle for reaching this edifice of supreme drama that is out-staged only by the utter magnificence of its surroundings.

217

But, with Cuzco, my railway journeying and dalliance on the tourist beat was, for the time being, over. The royal road of the Incas is not one of the sights of the city; it creeps out through an undistinguished housing estate to become the hard core for a dust road. My rucksack high on my shoulders, the crunch of my footsteps in the still air sounding like those of Francisco Pizarro's Spanish conquistadores, I made for the distant peaks on feet instead of wheels.

I was tempted back to the trains at Huancavelica partly because they were there and partly because of a painful crop of blisters. It was also the easiest way of getting to Lima where I intended to set up base my main assault on the Inca road project.

A glance at the rail system map of Peru will show you the route of the Central Railway as a lop-sided T with Lima at its base, running up to La Oroya at the junction of the cross piece. The main line runs from Lima through La Oroya to Huancavelica, its terminal on the right. A privately-owned railway runs from La Oroya to Cerro de Pasco on the left. My first journey was to Lima.

The Central Railway is regarded as one of the wonders of the Americas and the engineering of the route involved immense problems. The deep Rimac valley between Lima and La Oroya, the only feasible route to the central region of the country, narrows to a maximum width of about 656 feet. Within its limits the engineers had to find a way of climbing nearly 13,000 feet within a distance of less than 47 miles which is the length of the road that runs along the bottom of the valley. The twists and turns which the railway needs to gain height have made the railway considerably longer at 73 miles. To keep the gradient down to the necessary 1 in 23, the single track railway has to utilise the whole width of the valley, crossing frequently from one side to the other. Even this would be impossible without the use of the famous zigzags to gain height. Between Chosica and Ticlio, the heighest point of the line at 15,693 feet, there are six double and one single zigzags, 66 tunnels and 59 bridges to negotiate.

Construction of the line, which began in 1870, presented problems in addition to the geographical ones. A mysterious

218

disease killed off thousands of workers on and in 1877, Peru went bankrupt, which effectively held up completion until 1929. The chief interest of the Central Railway has always been freight, particularly since 1897 when the La Oroya copper mines opened. However the incredible journey still remains attainable to the traveller. Except for those unfortunates who suffer from altitude sickness and have to be given oxygen by the attendants on the train, all will marvel as I did at the ingenuity of the men who built this railway amidst some of the most rugged landscapes on earth.

Between Huancavelica and Huancayo, midway to La Oroya, the line is metre gauge. I travelled in a crowded railcar which whizzed along merrily before it broke down. A normally three-hour journey turned disconcertingly to one of ten hours. At least I was lucky to get a seat though I paid dearly for it by having a perpetually howling baby next to me dribbling all over my trousers.

The delay — much of it spent out on the track — resulted in a night on the tiles at Huancayo, an old market town that I could have found quite pleasant at anytime but two in the morning. The night was bitterly cold and I blessed a kindly bunch of vendors for allowing me to warm myself around their brazier. The night life of Huancayo is not without incident to judge from some of the prostitutes and shady characters who likewise came to warm themselves by the fire. The town finally redeemed itself in my eyes by displaying some ancient models of working steam locomotives surely not much younger than Robert Stevenson.

The 0700 to Lima was the Tren de Sierra and of more substance that the previous day's railcar. En route towards La Oroya the hilly scenery reminded me of north Wales and the industrial town into which we drew carried overtones of Port Talbot. La Oroya station was the usual jumble of humanity with everybody selling everything to everybody else. A wizened old man sitting with a basket of fruit between his knees caught my gaze. The fruits were about the size of oranges but a yellowish-green colour; I think they were chirimoya. I went over and entered into negotiations to buy some. Seeing my interest in buying, every vendor on the platform homed in on me and I found myself

219

ringed by eager, beaming Indian faces. My poor old man was edged out of proceedings so I pushed my way through the throng and made my purchase from him. It probably cost me more but I received a bonus of a great smile and a hug which made my day. Despite an over-abundance of pips, the chirimoya made good eating; a sweet rather fleshy fruit with a distinctive flavour. While I was sampling it, spitting pips out like a consumptive machine gun, the engine driver came over, tapped me on the shoulder and said, 'El Inglish, we go'. It was one of the few times in Peru I was given a title other than 'Gringo'.

All the way from Huancayo we had been climbing steadily though the gradients were not noticeable. Now the name of a station — Ticlio — came into view with its altitude (4,782 metres), prominently displayed on a board. Nobody in my compartment appeared to be affected by the height though oxygen-bearing officials haunted the corridors to help those that were. The line reaches its highest point in the tunnel between Ticlio and Galera and, thereafter, the train is off the leash and on the downhill leg of the journey. On the seat opposite a German breathed stentoriously, as I suppose I did too. In addition to their pale faces foreigners on this train are distinguishable by their heavy breathing.

The Andes are great humblers of men. They stretch the length of South America, forming a crenellated wall 4,500 miles long, draped at the northern end with vegetation and at the southern end with ice and snow. And down the length of this range, and on its slopes, lie untamed regions of snow, ice and fire, of dripping jungle and seared desert, of cloud cover and merciless sun, of intense heat and killing cold. This is the barrier that railway builders had to contend with when they planned and constructed the lateral lines that wind inland from the tropical coastline. As the pace of the Tren de Sierra slackened with the application of the brakes, a feeling of awe descended upon the whole train almost tangible in its intensity.

The Rimac Valley is not beautiful; it is savage, bleak and remorseless. The great walls and escarpments hem in the fragile track forcing it to curve, wind and dodge in a kind of desperate progress that is more like an escape. Where granite buttresses bar the way the line doubles back on itself, forcing the limping train to grind to a halt up against the canyon wall and reverse downwards the moment the hand-operated points have been switched by the guard. Forwards, backwards, forwards, backwards, slowly we spiralled down the valley. We all chattered inanely as the coaches traversed delicate lattice bridges over bottomless chasms and crept along the edges of sheer precipices on narrow ledges hacked from enormous cliffs of granite.

Nine hours after leaving Huancayo the valley flattened out and we entered upon a warm, tropical expanse of green countryside that had pushed aside the mountains to substitute terraced cultivation and urban development. Ahead lay the sea with Lima, the Peruvian capital, shimmering in the heat haze.

Ten days later I was to return by the same route as far as La Oroya. On this journey I travelled first class in a sudden fit of extravagance and lunched substantially on soup, salad, chicken and pudding for less than a pound while we dragged up the gigantic valley. At La Oroya I changed to the non-state-owned line to Cerro de Pasco on a crowded local full of friendly peasants and their livestock. With a bulging rucksack I was as loaded as they were and managed to share a seat with a substantial lady, each of us supporting one buttock on the wooden slats. The three-hour journey along the crest of the range cost the equivalent of 15 pence and at the village of Shelby, just short of Cerro, I disembarked. The altitude was 13,000 feet and it would be many weeks before I would descend again to lower and gentler climes.

I came down from the mountains in Ecuador, there to join the next railway link in the Andean chain. Many hundreds of miles of daunting, spectacular territory separate the Peruvian Central Railway from the Ecuadorian seaport of Guayaquil, the southern terminal of the Ecuadorian State Railway. After more than two months of backpacking and attempting to follow a road route that, at times, took me to rarified heights in excess of 20,000 feet I was, to put it mildly, somewhat dishevelled. I was also filthy, exhausted and happy as I tottered into Guayaquil which has the most unsavoury reputation of any town in Ecuador. Having unwittingly passed unscathed through the domain of the cattle

221

thieves of northern Peru I could raise no fear of the muggers of Guayaquil who give the town a reputation almost as unsavoury as that of Bogota in neighbouring Colombia.

The chief component of the Ecuadorian State Railway is the Guayaquil and Quito Line (misleadingly nicknamed the 'Good and the Quick') which connects the two major cities of the country, the former on the coast; and the latter 9,000 feet up in the mountains. Construction work began in 1871 but it was not until 1908 that the contractors completed the rare 3'6" gauge line. To traverse the 288 miles and 11,840-feet altitude tight curves and zigzags are incorporated. It has never been a commercial success and its resulting near-bankruptcy has given it a dreadful reputation for chaotic administration, breakdowns and derailments. Its rolling stock is antique and the fact that the railway continues to operate is probably more amazing than the fact that it was ever built. But for anyone interested in travelling impossible railways, who is not put off by an uncomfortable ride punctuated by possible disasters the 'G & Q' is a prize experience. 'The World's mightiest roller coaster' it has sometimes been called.

Guayaquil itself — Ecuador's second city though larger in terms of population than Quito — is something of a garden metropolis though its prosperity derives from the industry it encompasses. The odd thing is that the railway fails to enter the city, the terminus being at Durán on the east bank of the Guayas River though I should have thought the perfectly good road bridge linking Guayaquil with Durán could have been adapted to carry the single line too. Train tickets to Quito, however, cover the cost of the road toll on the bridge or the ferry crossing which, I suppose, is the next best thing.

At Guayaquil I made the mistake of catching the more expensive *autoferro* — a clapped-out railcar — which, amazingly, is the luxury vehicle of the line and the only sort to go right through to Quito. I ought to have boarded the cheaper and unreliable *tren mixto* which goes no further than Riobamba and then caught the *autoferro*. As it was, my train was full of tourists and a few Ecuadorian businessmen; not my favourite travelling companions.

Leaving Durán we whizzed across the broad fertile Guayas

Valley by fields of sugar cane, rice and split cane houses built high on stilts overlooking waterways speckled with thousands of water birds and big dugouts piled high with produce. After Huigra and the River Chanchán the line begins its zigzagging course within a narrow gorge and, past Sibambe, climbs the famous Nariz del Diablo (Devil's Nose), a perpendicular ridge rising in the gorge to a height of 10,600 feet. Another engineering challenge, this almost insurmountable obstacle was finally conquered by the building of a series of switchbacks on a 5½ per cent grade. First one way and then the other the train zigzags higher and higher to gain an altitude of 11,840 feet at Urbina. This small town lies at the foot of the snow-capped Chimborazo, a dormant volcano once thought to be the highest mountain in the world at nearly 22,000 feet. I was later to climb this considerable peak, lose my way and, but for the grace of God, end up as dead meat on its flank. Coming down the valley of the volcanoes to Quito the views from the train windows are probably the most spectacular to be seen from a railway anywhere in the world. One by one by one the towering volcanic summits of Carihuairazo — Altar, Tungurahua, the burning head of Sangay, and Catopaxi — appear in the clear atmosphere.

I made the full journey to Quito in sections, my first break being at Sibambe where I rode the branch line to Cuenca, Ecuador's third largest city. Here is a gracious town that has preserved its colonial air with cobblestone streets and picturesque old buildings. I stayed some days in the city, the climax of my sojourn being a long immersion in the warm but eye-stinging sulphur baths at nearby Banos. Back on the route of the Inca royal road I walked to Canar and to Ecuador's sole major Inca ruin, Ingapirca, a fortress complex all tidied and tarted up and not at all like the lonely ruins I had stumbled across in Peru which few 'gringo' eyes have seen.

Riobamba, the headquarter city of the Ecuadorian State Railway administration, was another destination. It was from here that I made my nearly ill-fated ascent of Chimborazo with the collaboration of the Asociacion de Andinismo de Chimborazo who lent me the necessary climbing gear. A town prone to earthquakes it has ageing, vaguely impressive buildings which give it

223

the inaccurate description of 'Sultan of the Andes'. Ambato, likewise on the railway to Quito, I also got to know a little though anything that might have been of interest historically was destroyed in a 1949 earthquake.

What Riobamba and Ambato might lack in charm is made up for in full by Quito. Few cities have a setting to match it. Although nearly three kilometres high — it is the second highest capital in Latin America — the mountains which circle it are higher still. Modern Quito extends northwards into a luxuriant plain; it has wide avenues, fine private residences, parks, embassies and villas. But the city's attraction lies in the old southwestern section where cobbled streets are steep and winding, and the houses are mostly Indian-made adobe brick with low red roof tiles, or whitened stone. Quito's heart is the Plaza Independencia, dominated by the usual grim-looking cathedral, this one sporting grey stone porticos and green tile cupolas.

Oddly enough it was the modern part of the town — and in the posh embassy sector — that I again fell victim to a pickpocket gang, this time on a crowded bus. I managed to retain my passport and a few last remaining travel cheques but lost my air ticket, credit cards and all my money. I made myself unpopular by yelling to the driver to stop, denying exit to all those wishing to alight and dragging aboard a reluctant policeman on point duty who felt impelled to line everyone up against the bus with their hands above their heads to be searched. Meanwhile the villains, who had escaped before the hullabaloo, simply melted into the horrifying traffic pandemonium that resulted from the now uncontrolled intersection.

Fortunately this incident occurred towards the end of my term in South America but, thereafter, my onward journey to Bogota was to be accomplished with the minimum of funds; enough only for basic feeding and none at all for hotel accommodation and transportation. Arrival at Quito had brought my Inca road project to fruition. I now had a new challenge; that of reaching Bogota on a shoestring and surviving the period up to the date of my scheduled homeward flight from that city.

The first move obviously was to get out of Quito; capitals are expensive luxuries and hotels — even the strictly no-star variety

— were emphatically out. The northward route towards Colombia offered Ibarra as the subsequent destination and, with a gratis railway ticket prized out of the Ecuadoran railway authorities that gave me free travel from Quito to Ibarra to San Lorenzo and back if I wanted to, I decided to take advantage of part of it. I would go as far as San Lorenzo but return to Ibarra ready for the final leg of the journey to Bogota. Neither of my bibles, the *South American Handbook* nor *Cook's International Timetables* could vouchsafe any information or timings of the Quito—Ibarra—San Lorenzo trains so I took it upon myself to find out since the only timetable Quito could produce was one dated 1925! (I subsequently reported my version of the timings at stations along the line and other details to the editor of *Cook's* who published them in later issues. Currently, I notice, services on this line are suspended.)

Ibarra is a friendly town neatly ringed by a mountain range, a volcano and a lake where Atahualpa, the Inca chief, is supposed to have drowned his Indian captives. I spent the first of two nights on the floor of the stationmaster's office with strident bells and telephones ringing unanswered all around though there was less than one scheduled train a day using the station. In the morning the staff arrived, stepped over my prostrate form wrapped in a sleeping bag and commenced their duties as if stray English sleepers on their floor were the most natural thing in the world. One wonders what would have been the reaction in the stationmaster's office at, say, Temple Meads. For breakfast I consumed half a pint of rum donated by the staff and half a cut loaf contributed by a local grocer.

My train, when it condescended to put in an appearance, promptly quashed any notions I might have entertained about sleeping cars and plush first class compartments. On offer was a little monster called an *autocarril*. Basically this was a vehicle that was born as a common o'garden British Leyland lorry ending a long hard life on flanged wheels and a fixed course.

The initial portion of the journey was very definitely second class. My ticket (first class) stipulated a reserved seat, but there were no seats to reserve. The cope bulged with people standing or squatting amongst bags of flower, chickens and a nanny goat.

225

We were classed as a *treno mixto* and the definition was accurate. In a tunnel we ran out of petrol and the nanny goat was sick over my sandals.

A few miles on the train ran out of track at the edge of the river Mira. The river had cut the line in two — literally — by having swept away the bridge. We all had to get out and cross (no more than four passengers at a time) using a temporary rope structure that swayed alarmingly above a seething brown torrent, to the second train the other side. I enquired when the flood had brought down the bridge and was told four years ago.

The second train was an old British Leyland bus and was a slight improvement on the lorry for having hard seats. At least it did for some, though for me, only one buttock benefitted. We moved like a bat out of hell along the badly laid and worn track, swaying from side to side in hair-raising fashion, while the driver talked animatedly to a girl by his side and I wished he'd watch where he was going. Several hours later we came to the stock joke of the run: a waterfall that descends directly upon the track. All those in the know had quietly closed their windows but of course I hadn't and so received a powerful deluge of cold water to huge guffaws of mirth. With the Mira Gorge behind us we hurtled through a steamy jungle and swept into San Lorenzo.

The seven-hour ride had installed a dream of prolonged immersion in the cool clean water of the Pacific but the soft beaches of my fevered imagination turned out to be fetid mangrove swamps while the balmy night disintegrated into a tropical downpour. I spent the night on the concrete floor of the tin-roofed ticket office of the main station being eaten alive by mosquitoes. Rarely have I come across so awful a place as San Lorenzo, a township of wooden shacks and a bazaar rotting in its own sweat. Not even my guide book dared call it 'quaint'.

My morning alarm clock was the arrival of the first passengers queuing for tickets over my sleeping bag (with me in it) and I was delighted to return to the train, even obtaining a whole seat to myself. Again the driver was a speed maniac. Not once did he slacken the pace even for the most excruciating bend. Around one of them, with his foot hard down, we ran over a yellow triangle placed on the track — the one piece of signalling apparatus on the entire line — and ploughed straight into a sea of mud obliterating the metals. As with the Baluchistan line in Pakistan a little passenger participation is expected on such occasions.

In pouring rain we emerged from our bus, were issued with shovels and put to work in company with the regular clearance-crew to clear the tracks from the sticky soil and boulders that had slid down from the hillside. Nobody except me appeared the slightest put out by being made to help and by the time we ran into the second landslide some hours later I was an old hand at the job.

Back across the Mira River obstacle, and aboard the old lorry waiting patiently for the 'connection' in the tunnel mouth, I returned thankfully to Ibarra. It was to be my last railway ride in South America.

The tracks start again at Cali, in Colombia, but since they do not link with Bogota, I had to complete my travels using thumb power. In this my efforts were not completely unsuccessful since I managed to make the Colombian capital without quite starving to death, and in time to catch the plane out.

My Andean railway travels were supposedly secondary to my expeditionary undertaking which was the *raison d'être* for my being in South America. And that's how it often is with train journeying, not always can one 'travel not to go anywhere' at the bidding of the world's railways; often the opportunity to 'take a train' is proffered by chance.

But even though they were secondary, the journeys I made on those trains were rich experiences in themselves and provided some of my most memorable train riding. So much *can* happen on a train or by way of a railway line.

If my own experiences have awoken the realization of what trains can offer then my chronicle will not have been in vain.

And this is surely the essence of it — that the potential for adventure on the world's railways is there — all *you* have to do is acquire a ticket and ride them ...